'Designing Sustainable Futures' is an important work that successfully encapsulates the urgency and necessity of integrating sustainability into our socio-technical systems. The authors' showcase innovative approaches to tackle our planet's most pressing challenges. A must-read for anyone committed to the cause of a sustainable future.

Ani Dasgupta, CEO of the World Resources Institute (WRI)

"This book is a generous field guide to the important work of designing the future. From how to build scenarios to how to foster collaboration, the importance of imagination and the rigor of spotting signals, it's an excellent guide for anyone who wants to create a better world while acknowledging equity and diversity of perspectives and disciplines."

Ramona Liberoff, Executive Director, PACE (Platform for Accelerating the Circular Economy)

Design has become strategic, so it is our responsibility, our duty to take the lead at a time when companies must change by finding greater meaning. For designers, it is embodying an ethical leadership in order to prevail in all economic, social and political actions. This is the purpose of "Designing Sustainable Futures" - to open new frontiers for design towards the most ethical positions of all organizations.

Christian Guellerin, Honorary President of the international association Cumulus

In 'Designing Sustainable Futures,' the authors adeptly navigate the complexities of our times with foresight and systemic thinking at the forefront. This book embraces a much needed multidisciplinary approach that can integrate anticipatory and regenerative concepts into actionable strategies for sustainability. It's an essential resource for anyone committed to shaping futures that are not only imaginable but viable, equitable, and within our collective reach.

Shermon Cruz, UNESCO Chair on Anticipatory Governance and Regenerative Cities

T0331362

This book is a profound call to action for designing belonging into the fabric of our future. It showcases how we can integrate diverse perspectives to imagine and co-create more sustainable futures, enabling us all to embody the changes we want. 'Designing Sustainable Futures' serves as an essential guide for anyone looking to contribute to a more inclusive, equitable, and resilient world.

Ibrahim Jackson, Chairman at Information Technology
Senior Management Forum (ITSMF)

Designing
Sustainable Futures

We are in a decisive decade that demands more inspired and informed practitioners who can use positive futures to rebalance the present. The book you hold seeks to be a thought-provoking approach to imagine, create, and lead the journey to a more sustainable world – where a spectrum of choices, including regenerative practices, await conscientious citizens, companies, and communities.

With this objective, and the intent to help reverse the megatrends of economic disparity, social injustice, and climate change, the Institute for The Future (IFTF) and the Design Department of the Politecnico di Milano came together to prototype an approach to prepare all practitioners who seek to leverage the future to infuse our present with more impact and agency.

Guided by global experts and inspired by a growing network of future-makers, the authors share essential insights from this emerging landscape, offering thought-provoking theory, innovative experiments, real-world experiences, and practitioner stories. We draw insight and inspiration from many contemporary theories and practices, including strategic foresight, experiential futures, speculative design, design fiction, systems design, participatory design, and transformative leadership, and an emerging entry augmented design.

Regardless of whether you have a design or management background, or want to create a for-profit or non-profit, this book enables professionals across industries, as well as students preparing for a career in strategy, innovation, or transformation, the knowledge, skills, and confidence to strengthen resilience and guide the transition to the more sustainable practices of a better world.

Vice-Dean and Professor Joseph Press holds a PhD in Design Technology and is the Vice-Dean of NACAA – an intercultural design institute in Hangzhou, China, founded by the China Academy Of Art and L'Ecole de design Nantes Atlantique (EDNA). Previously he was a futures architect at the Institute For The Future and visiting professor at Politecnico di Milano, in both the Management and Design Schools. For over 25 years, he has advised organizations in imagining, designing, and implementing more sustainable practices. He holds a SMArchS in Architectural Design and PhD from MIT in Design Technology. At POLI.design, he co-led the pilot program *Designing Sustainable Futures* and convened a creative community for the *Designing with Emerging Technologies* global seminar series. He has co-authored books on digital transformation, futures of working and living, and social entrepreneurialism. As Co-founder of MakeOurFuture, he actively assists organizations in the transition to a better world.

Professor Manuela Celi holds a PhD in Design and is Associate Professor at Politecnico di Milano. Engaged in the Design PhD Board and Rectors' delegate for talent development, she navigates diverse sectors by delving into the multifaceted realms of design-related knowledge. Proficient in teaching product design, metadesign, and design futures, she leads the FUEL4Design.org research project, merging design with humanities and speculative inquiry. Prof. Celi's insights, showcased in renowned journals like *Futures* and *The Design Journal*, manifest her fusion of anticipation with critical design, offering unusual perspectives for envisioning transformative futures.

Designing Sustainable Futures

How to Imagine, Create, and Lead the Transition to a Better World

Joseph Press and Manuela Celi

Routledge
Taylor & Francis Group

NEW YORK AND LONDON

Designed cover image: Natasia Taylor

First published 2025
by Routledge
605 Third Avenue, New York, NY 10158

and by Routledge
4 Park Square, Milton Park, Abingdon, Oxon, OX14 4RN

Routledge is an imprint of the Taylor & Francis Group, an informa business

Library of Congress Cataloging-in-Publication Data
Names: Press, Joseph, author. | Celi, Manuela, author.
Title: Designing sustainable futures: how to imagine, create, and lead the transition to a better world / Joseph Press and Manuela Celi. Description: New York, NY: Routledge, 2025. |
Includes bibliographical references and index. |
Identifiers: LCCN 2024029530 (print) | LCCN 2024029531 (ebook) |
ISBN 9781032588414 (hardback) | ISBN 9781032588384 (paperback) |
ISBN 9781003451693 (ebook)
Subjects: LCSH: Sustainable development. | Sustainable design—Economic aspects. | Sustainable design—Social aspects.
Classification: LCC HC79.E5 P6786 2025 (print) |
LCC HC79.E5 (ebook) | DDC 338.9—dc23/eng/20240718
LC record available at https://lccn.loc.gov/2024029530
LC ebook record available at https://lccn.loc.gov/2024029531

ISBN: 9781032588414 (hbk)
ISBN: 9781032588384 (pbk)
ISBN: 9781003451693 (ebk)

DOI: 10.4324/9781003451693

Typeset in Sabon
by codeMantra

To our past, present, and future students – together we can design more sustainable futures.

Contents

Foreword

We've entered dramatic times, living through eras akin to the French Revolution or the recent Arab Spring – heterogeneous realities where the next step is highly unpredictable. The plasticity of time allows for greater agency, a sliver of hope, perhaps leading the Secretary-General António Guterres in 2022 to outline the United Nation's several strategic foresight initiatives under the UN's "Be Prepared Cluster." Yet, we're simultaneously grappling with the difficult aspect of losing "Prama," the Sanskrit term for equilibrium. Particularly in the era of artificial intelligence (AI), our internal and external worlds find themselves drastically out of balance. This imbalance is both a challenge and a call to action for establishing a more dynamic equilibrium. We can't simply go back; we must create a new equilibrium, a dynamic one, to navigate these challenging times. The urgency is in forging what comes next.

However, our inclinations often tend toward the past – a nostalgia for a perceived state of equilibrium. This is evident in the resurgent calls for racial purity, medical purity, nature purity, and class purity. A return to what was is a natural human reaction when faced with disequilibrium. Take, for example, the decline of Ayurvedic science in favor of modern medicine. Ayurveda met the unique needs of South Asians but stumbled when pandemics like smallpox swept the region. My grandmother was the lone survivor among her siblings, a poignant example of the life-saving role of Western medicine. But standing still in the present, or maintaining "business as usual," is not an option. Our existing systems are woefully inadequate for tackling the multifaceted challenges of today – AI inequity, gender disparity, climate change, or the dysfunctional nature of nation-states. Therefore, the challenge is neither in reverting to the past nor in maintaining the present, rather co-creating a new dynamic equilibrium for the future.

Futures emerges not as a causative tool but as part of an ecology of interventions that contribute to meaningful change. Although the linear methods of 20th-century social science offer some insights, we now acknowledge that we're dealing with multiple variables interacting in intricate ways. Take, for instance, the work with law enforcement agencies. The Queensland Crime and Corruption Commission integrated foresight into their strategic planning, swiftly recognizing the potential of technologies like ChatGPT for organized crime. Anticipating new categories of crime such as greenwashing became central to their approach. What started as discussions around infrastructure financing at the Asian Infrastructure Investment Bank (AIIB) transformed into initiatives focused on climate and gender. The Asian Development Bank (ADB) has even gone on to issue the world's first gender bonds, aimed at supporting unemployed women in the private sector. While we can't assert a direct causative link, it's an excellent example of how foresight and futures studies can create ripple effects, catalyzing meaningful shifts in policy and action.

When the aspiration for a new approach disintegrates, the urgency of creating a new dynamic equilibrium is lost. In navigating the terrain of futures interventions, we must be keenly aware of the phenomenon of "future-washing" – you do a workshop, people get excited, but nothing changed Monday morning. I recall an episode with a bank: the most innovative minds threatened that unless there was a move to action, they would leave and set up their own fintech start-up.

My personal pursuit of avoiding stagnation and finding balance through futures work has unfolded through three distinct phases, each contributing to a sense of balance. The first phase involved planting the seeds, akin to Johnny Appleseed greening the East Coast, where I engaged with organizations like Interpol and law enforcement agencies. The second phase was about nurturing those seeds into trees, working on a variety of projects to anticipate new behaviors and encourage sustainable solutions, such as gender bonds. The third phase, which I find myself in now, is about creating a forest of foresight, where diverse approaches co-exist, contributing to a dynamic equilibrium, a new balance that we all strive to achieve.

Designing Sustainable Futures fits well within this third phase, aiming to fertilizing the ever-growing forest of futures work. It seeks to be an integrated approach to rebuilding balance on multiple fronts, toward cultivating a shared vision for a sustainable world. A collaborative effort of the Institute For The Future (IFTF) and the Design School of Politecnico di Milano, this work brings together futures and design to cultivate shared leadership, the aspiration of a world with more balance. Without claiming to have all the answers, it seeks to initiate dialogues about balance – between disciplines, between humanity and the Earth, and within our own communities. It's an invitation to invigorate practices like strategic foresight with speculative design and explore emerging practices like generative AI and storymaking. It aims to encourage us all to find a role in this complex adaptive system we're all a part of, with less a desire to drive the transition to sustainability, rather be part of a collective journey toward it.

Sohail Inayatullah

UNESCO Chair in Futures Studies at the Sejahtera Centre for Sustainability and Humanity

EXPERT ADVISORS

The authors would like to acknowledge the critical role of our *Expert Advisors* in nurturing the anticipatory perspectives and ensuring their relevance in writing this book. Their contributions, from both academic and professional communities, included content, insights, comments, and adjustments that significantly strengthened the result of our collaboration journey and seeded many more paths to explore together.

- Silvia Barbero, Politecnico di Torino
- Jacques Barcia, Institute For The Future
- Tommaso Buganza, Politecnico di Milano
- Jake Dunagan, Institute For The Future
- Jeremy Kirschbaum, Institute For The Future
- Anna Meroni, Politecnico di Milano
- Victoria Rodriguez Schon, Politecnico di Milano

Preface

At the beginning of 2021, we (Joseph Press and Manuela Celi) met over lunch in Milano. Initially sharing our teaching and research experiences from opposite sides of the Bovisa station, the conversation quickly moved to how we might inspire and prepare practitioners to confront the grand challenges of our time. Driven by a shared interest in futures *and* design to accelerate the transition to more sustainable practices, we saw an opportunity: How might we integrate the IFTF's 60-year history of strategic foresight with the Design School of Politecnico di Milano's centuries-old legacy of Italian design?

Building on our common commitment, Manuela's work with the European Union funded project Fuel4Design,[1] and guided by Lyn Jeffery of IFTF and Cabirio Cautela of Politecnico di Milano, we sketched the initial design of a new professional development course that would prepare professionals to imagine, design, and lead toward a more sustainable future. Given the breadth of our intentions and depth of the topics, we collaborated with experts from both IFTF and Politecnico di Milano to design and deliver a meaningful experience (see all the profiles in the Appendix). Essential to making our vision real was Victoria Rodriguez Schon, a PhD student from Argentina, who led the course delivery and contributed to its design.

The course came to be known as Designing Sustainable Futures. With a joint marketing effort, 15 participants from across the globe joined our educational experiment. In the Fall of 2022, we and our experts delivered nine online sessions. Using a speculative-project pedagogy, the faculty and participants collaborated to anticipate better future, create more sustainable experiences, and mobilize leadership for contributing to the UN's Sustainable Developmental Goals (SGDs). With feedback that was both positive and constructive, we decided to incorporate our collective learnings and sharpen the approach by writing a book.

The result, *Designing Sustainable Futures: How to Imagine, Create, and Lead the Transition to a Better World,* seeks to empower practitioners who want to contribute to the great transition. Because of the scale of challenges we face, this book is intentionally transdisciplinary, cutting across the emerging participatory practices of foresight, design, and leadership to trigger personal, organizational, and community transformation. We see this as a solid, but not solidified, foundation for further research and development. With that intention, we hope it inspires and empowers a new generation of changemakers to collaboratively design a better future for all.

Milano 2024

Joseph Press
Manuela Celi

Note

1   Future Education and Literacy for Designers (FUEL4Design) aims at developing knowledge, resources, and methods to help young designers designing for complex tomorrow. FUEL4Design builds on an extensive research programme conducted by the Oslo School of Architecture and Design, Politecnico di Milano, University of the Arts London, and ELISAVA, Barcelona. http://www.fuel4design.org

Introduction

We are in a decisive decade. The United Nations reported in 2023 that national climate action plans are insufficient to limit global temperature rise to 1.5 C (UN, 2023). This is despite an increase of sustainability-related measurement initiatives and reporting regulations[1] (Ruiz, 2023; Kotchen et al., 2023, Burley Farr et al., 2023). According to the World Bank, climate change is driven in large part by economic inequalities and social disparities across the globe (World Bank, 2023). These interdependences underlie the World Economic Forum's position that the top two risks in the next ten years are failure to mitigate climate change and failure of climate-change adaptation (WEF, 2023).

Policy and reporting requirements are a necessary, yet insufficient condition to reverse the megatrends of climate change, social injustice, and economic inequality. Therefore, a multitude of theories and practices from a wide range of disciplines have emerged with the intent to facilitate transformation to a better world. Innovation management frameworks like the technology adoption life cycle (Moore, 1991) and the "three horizons of growth" (Baghai et al., 1999) offer approaches to balance transformative innovation with core business sustainability. In change management, traditional methodologies like Kotter's eight-step process still dominate organizational change initiatives (Kotter, 1995). More recently, regenerative leadership has encouraged a shift from such traditional approaches to a focus on rejuvenation, sustainability, and holistic value creation (Hutchins and Storm 2019). Dr. Joel Carboni (2017) and others advocate for the criticality of a deeper understanding of systemic collaboration to face climate challenges.

DOI: 10.4324/9781003451693-1

In futures studies, Causal Layered Analysis (CLA) (Inayatullah, 1998) proposes a method to explore alternative futures by challenging underlying societal assumptions. Inayatullah and his team have documented numerous cases in over 30 countries, applying CLA across various sectors including government, education, health, and corporate strategy. *The Causal Layered Analysis (CLA) Reader 3.0* (Inayatullah et al., 2022) covers 30 years of transformative research (authors note – 4.0 is in process) and has garnered accolades from both practitioners and academics. CLA and many others showcase the versatility and impact of foresight interventions in informing policies, strategies, and sustainable development initiatives worldwide.

In the discipline of design, Transition Design (Irwin et al., 2015) and Don Norman's latest humanity-centered design (Norman, 2023) seek to redress the failures of design thinking by advocating for systemic societal change through sustainable and equitable solutions (Gaziulusoy & Oztekin, 2019). A significant contribution to repositing design for impact is *Design for Social Innovation: Case Studies from Around the World* (Amatullo et al., 2021). This groundbreaking work compiling 45 richly illustrated case studies spanning six continents

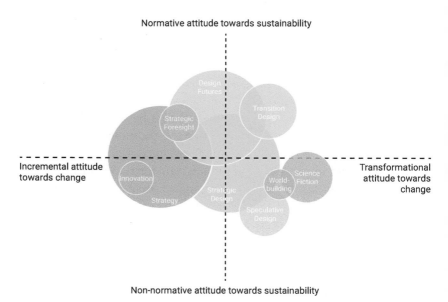

Figure 0.1 Mapping attitudes toward change and sustainability.
Source: Courtesy of Corina Angheloiu. With permission.

delves into how design is being utilized by organizations such as the United Nations, Australia Post, and governments in various countries to drive social change across diverse sectors, including public health, urban planning, economic development, education, humanitarian response, cultural heritage, and civil rights.

Despite the methodological commonalities and compiled cases, for anyone intending to design existing situations into preferred ones (in deference to the iconic yet cliched Herbert Simon seminal quote), a more aligned approach remains elusive. As illustrated by Corina Angheloiu (Figure 0.1), the archipelago of overlaps between the different sub-disciplines acutely reveals a need for greater coherency, and an opportunity for some simplicity, if we are to improve our attitudes toward change and sustainability.

In the landscape of theories and practices that aim to aid in understanding and directing the complexities of societal and organizational transformation, we see a pattern. After many years of advising change initiatives and educating its practitioners, we believe that the synergy of foresight, design, and leadership creates a potent space of opportunities to address the grand challenges we face. Most important for our intentions, as illustrated in Figure 0.2, we see sustainability – the confluence of climate change, social injustice, and economic inequality – at the nexus of a more integrated practice. Indeed, while many approaches explore the adjacent intersections – between futures and design in Design Futures; between design and leadership in design thinking; between futures and leadership in foresight training – we see *Designing Sustainable Futures* as an important iteration in our collective search for more meaningful methodologies for creating a better world.

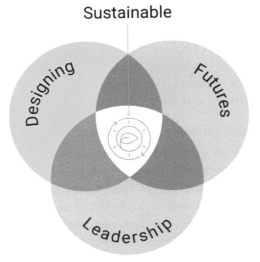

Figure 0.2 Designing sustainable futures – integrating disciplines with sustainability.
Source: Authors.

Designing Sustainable Futures, as the subtitle describes, explores some of the emerging practices of how to imagine, create, and lead the transition to a better world. It offers a framework to help us all integrate the deep, yet diverse traditions of futures, design, and leadership that have informed and inspired us all. *Designing Sustainable Futures* aims to open a broader space for more imaginative, participatory, and embodied experiences of a more sustainable world. We believe that the catalyst for transitioning to a more sustainable world begins with clarity among stakeholders on a possible, and preferred, future. This foresight provokes insights into what might be the solutions stakeholders need to co-create (i.e., design) in order for that future to become a reality. If foresight provokes collective insight, then stakeholders will be engaged in systemic change. Such a synergy enables us to be future-ready – ready to act today. Designing sustainable futures opens a three-dimensional design space circumscribed by imagining better futures, creating sustainable experiences, and leading the transition to a better world.

OUR FOUR FOUNDATIONAL PREMISES

Designing Sustainable Futures will explore the emerging practices of anticipating futures, designing experiences, and leading the transition. Our aim to weave the critical dimensions of designing sustainable futures into an integrated framework rests on four foundational premises: a holistic definition of sustainability; an explicit focus on the participatory and experiential nature of our three disciplines; the future is not singular, but plural; our present socio-technical environment is framed by four possible scenarios; finally, our educational objective to develop the futures literacy of all.

Sustainability Is a Spectrum

Often words lose their original meaning as more people use (and misuse) them. It might be argued that the term "sustainability" is one of those. First used in 1987, the Brundtland Report (World Commission on Environment and Development, 1987) defined sustainability as "development that meets the needs of the present without compromising the ability of future generations to meet their own needs." This definition framed sustainability within a global context, emphasizing the balance between environmental protection, economic growth, and social equity. Following the United Nations Millennium

Summit in 2000 (United Nations, 2000), the United Nations Conference on Sustainable Development (Rio+20) in 2012 set the stage for more inclusive and comprehensive sustainability goals (United Nations, 2012). Finally, in 2015, the United Nations Sustainable Development Goals (SDGs) were adopted by all United Nations Member States as part of the 2030 Agenda for Sustainable Development, offering a more holistic approach to achieving sustainability by addressing a wide array of global challenges (United Nations, 2015).

Despite the lack of progress toward the SDG targets set for 2030 (WEF, 2023), they remain a uniquely comprehensive framework for a better future. Addressing 17 critical areas for people and planetary improvement, this globally agreed blueprint is sufficiently clear, yet simultaneously ambiguous, to inspire changemakers toward a more equitable and sustainable world for all. Often misunderstood as isolated targets, their interconnectedness is vividly captured by the SDG Layer Cake model, which categorizes the 17 goals into three foundational layers: the biosphere, society, and the economy (Figure 0.3). This layering reflects the circularity emphasized in

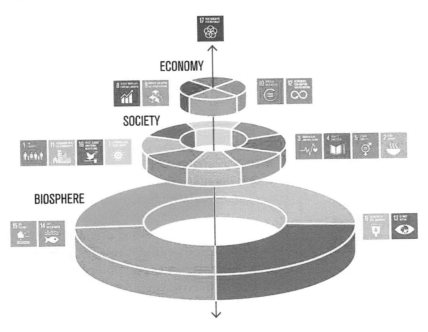

Figure 0.3 The SDGs wedding cake.

Source: Stockholm Resilience Center. Creative Commons.

Kate Raworth's Donut Model, which focuses on creating a balance between human needs and the planet's ecological boundaries. Both models serve as a vivid reminder that environmental sustainability is not an optional extra but the basis for all sustainable development (Raworth, 2017)

In addition to visualizing the interdependencies of the SDGs, we also recommend thinking full-spectrum about sustainability (Johansen et al., 2023). As illustrated in Figure 0.4, this means recognizing the full range of possible practices between net-zero and regenerative practices, rather than rejecting any option outright.

REGENERATIVE

NET ZERO

Figure 0.4 Thinking full spectrum about sustainability.

Source: adapted from Office Shock: Creating Better Futures for Working and Living. With permissions of authors.

Net-zero is positioned at one of the spectrum to encourage choices that seek a rebalancing emitted and offset greenhouse gases, primarily through carbon footprint reduction, energy efficiency, and renewable energy adoption. Regenerative practices, on the other end, aim to actively restore and rejuvenate ecosystems through more local initiatives like local agricultural production on cooperative farms. Practitioners should eschew rigid categorizations and instead adopt a more agile approach in order to tailor their sustainability strategies to the specific environmental, social, and economic contexts they face. The integrated perspective enabled by thinking full-spectrum offers a more effective and context-sensitive implementation of sustainability initiatives, ensuring a comprehensive approach to ecological stewardship. Therefore, even if the "sustainable" world is moving away from the language of sustainability and into more proactive language like resilience or regeneration, we will use the term sustainability to encourage practitioners to collectively explore the entirety of this spectrum

Introduction

Design Is a Dialog – Participatory and Experiential

Building on Herbert Simon's seminal *The Science of the Artificial* (1996, 3rd ed.), we position design as a social, co-creative activity yielding tangible, artificially created things. Unlike art, it is explicitly social, and therefore intrinsically both participatory and experiential. As researched in the IDeaLs Lab (Press et al., 2021), the design-driven dialog (Figure 0.5) encapsulates an epistemological process between an individual and others around an object or concept, driven by a continual oscillation between creating/shaping and learning/reflecting. Design in this model is dialogical, where the path from personal insight to collective consensus is characterized by a continuous interplay of reflection and shaping, both individually and together. The design object serves as a pivotal, and tangible, fulcrum for personal connection and collective evolution. Encapsulating the characteristics of a 'boundary object' – a collective reference point that contains meaning for both individuals and communities of practice – the design object acts as the nexus of a design-driven dialog because it is concrete enough for specific interpretations, yet flexible enough to be interpreted and employed distinctly by each individual or subgroup (Starr, 1989).

Neither linear or cyclical, the value of a design-driven dialog is less the physical output, rather the outcome of shared understanding. As illustrated in Figure 0.5, the infinite loop of a design-driven dialog reinforces our definition of leadership – a communal, emergent phenomenon where the co-creation of meaning within a community

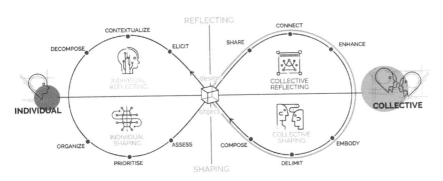

Figure 0.5 Design driven dialog. IDeaLS

Source: IDeaLs (Innovation and Design as Leadership): Transformation in the Digital Era. With Permission.

of practice leads to the establishment of a common direction, alignment of actions, and building of commitment (Darth et al, 2015). As people design, leadership emerges along the three axis:

1. Creation of Common Direction: In the design dialog process, the act of collective shaping involves bringing together diverse perspectives to create a shared understanding of the design object. This convergence of views establishes a common direction for the community, mirroring the leadership role of setting a collective course.
2. Alignment of Actions: Through both individual and collective shaping, actions are aligned as each member of the community contributes to and refines the shared object. This collaborative effort ensures that all actions are directed toward a cohesive end, fulfilling the leadership function of coordinating efforts toward a common goal.
3. Building of Commitment: The iterative process of reflection and shaping within the design dialog fosters a deep sense of ownership and commitment among participants. As individuals see their inputs and perspectives valued and incorporated, their commitment to the community and its objectives solidifies.

These dialogical interactions within design foster a creative and collaborative environment where leadership is a dynamic, collective orchestration of diverse contributions, aligning individual efforts toward shared understanding and goals.

Similarly, the design dialog infuses futures with participation by opening an environment for citizens to collaboratively shape potential futures. Referred to as *Participatory Futures* (NESTA, 2019), design accelerates the movement from a specialized domain to a collective intelligence exercise, enabling broader engagement in long-term thinking. Through a design dialog, public imagination can be scaffolded, as participants draw upon their knowledge and ideas to co-create vivid mental images of desired futures. This collective envisioning then translates into immediate, collective actions and behaviors, reflecting the shared aspirations for a preferable tomorrow. The design dialog acknowledges the multiplicity and malleability of futures, empowering individuals to comprehend the plasticity of the future and to act in innovative ways that prefigure those preferred outcomes. When the participatory nature of design intersects with futures studies, we can transcend traditional expert-driven models by fertilizing the ground with embodied experiences enabling participation to flourish at all levels of interventions in complex environments.

Since design permeates our three disciplines, *Designing Sustainable Futures* is intrinsically an experiential, participatory approach to long-term change. With embodied experiences embedded throughout, it circumscribes interventions in complex situations to nurture the emergent engagement, particularly over time. In all interventions, the more participatory and embodied the intervention is, the more responsibility practitioners have to manage and meet the increasing expectations of stakeholders. Designing sustainable futures is no different, so we position *Designing Sustainable Futures* as a socially informed scaffold to facilitate the transition toward more sustainable futures (Press et al., 2021).

Futures Are Plural, and Preferable

In the discipline of futures studies, the future is not a linear progression from the present but a complex interplay of multiple trajectories, informed by the past yet oriented toward various future scenarios. Encapsulated in the concept of the futures cone, and expanded in Figure 0.6, (inspired by Stead et al., 2019), this visual guide delineates a range of potential futures, from the probable to the provocative (Hancock & Bezold, 1994). The futures cone respects the instructive nature of the past, using it as a lens through which to view the spectrum of futures. This approach aligns with the work of Dator (2009), who introduced the concept of 'alternative futures,' emphasizing the importance of envisioning different possible futures as a means to better understand and influence the present.

When the future is not a singular, predetermined endpoint, it becomes a spectrum of potentialities. While some futures are more likely to occur, others, though less probable, may carry significant transformative potential (Bell, 1997). Understanding the breadth and depth of future possibilities necessitates a comprehensive exploration of potential, plausible, and preferable futures, not to predict what will happen, but to prepare for what could happen.

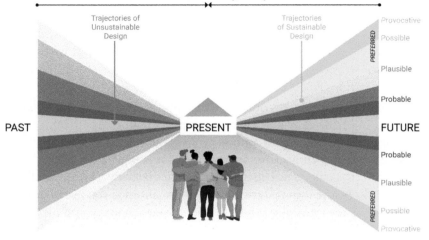

Figure 0.6 The futures cone revisited: preferred futures.
Source: By authors, inspired by Stead et al. (2019).

But what we do know is what is happening now. As iconoclastic architect Victor Papanek foresaw in 1971, (Papanek, 1971), our long-established modes of production, consumption, and disposal are profoundly damaging to the environment, economic equality, and social justice. Since we see the SDGs as describing a preferred future, we also believe that humanity cannot afford to continue in the same path as the past. Despite the challenges of the question "what does preferable mean, for whom, and who decides?" (Dunne & Raby, 2013), we also believe it is essential to avoid the relativist trap and start the hard work of designing preferable futures. To grapple this complex conversation, and the accompanying emotional effort, we propose a series of framing scenarios as catalysts for designing sustainable futures.

Scenarios Are STES (Socio-Technical-Ecological Systems)

Our world is complex, exemplary of the "wicked problems" described by Rittel and Webber (1973). These problems, particularly in environmental sustainability, are defined by their intricate interdependencies and resistance to simple solutions. To guide us in designing sustainable futures, we describe such complex environments as STES. The STES framework seeks to integrate social, technical, and ecological considerations (Hughes, 1987; Geels, 2004) by acknowledging the interplay between societal, technological, and environmental factors. This approach reflects with environmental science and sustainability studies, advocating for solutions that are comprehensive and recognize the interconnectedness of human, technological, and ecological systems (Folke et al., 2005; Berkes & Folke, 1998). It will also help us to clearly distinguish between more chimerical and singular visions of the future, most often rooted in technological 'solutionism' (Morozov, 2013)

While the framework aims to help practitioners grasp the complexity of our present condition, it also anticipates our preferences within a set of *probable* futures. As illustrated in the 2×2 matrix in Figure 0.7, we anticipate *socio* as a spectrum on the Y-axis, describing the paradigm and myths of how society organizes itself – ranging from individually based to more community based. Not represented, but implicit, is a point of view on how we govern (individual vs collective rights) and even how we consume (from selfish to sharing). The *technical* can be found on the X-axis, which includes economic models that use guide technological output, and is represented as the spectrum describing the systems and means of how we produce – ranging from global/mass-scale production to local/small-scale production.[2] Since we are exploring sustainable futures, *ecological* is the backdrop where these future scenarios will play out, so it is implicitly present rather than explicitly represented.

By centering designing sustainable futures on these two axes, we intentionally encourage practitioners and their stakeholders to circumscribe their future. This topography will establish the design problem space with a set of agreed cultural and economic assumptions. Each future will include a scenario description to contextualize the conversation, and a GenAI illustration to visualize the scenario, at each step of the designing sustainable futures journey. The illustrations are intended to offer readers a visual narrative through the book structure. More importantly, it also aims to evoke more embodied experiences of anticipation, design, and leadership. These are the author futures, to inspire the readers to create your own. By augmenting our creativity with genAI, we hope to demonstrate how design can turn sustainable futures into desirable futures!

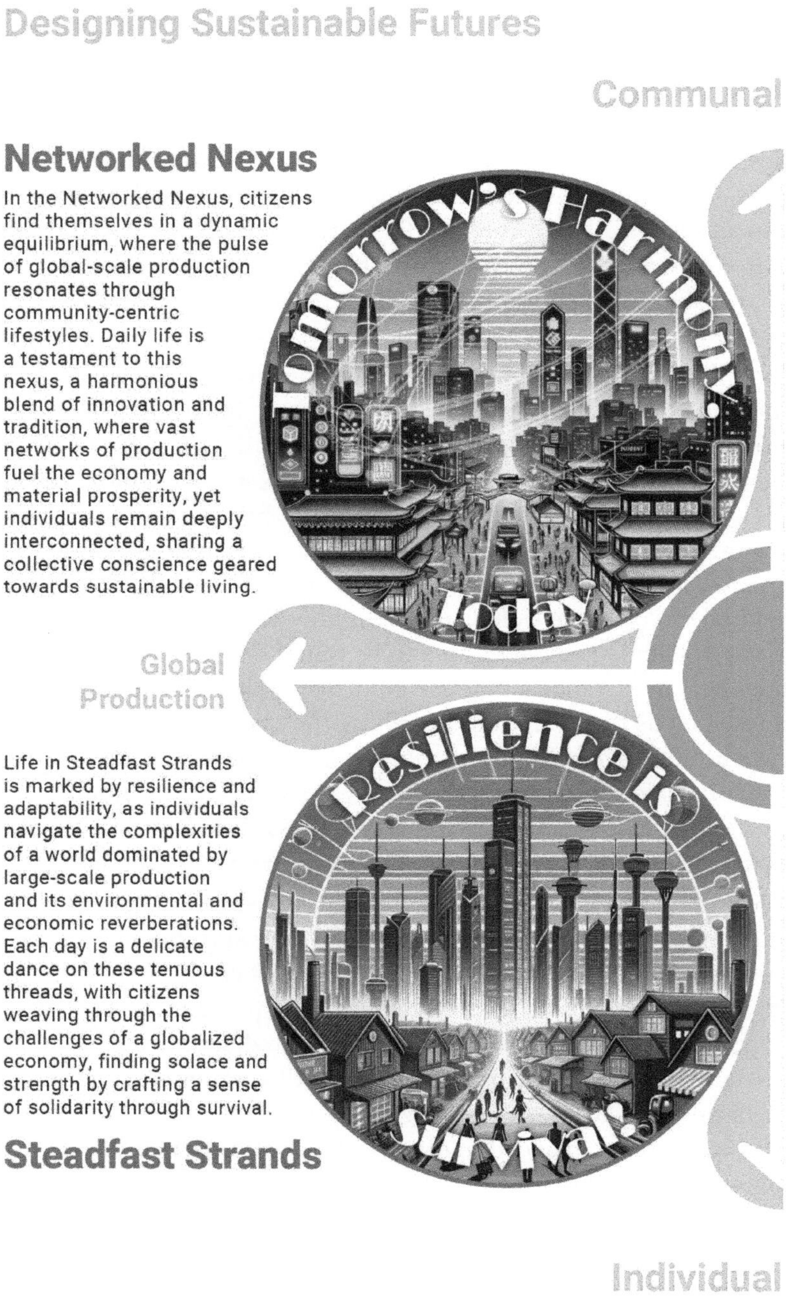

Communal

Networked Nexus

In the Networked Nexus, citizens find themselves in a dynamic equilibrium, where the pulse of global-scale production resonates through community-centric lifestyles. Daily life is a testament to this nexus, a harmonious blend of innovation and tradition, where vast networks of production fuel the economy and material prosperity, yet individuals remain deeply interconnected, sharing a collective conscience geared towards sustainable living.

Global
Production

Life in Steadfast Strands is marked by resilience and adaptability, as individuals navigate the complexities of a world dominated by large-scale production and its environmental and economic reverberations. Each day is a delicate dance on these tenuous threads, with citizens weaving through the challenges of a globalized economy, finding solace and strength by crafting a sense of solidarity through survival.

Steadfast Strands

Individual

Figure 0.7 Mapping the preferred scenarios of our socio-technical-ecological systems. *Source*: By authors.

Introduction

Regenerative Weave

In the Regenerative Weave, every day threads a rich tapestry of community life, interlacing the strength of local production with the warmth of communal bonds. Citizens live in a vibrant, interconnected network, where the resilience of the weave is felt in every shared meal, every local product, and every community decision. This resilient fabric safeguards and enriches their lives because it is beautifully interwoven into a sustainable, harmonious, and adaptable existence.

Local
Production

The cornerstones of the Quiet Revolution is in the local production and personal responsibility. Every aspect of life, from the locally sourced food to the small-scale businesses, contribute to this silent uprising. The power of these quiet revolutionaries are amplified by the agency of its small-scale, crafting a society that's revolutionary in both its simplicity and awareness of a better future.

Quiet Revolution

Society

Figure 0.7 Continued.

DESIGNING A SUSTAINABLE FUTURE FOR BANGLADESH

These generated scenarios actually resonate with the transformative trajectory of Bangladesh. A rare occurrence in futures studies, this story over 50 years in the making offers guidance on how we propose to navigate designing sustainable futures

Envisioning a Better Future

Following the devastating Liberation War in 1971, Sir Fazle Hasan Abed returned to a newly independent Bangladesh, a nation grappling with the aftermath of genocide and extreme weather events. Sir Abed, deeply moved by the dire situation, founded BRAC, a small relief operation in the remote village of Sulla. Its initial focus was on providing emergency aid, but Sir Abed's vision quickly evolved to encompass long-term development goals. He pioneered a community-based approach, recognizing that the most effective solutions came from understanding and addressing the needs of the impoverished. Sir Abed understood that sustainable futures for Bangladesh required more than just aid; they needed empowerment and self-sufficiency. BRAC, therefore, expanded its focus to include education, healthcare, and microfinance. These initiatives, especially the emphasis on educating girls and empowering women, became cornerstones of BRAC's approach. By integrating these elements, Sir Abed laid the foundation for a comprehensive development model that sought to uplift entire communities from the cycles of poverty. Sir Abed's legacy in cultivating a future-forward mindset in Bangladesh is a testament to his visionary leadership. His approach went beyond conventional development models, focusing on empowering individuals and communities to be architects of their own futures. This ethos of fostering self-reliance and resilience has become a guiding principle for sustainable development, inspiring similar initiatives globally to architect better futures for all people.

Designing Sustainable Solutions

Building on the future of a better Bangladesh, in December 2008 Prime Minister Sheikh Hasina announced the Digital Bangladesh Vision aimed at delivering improvements across the country by closing the digital divide (Zunaid Ahmed Palak, 2023).

Anir Chowdhury emerged as a pivotal figure in making the Vision real, by establishing the Aspire to Innovate (a2i) program (formerly known as Access to Information). Under Anir's leadership, a2i's innovative approach focused on creating sustainable and scalable solutions within the public sector by nudging the Bangladesh government to transition from being merely a service provider to a facilitator of inclusive services. Through public-private initiatives, a2i played a crucial role in streamlining government services by simplifying, digitizing, and decentralizing the delivery of public services. a2i has won multiple awards, and saved billions of dollars and hours, sponsoring 1,000s of female intrapreneurs. This approach mirrored the ethos of BRAC, adapting it to the digital age and furthering the vision of transforming and modernizing Bangladesh's public infrastructure.

By promoting a culture of frugal, citizen-centric innovation, the capacity of civil servants to leverage technology encouraged public services to be more inclusive, affordable, reliable, and easier to access. a2i's subsequent digitalization of processes and introducing e-governance reduced bureaucratic barriers, making services like obtaining legal documents and business licenses simpler and more efficient. Guided by Anir's foresight and design of cultural and digital experiences, a2i significantly reduced time, costs, and number of visits for citizens, exemplifying a successful integration of technology in governance. a2i has launched digital initiatives like 'Noipunyo' and 'Smart 333' to enhance public service efficiency. Anir's contributions continue in the refreshed vision of 'Smart Bangladesh' by 2041. Soon to become an autonomous national innovation agency, a2i will continue its impact by cultivating more sustainable growth via systemic solutions, demonstrating how visionary design and digital innovation can be effectively utilized to enhance transparency, efficiency, and citizen engagement.

Educating Leadership for a Better Future

As a2i began reshaping governance in Bangladesh through digital innovation, Shakil Ahmed also stepped into its radar. His approach and focus on transforming the education sector were deeply influenced by Sir Abed's philosophy and Anir's work in innovation in technology and governance. Shakil's transformative journey in the education sector of Bangladesh began with a pivotal moment: attending a futures thinking workshop led by Sohail Inayatullah, when he was working at the BRAC Institute of Educational Development in 2013 to co-create three scenarios for BRAC University in 2030 (Inayatullah, 2015). This experience profoundly influenced Shakil, igniting a passion for integrating futures thinking into education. His goal was clear: to embed futures thinking into the education ecosystem and governance, thereby equipping the next generation with the tools to envision and shape their own futures. Given a2i's appetite for innovation, Shakil was able to propose a series of futures thinking workshops in 2017–2018 on the Futures of Education in Bangladesh in 2041 to a2i, when it was part of the Prime Minister's Office. The ideas discussed during these workshops, the relationships created among participants, and the corresponding publication from the workshops enabled Shakil to participate during the National Curriculum transformation in Bangladesh, since 2021.

Shakil's commitment to embedding futures thinking in education materialized with the introduction of a new subject for sixth-grade students. Life and Livelihoods was an opportunity to integrate aspects of futures thinking into the curriculum and its new cover (Figure 0.8). Due in part to educational leaders who were already grappling with questions of how students can prepare for the future, the new curriculum contributed significantly to the broader educational reforms. As a symbolic shift toward preparing students to engage with and shape their futures proactively, the textbook and teacher guide became tools in equipping young minds with the skills and perspectives needed to navigate and influence a rapidly evolving world. Under Shakil's guidance, content for the textbook and teacher guide was developed emphasizing skills essential for future readiness, such as adaptability, strategic thinking, and collaborative problem-solving. These shifts aim to enhance academic learning and also to cultivate a generation capable of leading and innovating in an increasingly complex world.

Although no single act can explain Bangladesh's transformation, the cumulative impact of Sir Fazle Hasan Abed, Anir Chowdhury, and Shakil Ahmed in *Designing Sustainable Futures* for Bangladesh indicates a cohesive narrative of how to design sustainable futures. Sir Abed's envisioning of better futures through BRAC's community initiatives, Anir's co-creation of experiences via a2i's digital

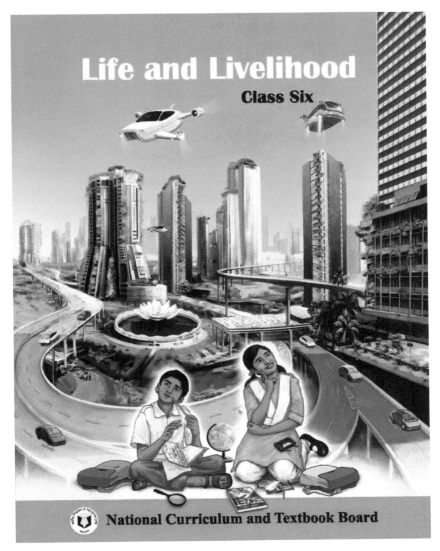

Figure 0.8 Life and livelihoods – sixth-grade textbook cover.

Source: Bangladesh National Curriculum and Textbook Board. Reprinted with permission.

innovations, and Shakil's infusing educational pedagogies with futures thinking collectively demonstrate the dynamic interplay of three essential dimensions: futures, design, and leadership (particularly preparing the next generation through education). By embodying the principles of envisioning, designing, and leading, their synergistic efforts have cultivated a new generation, ready to face global complexities with foresight, creativity, and leadership. By preparing the next generation, they have set a powerful example of how strategic, holistic approaches can empower of Bangladesh's youth to become active architects of sustainable futures.

These changemakers – and all the others who contributed to Bangladesh's transformation – can be considered as "network entrepreneurs" because they lead system-level, collaborative efforts (Sawyer & Wei-Skillern, 2015). This is emblematic of a broader definition of leadership, where the impact of these network entrepreneurs enabled stakeholders to thrive across the country. Sir Abed's work laid the groundwork for community-led transformation, Anir's digitalization efforts streamlined government processes and Shakil's educational contributions preparing future generations. Their collaborative efforts provide a blueprint for the leadership of global systemic change, demonstrating how diverse approaches to envisioning, designing, and leading are essential in crafting sustainable futures.

We see such leadership as an opportunity to integrate futures thinking, design, and leadership in other contexts, emphasizing the synergy of these domains to address the global challenges facing us all.

OUR ASTROLABE – NAVIGATING THROUGH DESIGNING SUSTAINABLE FUTURES

The preferred scenario of Bangladesh, or at least the one that emerged, did so because it impacted many domains that relate to SDGs, including but not limited to poverty, work, education, industry, partnerships, etc. The interdependencies of the collective impact are complex, making an a posteriori analysis comical. However, we do see the SDG layer cake as offering a lens to assist in designing sustainable futures with greater clarity, and with increased simplicity (Figure 0.9).

To guide us into the preferred scenarios of Designing Sustainable Futures, we are inspired by the spirit of Buckminster Fuller 1969 classic *Operating Manual for Spaceship Earth*. Like the **mariners** of old who used an Astrolabe to navigate the seas, we reuse this visual metaphor to help us maintain clarity while avoiding the traps of certainty in these unchartered waters. The mariner's Astrolabe symbolizes the harmony between human innovation and the natural world, guiding navigators across tumultuous seas by aligning celestial patterns with earthly coordinates. As Figure 0.10 represents, our Astrolabe includes the three layers of the SDG cake to set your direction, which acts as inspirational yet distant navigational star.[3] As a metaphor for designing sustainable futures, our Astrolabe represents our need to navigate complexities with precision and adaptability, ensuring our journey toward sustainability aligns with the universal principles of balance and interconnectivity.

Figure 0.9 Our Astrolabe: a navigational metaphor.

Source: By authors.

Further developing our visual metaphor of an Astrolabe, Designing Sustainable Futures is organized to structure theory, methods, and mindsets. Not to imply a linear process, the wayfinding map (Figure 0.10) aims to guide designers, educators, and leaders to anticipate, create, and lead transitions to flourishing futures via an SDG. Let's explore the regions charted by the Astrolabe:

Part I: Anticipate Better Futures: In Part I's three chapters, we build critical foresight skills to systematically analyze forces shaping the future and envision plausible, possible, probable, and preferable futures. **Chapter 1: Experiencing Foresight,** guided by foresight expert Dr. Jake Dunagan of IFTF, introduces strategic foresight methods including signals, drivers, scenarios, and assumptions mapping. You will gain skills to evaluate change forces and alternative futures. This chapter develops literacies in analyzing

Economy ▬▬▬▬ Society ▬ ▬ ▬ Biosphere

Figure 0.10 Designing sustainable futures – territorial map.
Source: By authors.

uncertainty, complexity, and speculation by embodying strategic forecasting. **Chapter 2: Speculating Futures**, guided by speculative design expert Manuela Celi, explores how speculative design informs and influences imagining future experiences. You will learn to map design's role in creating preferred futures. This chapter cultivates skills in speculative imagination and critical reflection on the norms, values, and assumptions that influence - often limiting - our capacity to envision better futures. **Chapter 3: Generating Visions**, advised by Jeremy Kirschbaum of IFTF, examines how generative technology like AI can enable collective visions and shared leadership. This chapter will prepare you to ethically and responsibly augment design using emerging tech. You will develop a more discerning attitude when using in technology for participatory futures. Part I equips learners with critical foresight methods to systematically analyze forces shaping the future. Through forecasting, speculation, and generative technology, these chapters provide tools to envision plausible, possible, and preferable futures.

Part II: Create Sustainable Experiences: Equipped with critical foresight methods, Part II's three chapters focus on designing tangible, experiential artifacts of sustainable futures. **Chapter 4: Building Worlds**, led by futurist Jacques Barcia of IFTF, applies science fiction worldbuilding to design solutions across the SDGs. You will develop scenario-creation skills linked to research-based insights essential for ideating and prototyping future scenarios. **Chapter 5: Shaping Systems**, taught by systemic thinker Professor Silvia Barbero of Politecnico di Torino, introduces Systemic Design's holistic methodology to create meaningful experiences within complex contexts. You will gain insights on how to see to relationships and perspectives within sustainability challenges. This chapter develops systems thinking and human-centered design competencies. **Chapter 6: Designing Fictions**, guided by design researcher Victoria Rodriguez Schon, explores Design Fiction as an approach to make critical concepts tangible through prototyping. You will learn to spark conversations about preferable futures through artifact creation that make sustainability solutions tangible and actionable. Part II facilitates the transition from analysis to action, providing human-centered design methods to make sustainability solutions experiential and tangible. Learners develop skills to design systemic interventions that address complexity.

Part III: Lead the Transition: With foresight and design skills developed, Part III's three chapters provide approaches to leading change through engagement, storytelling, and activation. **Chapter 7: Cultivating Collaboration**, led by participatory design expert Professor Anna Meroni of Politecnico di Milano, promotes Participatory Design to engage stakeholders in co-creating visions. You will learn facilitation methods for equitable, participatory processes. This chapter develops skills in stakeholder engagement, facilitation, and movement building. **Chapter 8: Making Stories,** taught by storytelling expert Professor Tommaso Buganza, introduces Storymaking to craft personal and systemic narratives that motivate change. This chapter builds skills for transformative storytelling across media. You will be able to craft compelling stories that engage values and perspectives. **Chapter 9: Mobilizing the Transition,** guided by Futures Architect Professor Joseph Press, shares the IDeaLs research to catalyze change for individuals, organizations, and societies. This chapter shares insights and techniques to increase agency by scaling collective leadership through shared visioning, co-creation, and conscious engagement.

By following the Designing Sustainable Futures' Astrolabe into your preferred future, you can expect to increase your understanding of strategic foresight, human-centered design, and social innovation to navigate complexity and catalyze sustainable futures. Blending speculative imagination, participatory engagement, and change activation, Designing Sustainable Futures inspires agencies to initiate transformations across industries, communities, and generations. When we shape futures together, another world emerges.

FUTURES LITERACY AS A CORE CAPABILITY

The future is not about what you have to do in the future.

It's about what you have to do now to create the future.

Vijay "VG" Govindarajan, Distinguished Professor,
Tuck School of Business, Dartmouth

At the center of any methodology, and the crux of all tools, is the practitioner's mindset. Inspired by the leaders of Bangladesh's transformation, and the many other stories and practitioners researched for this book, we see Futures Literacy as a critical mindset for designing sustainable futures. As developed by Riel Miller and spread across the globe by UNESCO (Miller et al., 2014, Miller, 2018; Cagnin et al., 2015), Futures Literacy elevates traditional forecasting by empowering individuals to imagine futures in order to influence the present with a spectrum of possibilities. As Miller describes, the future enables us to see the world differently. By increasing the awareness of today, Futures Literacy encourages what UNESCO Chair in Futures Literacy Loes Damhof calls "radical hope" (Damhof & Gulmans, 2023). With a strong resonance with what Christiana Figueres and Tom Rivett-Carnac, architects of the 2015 Paris Climate Agreement call "stubborn optimism" (Figueres & Rivett-Carnac, 2020), Futures Literacy will be essential for designing sustainable futures.

Recognizing plurality over prediction, and preferable over perfunctory, developing a Futures Literacy requires a dedication to deep inner work (as illustrated in the *Inner Development Goals*). The core capacities of enhancing perception, embracing complexity, and raising agency involve humility and openness to understanding the forces that shape potential futures and use this knowledge to reveal, reflect, and reframe one's anticipatory assumptions. Strengthening the anticipation and tolerance for emergence also demands a growth mindset, and a high penchant for neuroplasticity, in order for the emancipatory power of Futures Literacy to be activated.

With these developmental aspirations for all who seek preferable futures, rather than adhere strictly to Futures Literacy, we adapt the key competencies *Designing Sustainable Futures*. As illustrated in Figure 0.9, we begin in Chapter 1 by exploring how to **Experience Foresight** in ways that help us to anticipate and evaluate multiple futures. Such embodied experiences develop the ability to apply the "precautionary principle," to assess the consequences of actions and to deal with risks and changes. Chapter 2 examines how to **Speculate Futures** that question how narratives of the futures may inform and increase futures awareness. Learning how to **Generate Visions** in Chapter 3 explores how emerging technology megatrends can increase awareness and anticipation by raising the levels of creative confidence to new heights. Practitioners who are more confident to express their imaginations will be more prepared, and even feel more agency, to build more inclusive and sustainable worlds (Figure 0.11).

As we move into Part II: Creating Sustainable Experiences, we **Build Worlds** to develop our abilities to apply different problem-solving frameworks to complex sustainability problems and develop viable, inclusive, and equitable solution options that promote sustainable development, integrating the abovementioned competencies. As we **Shape Systems**, we develop the abilities to recognize and analyze relationships across complex systems. Those who can see the systems embedded within different domains and at

Figure 0.11 Futures literacy mosaic for designing sustainable futures.
Source: By authors.

different scales are more likely to be able to deal with uncertainty. To **Design Fictions** is to exercise the ability to learn from others, because the design object begs us to the needs, perspectives, and actions of others. The design dialog demands we go beyond mere empathy toward deeper presencing within a social synapse with others, essential to engage in participatory problem solving.

Part III: Mobilizing Leadership depends on knowing how to **Cultivate Collaboration**. The personal awareness required for real collaboration requires developing the capacity to understand and reflect on the norms and values that underlie one's actions. Enlightened practitioners are able to negotiate a plethora of priorities, values, principles, goals, and targets, in a context of

Introduction

conflicts of interests and trade-offs, uncertain knowledge, and contradictions. The practices of how to **Make Stories** develop the abilities to question norms, practices, and opinions. Given the role of stories in personal narratives and cultural myths, to consciously make a story of the future is to deeply reflect on own one's values, perceptions, and positions in a complex present. Lastly, those who understand the mysteries of how to **Mobilize Leadership** will have the ability to reflect, react, and revise one's own role in the local community and global society. Cultivating such connections with authenticity and patience is a limitless literacy for anyone embarking on the journey of designing sustainable futures.

By integrating Futures Literacy, Designing Sustainable Futures aims to spark curiosity and desire to further develop this core competency. At the end of each chapter, you will find suggestions for practitioner's journal entries, and stories of practitioners and their practices. We also share sources for additional inspiration, which ideally will trigger readers to curate even more knowledge as the wealth of resources continues to expand.

ARE YOU DIFFERENT?

...if you're not different, you are not able to envision another future, another world.

Greta Thunberg, Climate activist

As a final thought before designing sustainable futures, consider how different you are – do you want to *imagine* a more sustainable world, do you want to *create* more sustainable experiences, and do you want to *lead* together the transition to more sustainable practices?

If your purpose or raison d'etre aligns with any or all of these, then designing sustainable futures will be a valuable contribution to your mission. Learning how to apply strategic foresight, speculative design, and collective leadership is a necessary, but not sufficient condition to bring a more sustainable future closer to the present. The knowledge, skills, and confidence to navigate the uncertain future and drive the transition to a more sustainable future requires a deep conviction and steadfast resilience.

Designing Sustainable Futures is not intended to be linear or exhaustive, rather a tasting menu at the crossroads of a plethora of emerging practices. Our hope is that this will contribute to inspiring a new generation of leaders to collectively accelerate the transition to more sustainable practices. This transition is for the sake of people and the planet, enabled by communities who are interested in cultivating the commons rather than extracting from it. It aims to inspire those brave enough to make the choices for better futures.

Along our way, you will find many resources; here are a few to begin our journey:

- Fuel4Design – Future Education and Literacy for Designers (www.fuel4design.org)
- IFTF_Equitable_Futures_Toolkit (www.rb.gy/4w0jjh)
- Metafuture: Futures Studies (www.metafuture.org)
- UNESCO Chair In Futures Studies (www.flagship.iium.edu.my/unesco/)
- UNDP RBAP Foresight Playbook (www.rb.gy/qtt0bs)
- Nesta Participatory Futures (www.nesta.org.uk/project/participatory-futures/
- OECD Actionable Futures Toolkit (www.oecd-opsi.org/toolkits/actionable-futures-toolkit/)
- UK Government Futures Toolkit (www.gov.uk/government/publications/futures-toolkit-for-policy-makers-and-analysts)
- Centre for Strategic Futures (csf.gov.sg)
- Inner Development Goals (www.innerdevelopmentgoals.org)

Buon Viaggio!

Notes

1   Initiatives include Science-Based Targets initiative (SBTi), International Sustainability Standards Board (ISSB), Corporate Sustainability Reporting Directive (CSRD), Empowering Consumers for the Green Transition (EU website), to name a few. In the USA, the Federal Sustainability Plan focuses on climate change and includes partnerships, workforce development, and even equity-focused operations that aim to redress social and economic inequalities.

2   Ramona Liberoff, Executive Director, Platform for Accelerating the Circular Economy, encourages us to explore the choices along this spectrum in ways that encourage new descriptions of production methods (like circular design) and economic models (such as cooperatives) in more innovative ways. The current resource-centric descriptions of fulfilling human needs seem to be about closed product loops and recycling rather than the alternative business models, which will be needed more sustainable futures.

3   We intentionally are not referring to a specific star, like the North Star, to encourage everyone to focus on their own celestial viewpoint.

Part I

Anticipate Better Futures

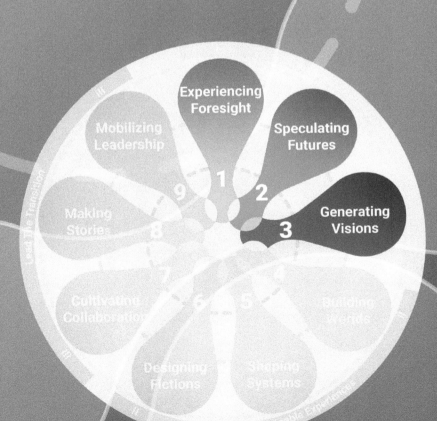

Part I of Designing Sustainable Futures explores the pivotal role of anticipation in catalyzing societal transformation toward sustainability. Rebecca Solnit (2004), an American writer and activist writes "What we dream of is already present in the world... (so) the future is determined in part by the stories we tell in the present." Solnit and others like her underscore the urgency of developing robust capabilities for anticipating future complexities. Well-crafted forecasts are indeed a necessary enabler to steer signals and trends toward sustainable futures. However, given the challenges of mobilizing for action in the present, anticipation is a necessary but insufficient condition for change. Despite the pressing need to anticipate more sustainable futures, our vision of the future is frequently obscured by a litany of cognitive biases, cultural habits, and institutional incentives. This is precisely where anticipating better futures is essential – dreaming can open new vistas for all the levers of designing sustainable futures.

Accordingly, we begin with Chapter 1 focusing on *Experiencing Foresight*, exploring how emerging foresight practices amplify the mechanisms of imagining futures. Informed by the work of Jake Dunagan, we share approaches that enable cultivating collectively the signals of change in ways that encourage crafting collective visions or probable, possible, and even preferable futures. Readers will gain insights into how more embodied forecasting can be a catalyst for anticipating sustainable futures. Chapter 2 then delves into *Speculating Futures*, harnessing the imagination-activating nature of design. With Professor Manuela Celi, we learn speculative approaches that reveal assumptions, challenge norms, and expand mindsets. This chapter shares methods to critically assess present trajectories, triggering alternative futures that can promote sustainability. Speculative design concurrently reveals the profound changes in ethics, policies, and lifestyles needed for transformation, thereby preparing stakeholders to think, and also act. Chapter 3 expands the potential of anticipation by investigating how emerging advances in artificial intelligence (AI) amplify *Generating Visions*. Guided by Jeremy Kirshbaum, we explore how generative AI augments the visual stories of more sustainable futures. Readers will gain insights on how to make sustainability more tangible at scale and across diverse sets of stakeholders. While

DOI: 10.4324/9781003451693-2

AI is still evolving, we see it as a potential supercollider of collective imagination for converging on shared aspirations of better futures.

Part I offers both theoretical perspectives and practical techniques to activate our imagination. As we immerse in foresight, speculative design, and generative AI, we can ask ourselves how might these capabilities empower practitioners to play an active role in building an equitable and sustainable tomorrow.

Let's explore the preferred future scenarios that could emerge if we anticipate better futures.

Networked Nexus

In the Networked Nexus, citizens find themselves in a dynamic equilibrium, where the pulse of global-scale production resonates through community-centric lifestyles. Daily life is a testament to this nexus, a harmonious blend of innovation and tradition, where vast networks of production fuel the economy and material prosperity, yet individuals remain deeply interconnected, sharing a collective conscience geared towards sustainable living.

Global
Production

Life in Steadfast Strands is marked by resilience and adaptability, as individuals navigate the complexities of a world dominated by large-scale production and its environmental and economic reverberations. Each day is a delicate dance on these tenuous threads, with citizens weaving through the challenges of a globalized economy, finding solace and strength by crafting a sense of solidarity through survival.

Steadfast Strands

Individual

Regenerative Weave

In the Regenerative Weave, every day threads a rich tapestry of community life, interlacing the strength of local production with the warmth of communal bonds. Citizens live in a vibrant, interconnected network, where the resilience of the weave is felt in every shared meal, every local product, and every community decision. This resilient fabric safeguards and enriches their lives because it is beautifully interwoven into a sustainable, harmonious, and adaptable existence.

Local
Production

The cornerstones of the Quiet Evolution is in the local production and personal responsibility. Every aspect of life, from the locally sourced food to the small-scale businesses, contribute to this silent uprising. The power of these quiet evolutionaries are amplified by the agency of its small-scale, crafting a society that's evolutionary in both its simplicity and awareness of a better future.

Quiet Evolution

1

Experiencing Foresight

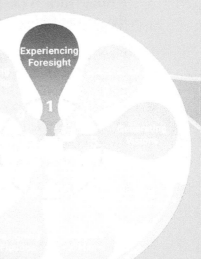

Our initial departure point for anticipating better futures is foresight, the set of practices that include collecting signals, understanding trends, and forecasting scenarios of plausible changes. We will venture from the basics of strategic foresight into the emerging practices of experiential foresight. Guided by the IFTF's Jake Dunagan, and informed by his work and others to expand foresight into more embodied experiences, we will see that such practices are essential for designers of more sustainable futures. When "experiential" foresight connects stakeholders deeply to a future, it becomes a critical catalyst for engagement through the journey toward more sustainable futures. Embodied experiences – as opposed to more intellectual, or cognitive activities – are seen as a catalyst for changing people's minds and specifically about sustainability-related topics such as climate change (see Ballew et al., 2022; WEF, 2022). It is in these shared experiences, we see an opportunity to amplify the learning of a competency fundamental for sustainability, UNESCO's anticipatory competency, namely "the ability to comprehend, assess, and formulate visions of various potential, likely, and desirable futures." With these simulated encounters and experiences, we can expand our comprehension, heighten our readiness, and augment our capacity to steer the course toward more sustainable futures.

THE EVOLUTION OF FORESIGHT

The origins of the foresight discipline, dedicated to contemplating prospective futures, finds its intellectual lineage in utopian writings such as the ancient Indian text Ramrajya, the work of the ancient Chinese philosopher Mozi (also known as Mo Tzu), and Plato's ideal city-states in the Republic. In the 19th century, science fiction expanded these seemingly human tendencies with the signals of industrialization. Although these early authors may not have explicitly identified themselves as practicing foresight, their forward-thinking narratives undeniably ignited the flames of our collective imagination into the future. These literary works diverged substantially from their contemporary realities, challenging preconceptions, common practices, and societal norms. They presented alternative futures that stretched the boundaries of

DOI: 10.4324/9781003451693-3

imagination, laying the groundwork for the formal development of the foresight discipline.

During the Cold War era, the discipline underwent significant formalization, a transformation characterized by a blend of geopolitical tensions and rapid technological advancements. A key figure during this period was Herman Kahn of the RAND Corporation, who integrated statistical analysis with intuitive insights to develop foundational methodologies for foresight. Kahn's work underscored the imperative of structuring an approach to envisioning and preparing for a range of possible outcomes. This methodological rigor laid a cornerstone for what would later evolve into the increasing use of foresight for strategic choices.

As foresight was inching closer to the growing industry of consulting, the discourse surrounding strategic foresight sprouted a new strand toward sustainability. In 1972, the publication of *The Limits to Growth* by the Club of Rome spotlighted the consequences of unchecked economic growth on environmental sustainability. A key contribution to the impact of this report was the World3 model. Developed a few years earlier by Jay Forrester, an engineer and systems scientist, it was the first time computer simulations were used to analyze long-term global trends in population, economics, and the environment. The resulting widespread debate on sustainability and the future of the planet shifted foresight's focus from a preoccupation with political and economic prospects to a more nuanced understanding that also embraced environmental and social dimensions. The report catalyzed the incorporation of sustainability considerations into foresight methodologies, steering the discipline toward a more globally conscious and resilience-oriented approach.[1]

Emerging against the backdrop of the burgeoning field of futures studies in the mid-20th century, the work of Dutch futurist Fred Polak brought a renewed focus on envisioning desirable futures. Polak's seminal book, *The Image of the Future*, articulated the motivational power of optimistic, idealized future visions in driving societal change. As a response to the horrors of World War II, Polak emphasized the necessity of a sustainability ethic grounded in intergenerational responsibility and highlighted the dangers of dystopian visions that could lead to societal fatalism and inaction.

It went on to inform and inspire the pioneering methodologies of futurists like Bertrand de Jouvenel and Herman Kahn, and generations of practitioners seeking to create a better world through futuring.

Elise Boulding expanded on Polak's foundational theories by providing a comprehensive model analyzing how societal images of the future emerge and in turn shape human behavior. Her concept of the "two-hundred year present" suggests a helpful timespan for envisioning sustainable futures, linking past, present, and future generations. As Boulding argued, developing a long perspective that acknowledges our interdependence with both ancestors and descendants can motivate responsibility and action on issues like climate change that impact far-future generations. Her model reinforces Polak's conviction that images of desirable sustainable societies can galvanize collective efforts to make that vision a reality. But enacting these shared images relies on individuals adopting an expanded temporal perspective and ethics of intergenerational care.

Both Boulding and Polak's work highlights the motivating power of positive future images and the dependency on the individual's temporal location, both physically and cognitively. Richard Slaughter (1991) found that reinvigorating anticipation capacity can occur through accessing cultural resources, critiquing images, running innovative workshops, and renegotiating problematic assumptions. When individuals take an active role in creating preferred futures, Slaughter observed, individuals and groups can rediscover motivational power to drive sustainability efforts. This is where the experience of foresight opens a new opportunity to engage people for better futures.

FOUNDATIONS OF FORESIGHT

An important contributor to codifying and democratizing foresight globally is the IFTF. Spun out of the RAND Corporation in 1968 as an independent nonprofit research organization, IFTF's many tools and training provide an essential foundation for foresight practitioners.

Fundamental to foresight practices are *signals and drivers*. Signals serve as preliminary indicators for emerging trends and transformations. Consider the increasing application of blockchain technology in ensuring sustainable supply chains. Such signals, often manifesting as minor yet impactful innovations or societal shifts, act as elemental constituents for anticipatory and future-oriented inquiry. Even though they might initially appear localized or of limited scope, the latent transformative capacity of these signals in the socio-economic sphere is substantial. Drivers, or trends, have the potential to either amplify or attenuate the influence of these early signals. For example, tax incentives enacted by governments to stimulate sustainable housing can be understood as a driver with the potential to transform a localized signal into a far-reaching societal transition. A signal-turned trend is the ascent of Environmental, Social, and Governance (ESG) criteria in reporting. Initially, related reporting was driven by local consumer demand or a company's brand identity. As sustainability increasingly became a societal priority, a driver of change, the EU made it into legislation. Drivers help foresight practitioners to leverage signals that may be in their formative stages or restricted to specific locales into increased clarity on potential future.

If signals provide raw materials for constructing visions of sustainable futures, and drivers act as the landscape that shapes visions, then systemic frameworks offer a simple yet comprehensive lens through which their complex interactions can be cultivated. One such framework is STEEP – Social, Technological, Economic, Environmental, and Political. This simple yet powerful analytical tool the influence of systems on individuals and organizations (Schwartz, 1991). As an example, the mapping of SDG 11 (in Figure 1.1) using the visual metaphor of a subway map provides a comprehensive understanding and enables a nuanced dialogue among stakeholders in an STES. The STEEP framework, when combined with signals and drivers, builds the basics of foresight that are essential for practitioners to anticipate sustainable futures.

Experiential Futures, as formulated by Candy and Dunagan, takes foresight a step further by connecting abstract possibilities with immersive experiences through storytelling, interactive interventions, and even imagined worlds to simulate future scenarios (Candy, 2010). It utilizes materiality and performance to enhance

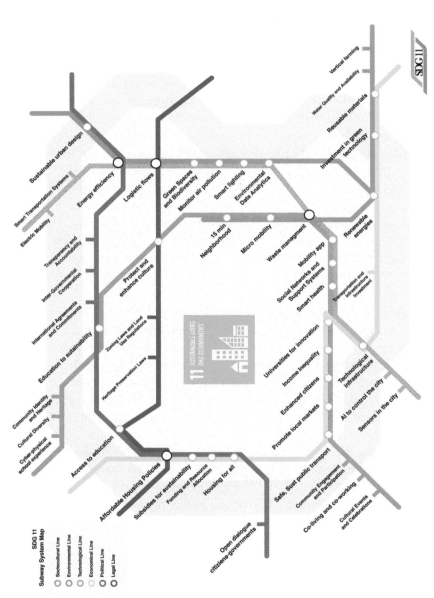

Figure 1.1 SDG 11 System subway map.

Source: Reprinted courtesy of Daniela D'agostino, Giorgia Lucini, Nicolas Torlaschi, Muhammad Arif Abdurrahman and

foresight's social impact (Candy & Kornet, 2017) by rendering glimpses into possible futures more tangible. The intent is to foster deeper connections by eliciting emotions – awe, joy, worry, and even discomfort – and stimulate creative dialogue about the future (Hayward & Candy, 2017).

With the goal to ignite emotional responses that reveal more about our shared human experience than what is possible with intellectual contemplation alone, Candy and Dunagan propose augmenting foresight with more embodied experiences. Embodied cognition, in contrast with disembodied views of cognition (Wilson & Golonka, 2013), suggests that our conceptual knowledge is shaped by bodily experiences (Shapiro, 2019). Embodied cognition research demonstrates that imagination and metaphor are grounded in physical interactions (Lakoff, 2015). These insights resonate with Polak and Boulding's emphasis on tangible future images as motivational. Envisioning sustainable futures through embodied metaphor, not merely data, makes ecological caring more intuitive. It also supports their views of sensory future images inspire commitment. Enabling groups to physically enact positive futures strengthens the collective purpose to achieve these visions. Walking through visualized sustainable cities triggers visceral responses unavailable to detached analytic minds (Abrahamson & Sánchez-García, 2016).

To aid practitioners in creating experiential futures, Candy and Dunagan created the "Experiential Futures Ladder" (Candy & Dunagan, 2017).

As illustrated in Figure 1.2, the Ladder acts as a guide to catalyze, capture, and analyze the foresight generated in a potential future. Acting as a "design brief" structuring an intervention's intentions, the *subject* at the top holds broad concepts like "sustainable world." This provides the setting, or frame, for the futures intervention. Moving down a level, practitioners create specific stories or *scenarios* within that theme. To incorporate the complexity of STES, we have added *systems* to acknowledge the underlying influences of the scenario, and what will inform the next rung, *scenes* designed to establish a stage for life to unfold in the imagined future. At the base are carefully crafted artifacts – *stuff* with symbolic meaning that are designed to make the future tangible, and also meaningful. For example, designers might introduce an algae-powered car

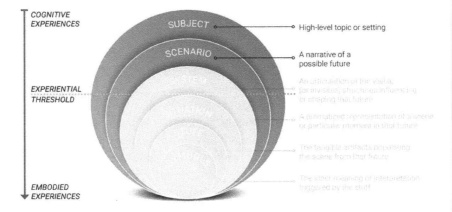

Figure 1.2 The Experiential Futures Ladder, spotlight on the subject.
Source: Adapted from Candy and Dunagan (2017).

or a tide-powered desalination gadget. We will explore these seemingly far-fetched objects in more detail in Part II, suffice it to say that now they are designed to elicit intrigue, skepticism, and optimism – reactions that drive deeper reflection. Their power comes from novelty and also from sparking conversations about what is important for stakeholders in the futures they want to create.

Embodied experiences, according to Dunagan, are a major part of the foresight ecosystem, but not the solution to the limitations of foresight. Making futures more visible, tangible, interactive, and even explorable reveals how current societal patterns, policies, and behaviors could shape future realities. These difficult questions require adept facilitation in safe spaces. Like any intervention in STES, the more embodied the experience is, the more responsibility practitioners of change have for ongoing engagement. Wrestling with complex issues collectively can act as a catalyst for change if there is clarity on the path of a futures intervention, as Futurist Anab Jain says "By putting ourselves into different possible futures, by becoming open and willing to embrace the uncertainty and discomfort that such an act can bring, we have the opportunity to imagine new possibilities." (TED, 2017).

The Experiential Futures Ladder ultimately leads to co-creating new *stories* about the future. Stories are the catalysts for even broader and deeper change, both individually and collectively.

Because stories help to transition from thinking present-forward to thinking preferred-futures, they are and will be an integral part of designing sustainable futures. For example, in a series of annual workshops started in 1993 on the Swedish island of Askö in the Baltic Sea, and organized by the Beijer Institute of Ecological Economics, a future of "earth stewardship" has guided a unique cooperation between internationally leading ecologists and economists throughout the years to shape a sustainable future through interacting policy and norm shifts (Chaplin et al., 2022). Our innate need for stories can empower us all to forecast more sustainable futures. As we set out on systemic transformation, enhancing our thinking about the possible, plausible, and even provocative futures becomes a necessary catalyst for change. It can enhance our adaptability and preparedness for the future, fostering resilience in the face of unpredictable climate turbulence. When we increase our capacity to anticipate the future, we anticipate the social changes, economic shifts, and of course the actions needed for a more sustainable future.

FOCUS ON EXPERIENCING FORESIGHT

For futures studies to impact mainstream culture and contribute to civilization-scale "social foresight" it must be capable of bridging the "experiential gulf" between abstract possible futures, and life as it is directly apprehended in the embodied present.

(Candy & Dunagan, 2016)

With our shared intention to emphasize and catalyze the focus on experiential interventions, particularly in the early stages of stakeholder engagement, we propose to focus Experiential Futures as a tool for engaged *foresight* – visualizing understandings, revealing assumptions, and increasing awareness. This resonates strongly with our initial definition of designing sustainable futures as co-creative actions with others that lead to tangible and shared sustainable solutions, and therefore intrinsically experiential. "Guerrilla interventions," for example, are a powerful experiential foresight because in these interventions, participants encounter unexpected scenarios in their daily lives – revealing rituals and aspirations. The surprises, though initially unsettling, become a significant learning opportunity, a chance to see the future differently, through a new lens, on the path to converging on a shared vision of the future.

Such provocative experiences to increase foresight on the potential outcomes of current unsustainable policies and behaviors simultaneously reveal the transformations that eco-friendly innovations and enlightened practices could catalyze (Chakrabarti & Mason, 2016). Participants might explore a grimy, run-down city suffering from the effects of climate disaster and pollution. Or they might explore the urban paradise flourishing with green technology, enlightened policies, and circular systems. This anchors abstract threats and opportunities in tangible sensations that reveal stakeholders' shared hopes and fears. With sustainability as the focus, experiential foresight reveals the signals of how current societal patterns and behaviors might potentially evolve in the future. For instance, are current trends of excessive consumption and waste compatible with a circular economy? Will political divisions and delaying tactics hinder progress on climate solutions? Visualizing various pathways forward brings the cascading implications to life and inspires timely action (Chakrabarti & Mason, 2016). For example, catching sight of futuristic objects like mixed reality goggles or algae packaging in a familiar store would arouse curiosity and challenge assumptions. Such interventions make sustainable futures tangible by revealing the signals and drivers of today.

Sharpening the focus on experiences in foresight seeks to amplify the insights and longer-term impact of designing sustainable futures. The refocus also reflects constructivist ethnographic and design research practices, such as Candy and Weber's Ethnographic Experiential Foresight (2017). The tangibility of experiential foresight makes us more aware of the present, ideally motivating and preparing us to take action to drive change. In the intervention Plastic Century (2010), we see clearly how experience renders foresight with more meaning.

With the objective to create an experience for the CA Academy of Sciences for World Oceans Day 2010, the foresight team set out to create an experience for participants to learn about their own levels of awareness and willingness to take action on ocean

Figure 1.3 Plastic century: interactive installation at California Academy of Sciences.

Source: Project by Stuart Candy, Jake Dunagan, Sarah Kornfeld and Wallace J Nichols, San Francisco 2010. Photo by Mike Estee.

pollution (Figure 1.3). The setting is the exponentially escalating plastic pollution crisis in our oceans. As global plastic production has skyrocketed, more and more plastic waste has flowed into marine environments through rivers, stormwater systems, and even winds carrying land litter out to sea. This has resulted in massive accumulations of plastic gathering in floating garbage patches and littering beaches worldwide. The environmental and public health impacts of this plastic epidemic have been disastrous. Microplastics are entering the marine food web at all levels, causing animals to suffer from malnutrition and chemical accumulation. Seafood consumption also risks human health as people ingest plastic-contaminated fish and seafood. With more plastic waste pouring into oceans than can be collected, the crisis continues to expand unchecked

The imagined *scenario* follows current trends of rampant plastic production and improper waste disposal, leading to over 250 million tons of plastic pollution in the ocean by 2030. Since plastic takes hundreds of years to degrade, the accumulation in marine environments is expected to continue exponentially given projections of plastic growth. The results would be devastating – more plastics than fish in our seas, with plastic waste littering even the most remote beaches and concentrations of suspended microplastics threatening entire marine ecosystems. Avoiding this scenario will require immense efforts to completely rethink plastic lifecycles, manage waste, curb unnecessary usage, develop alternatives, and redesign systems.

There are three main interconnected *systems* perpetuating the ocean plastic crisis that interventions must target. First, the maritime economy finds it cheaper to dump waste irresponsibly rather than invest in recycling infrastructure. Second, international geopolitics makes enforcement of ocean waste regulations extremely difficult across borders. Countries are reluctant to restrict plastics without global agreements. Finally, individual consumption patterns prioritizing convenience sustain demand for wasteful plastic packaging, single-use items, and ignorance about recycling. Though awareness is growing, most consumers continue using cheap disposable plastics out of habit. Tackling these systemic drivers across businesses, governments, and individuals is crucial to averting a plastic-filled future.

The immersive *situation* envisioned was a series of four clear open-top water coolers filled with increasing amounts of plastic waste, labeled with the years 1910, 1960, 2010, and 2030. The 1910 cooler had little plastic (reflecting the dawn of industrial plastic materials), but the amounts escalated over time, with the 2030 cooler overflowing to symbolize the exponential quantity projected if current plastic waste trends continue. The viscerally repulsive landscape of the 2030 cooler overflowing with mixed plastic trash provoked reactions of disgust and unease about the future, especially when participants were invited to drink from glasses placed near the coolers. This personalized the potential health impacts of rampant plastic pollution. The scene made the scenario of a future ocean devastated by orders of magnitude more plastic waste feel tangibly real and present to participants.

The *stuff* in Plastic Century was simple, but laden with symbolic meaning to create an embodied experience. The clear water coolers filled with different colored and labeled plastic waste items created a powerfully repellent landscape symbolic of projections. The nearby drinking glasses invited participants to react viscerally to ingesting plastics. Supporting signage labeled each cooler's year and plastic amount. This visually arresting setup required little explanation to instantly convey the scenario. The minimalist approach focused maximum impact on visualizing the data and eliciting emotions to motivate change.

Through this structured approach, the seemingly abstract or speculative elements of the experiential futures stories can be connected to the concrete and pragmatic aspects of decision-making and action. This approach uncovers potential challenges and opportunities while underscoring the implications of today's decisions on future generations, potentially increasing the likelihood of committing to more sustainable practices.

When experience amplifies foresight, it often does so by instilling a palpable sense of urgency. As experienced at Plastic Century, the future is not a distant objective, but a call for action now. In an intervention at Findlay, Ohio USA, Dunagan led a team to imagine an artifact meant to further conversations (and possibly inspire) better collective action toward opioid abuse. Created in a workshop in 2018, the Findlay Plan (Figure 1.2) was envisioned by Lydia Mihalik (mayor), Owen Carstensen (artist), Travis Kupp, and Jake Dunagan, to tell a story of a future where the town deployed effective holistic strategies, like access and affordability to treatment drugs, behavioral therapy, counseling, and a treatment-first approach, to empower the community to come together to make treatment a community-wide activity (Figure 1.4).

The Findlay National Monument poster tells a story that the people of Findlay ultimately saved themselves and created a model that inspired the world. This poster represents the triumph of the Findlay Plan, announcing the unveiling of a monument showing one resident reaching out to help another, symbolizing the collective defeat of addiction. Findlay is known as "Flag City," and flags were a key component of how helpers and those who needed help would find each other. This future empower any person who needed help would fly or wear a red flag. A person who was willing to help – anyone, anytime – flew or wore a blue flag. Those in recovery or those not able to help but who wanted to show their support flew

Figure 1.4 Findlay national monument poster.
Source: Courtesy of Owen Carstensen (2018). Reproduced with permission.

or wore a white flag. Soon, Findlay was covered in red, white, and blue. Those who needed help could find their blue helpers. Those in desperate need could hold something red and find helpers all around. The white was the beautiful background of a community coming together to save each other.

The Findlay Plan exemplifies how experiential foresight using the experiential futures ladder can script potential futures grounded in present realities, bring to life the systematic interconnections, and make plausible proposals. Such a story is designed to serve as a cognitive sandbox, spaces where we can safely explore, experience, and learn from possible futures. Environmental and social challenges often necessitate us to contemplate consequences that extend beyond our immediate realities and into a future we may not live to witness. Experiential foresight revealed the mechanisms that were inhibiting change because the stories described what overcame those same challenges. It enables stakeholders to overcome temporal barriers to empower thinking (and planning) about what could impact of today's decisions. By immersing ourselves in these future scenarios, experiential foresight narratives can stimulate profound reflection, inspire sustainable behaviors, and cultivate a lasting commitment to more sustainable practices.

EXPERIENCING FORESIGHT IN GAMEPLAY

As experience develops anticipatory capabilities, gaming offers another opportunity for more meaningful foresight. Gaming has been experiential since humanity started "playing." With the rise of climate-change games including Climate Fresk, SustainAble, Daybreak, and New Energies from Catan Studios, there is an important trend for how games will contribute to experiential foresight (McGonigal, 2022). For example, recent observations of students participating in the World Climate Simulation from Climate Interactive, the MIT Sloan Sustainability Initiative, and the UMass Lowell Climate Change Initiative – a game modeled after the UN where participants representing different nations create a global climate agreement – saw gains in the participant's climate change risk perception to the simulation and reported gains in collective efficacy as a result (Hensel et al., 2023).

The potential gains from gaming resonate with the work of Taqi Shaheen and Sara Khan Pathan, artists and change practitioners based in Karachi, Pakistan. Working with the community on a nearby island of Bhit, they saw a need to foster a deeper understanding of the community's multi-generational relationship to their land and sea and also trigger envisioning and creating sustainable change. This small fishing community has contended with "scarcity of natural resources, excessive dredging, sea level rise, deforestation, oil spills, overfishing, coastal erosion" and industrial encroachment (BBC Podcast, 2022). The community, as a prototypical coastal settlement, is on the "first line of defense" and often the first hit by calamities like floods. The indigenous residents rely on fishing for their livelihoods, but decades of environmental degradation, climate change impacts, and lack of investment in local infrastructure have threatened their way of life. Without access to fish or alternate sources of income, the community struggles to survive. Children often forego schooling to join their fathers fishing just to make ends meet. The systemic challenges span ecological, economic, political, and social realms, intertwined in complex ways. There is an urgent need to engage with the community to reveal the historical and cultural narratives that may create hope and agency, particularly for the next generation, for facing present-day crises threatening their livelihoods (Figure 1.5).

Figure 1.5 Top images: film stills from a documentary by Taqi Shaheen and Sara Khan Pathan on participatory sessions at Bhit Island near Karachi (2014). Bottom Image: Playtests with the community kids, Bhit Island by Taqi Shaheen and Sara Khan Pathan (2022).

Shaheen and Pathan decided to collaborate on an approach to engage with the islanders, learn their stories, and explore how art and design could catalyze systemic change, which faces immense systemic challenges. As Shaheen explains, their intention was not to conduct a detached "parachute research" project. Rather, the duo aimed to develop a real understanding of the community's culture, past traumas, and future hopes through empathy and deep listening. As they spoke with local children in hands-on educational activities about the island's ecology, they discovered many students later dropped out of school to become fishermen themselves. This sobering reality led Shaheen and Pathan to focus on creating "imaginative interfaces" that could reveal the social complexities at play and stimulate discussion about potential solutions.

To immerse players in the systemic challenges facing the Bhit fishing community, Shaheen and Pathan designed an interactive board game called Machi Wachi. The name derives from the local Kutchi language, with "Machi" meaning fish and "Wachi" meaning everything else. The game is set in a near future where resources are scarce. Players take on the role of islanders navigating choppy seas to catch fish while confronting storms, dredging, and other calamities. The game mechanisms require collaborating to survive with limited natural reserves of fish, water, mangroves, and more. Each player has a tribe of islanders and boats to traverse sea routes laid out on the game map inspired by the island's geography. The goal is to secure enough resources to place three "anchors" on the sustainability track before other players, signaling your community has successfully adapted to withstand crises. Players must make strategic decisions about where to fish when to reinforce sea walls, how to avoid border conflicts, and how to balance short-term needs with long-term sustainability. Authentic artwork and real portraits bring the islanders' stories to life. The game integrates real scenarios like storm warnings and utopian dream cards based on interviews with the community. As Shaheen says, "You have to address all of those stakes. And hence the learning emerges out of it, rather than you are thrown in with all of these bits of information..." (Figure 1.6).

Machi Wachi exemplifies how games serve as "cognitive sandboxes" for experiential foresight. This experiential nature of the

Figure 1.6 Machi Wachi: an environmental strategy board game by Taqi Shaheen and Sara Khan Pathan (2022).

game fosters systemic understanding organically through play. The interactive roleplaying makes abstract threats feel viscerally real. As players navigate scarce resources and calamities turn-by-turn, they gain empathy for the difficult tradeoffs facing islanders. The game mechanics require collaborating to survive, promoting systems thinking. For instance, drawing "storm warning" cards makes the danger of floods tangible, revealing how environmental factors shape islanders' lives. Character cards with backstories and portraits humanize the community members. Players see how political borders impose risks, as fishermen can accidentally cross into disputed territory. The game integrates real scenarios from interviews with residents, like aspirations to move into multi-story apartments on reclaimed land. Visualizing diverse perspectives helps players grasp the social complexities, which is critical for collective learning. Since the game reflects diverse subcultures it foster empathy across locales. By experientially navigating scarce resources and crises, players gain systemic insight organically. The immersive simulation motivates collaborative solutions, like youth appreciating elders' flood survival knowledge. Making socio-environmental challenges concrete enables creative adaptation strategies (Figure 1.7).

Moving forward, Shaheen and Pathan aim to build on the experiences of Machi Wachi's experiential foresight by expanding

Figure 1.7 Playtests with community members and politicians by Taqi Shaheen and Sara Khan Pathan (2022).

its reach. They plan to partner with coastal communities worldwide to customize the game's scenarios and characters. Across the water in Karachi, where many public parks have been lost to commercial and housing development projects, the game is an opportunity to imagine and develop foresight on possible futures for a rapidly growing, complex city. The designers also intend to develop a digital version of Machi Wachi. This will enable broader access to the game, allowing players globally to gain systemic understanding of coastal communities' realities. The digital game also creates opportunities to gather data and quantify insights across populations. Additionally, Shaheen and Pathan hope to inspire a genre of experiential foresight games tackling sustainability issues. They believe leveraging art, storytelling, and interactivity can strengthen public engagement and awareness. Games like Machi Wachi reveal shared human experiences, transforming players from bystanders to active participants in shaping resilient futures. However, as Casey Crownhart writes: "A simple game that crowns a winner may be more playable, but it doesn't represent how complicated the climate crisis is, or how urgently we need to address it." (Crownhart 2024).

EXPERIENCING FORESIGHT: A PRACTITIONER'S POSSIBLE JOURNAL ENTRY

Foresight that includes the foundational frameworks, gaming, or other embodied experiences stimulates our awareness of the assumptions we hold about the future. This is the first step in increasing our anticipatory capacity because it stimulates a different epistemology for understanding and relating to alternative realities. When practiced collectively, foresight encourages us to co-conceive a variety of futures, assess their consequences, and inform our choices for changes. Within the context of sustainability, foresight underscores the need to envision alternative futures collectively by the stakeholders

Figure 1.8 Designing sustainable futures literacy: experience foresight.

Source: By authors.

of that future. By emphasizing the experiential in the foresight process, we aim to encourage 'fore-acting' – taking a proactive approach to create a more sustainable world. Since foresight fosters a sense of agency, the more embodied the experience is, the stronger our sensibilities for a more sustainable world will be.

Foresight empowers practitioners to expand the status quo parameters and adopt new, embodied ways to design sustainable futures. By strengthening our anticipatory competencies with experiential foresight, we can collectively envisage and realize preferable futures that proactively transform society rather than reactively respond. Experiential foresight leverages the potency of sensory and emotional involvement to inhabit possible futures. These simulated encounters heightens our readiness, expands our comprehension, and augments our capacity to steer the course toward more sustainable futures. By enhancing our anticipatory capabilities with experience, we are also empowered to shape-shift as needed along the journey, between futurist and facilitator, and synthesizer and storyteller. As our interventions expand to include more immersive experiences that emotionally and sensorially engage us with potential futures, we elevate our readiness, challenge our cognitive biases, and broaden our perspectives, ensuring more informed and strategic decision-making.

Enhancing our anticipatory capacities through embodied experiences also increases our sense of being, by being ready to be "…surprised by simulation rather than blindsided by reality." (Dunagan & Candy, 2016). To future develop your futures literacy *experience foresight* (Figure 1.8), check out these resources:

- OECD OPSI Actionable Futures Toolkit (www.oecd-opsi.org/toolkits/actionable-futures-toolkit/)
- The Future Is Ours: Strategic Foresight toolkit – | Save the Children' (https://resourcecentre.savethechildren.net/pdf/strategic_foresight_toolkit_online.pdf/
- EU SEP: Horizon Scanning Toolkit (www.sepa.org.uk/media/367059/lsw-b4-horizon-scanning-toolkit-v10.pdf)
- ESPAS Strategic Foresight Primer (https://espas.secure.europarl.europa.eu/orbis/system/files/generated/document/en/epsc_-_strategic_foresight_primer.pdf)

- Singapore Government Driving Forces Cards (https://www.csf.gov.sg/media-centre/publications/csf-df-cards/)
- CIFS Using the Future (https://cifs.dk/news/new-scenario-report-using-the-future/)
- World Climate Simulation (www.climateinteractive.org/world-climate-simulation/)
- SustainAble (www.sustainable-sim.com)
- CATAN- New Energies (https://www.catan.com/catan-new-energies)

As we conclude this exploration of experiential foresight and its role in shaping sustainable futures, we seamlessly transition into the next phase of our journey. In Chapter 2, "Speculating Futures," we delve deeper into the speculative aspects of foresight. This next chapter opens a world where we speculate on potential futures, to imagine what might be and to critically examine and creatively engage with the possibilities that lie ahead. Here, we will explore how speculative thinking can further amplify our anticipation capabilities.

Note

1 Important to note for our reflections Herbert Simon`s comment that "The Club of Rome report predicted both too much and too little. It predicted too *much*, because its specified doomsday dates are not believable, and if believable, would not be important. We do not want to know when disaster is going to strike, but how to avoid it… For most design purposes, that is as much prediction as we need." (Simon, *The sciences of the artificial*, 3rd ed., p. 147)

2

Speculating Futures

Speculating
Futures

2

As we strengthen our ability to forecast futures with experiential foresight, speculating what those futures could be amplifies our anticipatory capacity for designing more sustainable futures. Guided by Professor Manuela Celi, in this chapter, we will explore how speculating what a future could be concurrently creates the context for change. Speculative design draws from the traditions and practices of design research, design futures, Design Fiction, and scenario building to spark our collective imagination. Because design is at its core, speculation is inherently a participatory activity, as the designed object – whether it be scenario, story, or forecast – is shared at the nexus of the creator's and stakeholder's experience. This epistemological position encourages speculative design practitioners to question the dominant assumptions and propose alternative ways of working with them (Design Council, 2006). By visualizing possible futures, we will learn about an important complement to our experiential foresight practices, which activates both the setting and scenarios in experiential futures ladder.

As we delve into the theory and practice of speculating futures with design, we will further develop the abilities to acquire and hone the strategic skills to collaboratively devise and execute innovative actions that promote sustainability locally and beyond (Miller, 2018). These practices are exemplified in the practices of Cherry-Ann Davis, a maker and creator, storyteller, and an independent researcher with a specialization in hybrid ethnography, focusing on Pan African narratives. Speculating futures encourages us all to design for critical thinking and acting, essential elements in our journey to design more sustainable futures.

DESIGN AND FUTURES: INTERTWINED STORIES

Herbert Simon's definition of design, which underscores the effects and outcomes of design actions, emphasizes the transformative nature of the discipline. This viewpoint aligns with a shift in future thinking, referred to as "futures design culture," which includes both creative making and critical analysis. This culture at a collective level, and mindset at an individual level, increases the capacity for anticipatory making within design practice because it enables the understanding and creation of affordances that address emerging complexities. By incorporating future thinking into the design process, designers actively shape potential futures,

DOI: 10.4324/9781003451693-4

as Professor Ruha Benjamin reminds us to "Remember to imagine and craft the worlds you cannot live without, just as you dismantle the worlds you cannot live within." (Benjamin, 2019).

The intersections between design and foresight methodologies offer a rich space for enhancing our collective comprehension of the present, past, and future of a sustainable world. Given that designers and design researchers are perpetually navigating a world marked by complexity and unpredictability, the relationship between design and futures is of particular significance. It becomes imperative to acknowledge the escalating significance of forging a robust link between design and the ability to anticipate, a concept we could term anticipation-focused exploration.

While traditional future studies tend to be more connected to policy-level discussions and may be less visible due to their intangible nature, design, on the other hand, is often perceived as concrete and material, manifesting in products and services. Design is intimately linked with the creation of theories and models that reconcile beliefs and desires. Furthermore, design possesses the vital capacity to anticipate the alignment between theories and models, which can only be confirmed through experimentation or the actual manifestation of the designed artifact. The conceptualization of futures thinking, creation, and critical analysis in terms of anticipation has led to the incorporation of knowledge and experience from design into the task of shaping futures. Design can be seen as an "ars anticipandi," offering a framework for investigating and predicting future possibilities.

These differences lay the groundwork for a robust collaboration between the two fields. By capitalizing on their unique skills, we can stimulate the expansion of design action informed by insights from future studies and foresight viewpoints. Simultaneously, design can give physical form to future concepts derived from other disciplinary angles. Design's capacity to predict future outcomes may not be a surprise to futurists, but it becomes intriguing when examined from a cross-disciplinary standpoint. There is value in the ability of design to project results by leveraging past experiences and drawing from current situations and challenges. What distinguishes design is its unique ability to convert these interventions into tangible and intangible forms (Margolin, 2007).

As two distinct epistemologies – ways of knowledge creation and sharing – the design and futures dialog reveals the breadth and depth of sustainability problems and solutions. With design as constructivist, and futures more inductive, then imagination connects in the service of expanding anticipation. As narrative plays a significant role in both combining the complementary storytelling perspectives delivers narratives with more richness and rigor. Because the future, like the present, contains a cultural domain, designers who conceptualize more responsible futures can weave in the deeper meanings that come with cultural constructs. Futures encourages designers to surpass conventional design limitations and prompt critical reflections on the state, particularly about production and consumption, key levers of a more sustainable world. Design can help Futures to go beyond what Sohail Inayatullah refers to as "futures theatre" – futuring without impact – by more embodied experiences. Similarly, futures can help design go beyond the "post-it parties" of design thinking by engaging deeply in the collective imagination in future-oriented narratives.

This convergence of specific design-centric knowledge systems with the growing future literacy observed across various disciplines, especially among design scholars and practitioners, prompts inquiries about our ability to influence the future. Despite the shared challenges encountered by both fields in securing recognition within the academic sphere, they share considerable similarities. For instance, as a discipline, design has struggled to be recognized as a subject worthy of study and exploration, despite its long-established tradition. In a parallel manner, future studies also face challenges in earning acceptance from the scientific community due to their association with order and chaos.

Over the past decade, design-based inquiry has transitioned from being primarily focused on professional education and practice to becoming an emergent and multifaceted research domain in its own right. This research domain emphasizes future thinking, social innovation, and the creative, cultural, and socio-technical aspects of creation. It also investigates the connections between design tools and research methodologies. Indeed, a broad array of tools and methods available for Designing Futures (see a partial list at the end of this chapter) which are utilized at various stages of the process, such as research, conceptualization, and visualization, similar to the Metadesign approach (Fischer & Giaccardi, 2006). However, we believe that there is no single correct methodology when overlapping Futures studies and Design studies. This plurality is also a significant aspect, revealing that there is just one possible trajectory, but that each individual harbors multiple visions.

An example of this intersection is the analysis of trends. Since they signal the direction of changing behaviors, trends are a key factor in futures studies, yet perhaps even more so in Design Fiction. Trend research identifies minor, weak signs that could potentially trigger larger shifts in society and culture, fueled by external factors and drivers of change. Interpreting these along the timeline allows for the understanding of how these novel and varying behaviors might impact people's values, ideas, consumption patterns, and so on. Designers are instrumental in interpreting and converting these insights into specific frameworks that encompass both tangible and intangible qualities, ranging from beliefs and priorities to aesthetic codes.

The trends timeline is an example of a tool that exploits the intersection between design and futures. It is a graphical depiction of the evolution and interplay of various trends over a period of time. This tool enables professionals to monitor the progression of trends, recognize patterns, and understand their influence on industries, markets, or society. A typical trends timeline is composed of chronological markers that highlight significant events, developments, or shifts across different domains. Through the analysis of a trends timeline, professionals can glean insights into the emergence and maturation of trends, spot potential convergences or divergences, and anticipate future opportunities or challenges tied to these trends. It proves to be an invaluable instrument for strategic planning, innovation, and maintaining a competitive edge in a swiftly changing landscape.

Drawing from firsthand experience, the Fuel4Design project[1], funded by the European Community, engaged multiple European universities with design futures-oriented courses to work on theoretical and practical outputs on futures literacy, specifically in relation to design futures education. This two-year project resulted in the creation of a series of templates, designed as supporting guides for educators to incorporate into their curriculum. The team at Politecnico of Milan put these templates to the test in a variety of courses, including the Polimi Future Fiction's course from the Integrated Product Design Master's Degree program.

Typically introduced in the early stages of a design future project, following broad research of weak signals exploring the present context, the Timeline tool provides a broader understanding how trends are rooted in past actions and how they can develop in the future, enabling the imagination to project multiple evolutionary paths. It does so by charting representative trends and tracking their progression over time. Its flexibility and openness offers users to adapt it to how they see fit. Users can define a specific time frame, starting from the present or the recent past, and can even create multiple timelines that diverge at key moments in time, thus constructing a shared narrative through visual strategies. The tool's strength lies in its exploratory nature, particularly in terms of visualization, narrative creation, and envisioning possibilities (Figure 2.1).

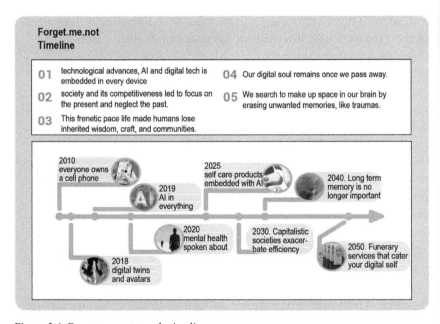

Figure 2.1 Forget.me.not trends timeline.

Source: Polimi future fictions (2019). With permission.

Part I: Anticipate Better Futures

DESIGN FOR CRITICALITY

As design and futures methodological branches become even more intertwined, their roots remain deep in speculation. Critical design, rooted in the Greek origin of "kritikós," denotes a discerning and judgmental approach aimed at dissecting and analyzing elements to make informed judgments. This process involves the deconstruction and examination of worldviews and phenomena, emphasizing questioning and interrogation rather than adopting a negative viewpoint. Critical design embodies a stance of scrutiny and analysis, focusing on revising perspectives and understanding rather than following a predefined process.

Many scholars trace the origins of Critical Design back to the Italian Radical Design period, which emerged in the late 1950s as a response to the Italian economic miracle. This movement, also known as Anti-design or Linea Italiana, challenged traditional values and rejected market-driven approaches to design. This avant-garde movement, comprised of groups like Archizoom, 9999, Superstudio, and U.F.O., and individual contributors such as Alessandro Mendini, Ugo La Pietra, and Riccardo Dalisi, crafted utopian and dystopian future visions as forms of critique and provocation (Figure 2.2). These groups produced projects

Figure 2.2 A Journey from A to B by Superstudio (1971) shows a satirical glance at modernist utopias, hailed as civilization's zenith over twenty thousand years (Ambasz, 1972).

Source: Public domain, reprinted under Creative Commons.

and products that defied mass production and consumption norms, focusing instead on intellectual and symbolic value. They introduced symbolism and emotional engagement into their designs, transcending utilitarianism and industrial functionality. Fiona Raby notes that the Critical Design approach builds upon the attitude of the Radical Design movement from the 1970s, which questioned the prevailing values of the time. The connection between Critical Design and the Radical Design movement is widely acknowledged in the literature and serves as a foundational reference point for understanding the evolution of design paradigms (Figure 2.3).

In the outstanding 1972 exhibition at MOMA titled "Italy: the New Domestic Landscape, " curator Emilio Ambasz identified three primary streams within Italian design practices at that time. Ambasz characterized these movements as counter-design, which encompassed the reformist, conformist, and even antagonist perspectives. The exhibition portrayed Italy as a microcosm where the possibilities, limitations, and critical issues of contemporary design converged. Ambasz emphasized the importance of philosophical discourse and social and political involvement in

Figure 2.3 Image by Superstudio exhibited in 1972 in Italy: the new domestic landscape at MoMA (Ambasz, 1972).

Source: Public domain, reprinted under Creative Commons.

effecting structural changes in society. This definition underscores the significant impact of radical design movements and their role in sparking discourse and transformation within design practices as epitomized in these quotes:

> Culture, and the making of culture, the formal act of doing so, doesn't mean expressing oneself through allegory or metaphor. It is a political right, not a subject for linguistic criticism. It is the task of rediscovering and asserting those physiological capacities that are linked to the body's material substance and the electrical energy of the nervous system. Thanks to these, the making of art or the making of culture take on a meaning quite complete in themselves, like a kind of liberating psycho-physiotherapy.
>
> (Ambasz, 1972, p. 234)

> The self-production and self-consumption of culture imply the ability to free oneself from all those repressive systems that 'official culture' has woven around us, by attributing an infinite variety of 'values' and 'meanings' to the reality around us and thus, in fact, taking away our freedom to modify that very environment at will. Our task, then, is to reduce to zero the moral weight of things, methodically questioning all the patterns of religious, aesthetic, cultural, and even environmental behavior.
>
> (Ambasz, 1972, p. 235)

Consequently, speculative design first emerged in the early 21st century; it sits at the intersection of design, philosophy, and anticipation. Its theoretical underpinnings are deeply rooted in the philosophy of science and epistemology, particularly in Karl Popper's philosophy. Popper, known for his work on the philosophy of science, emphasized the importance of falsifiability in scientific theories, arguing that no number of experiments could ever fully prove a theory, but a single counter-example could disprove it. This philosophy resonates with speculative design's approach to exploring multiple possible futures without committing to a single, definitive outcome.

Speculative design evolved from its early practices of the Italian Radical to its contemporary conceptualization by designers Dunne and Raby. In their influential book *Speculative Everything* (2013), design becomes a means of speculating about how things could be. This approach was a departure from designing for the world as it is to imagining how it could be, encompassing the broader scope of social, political, and environmental implications. Studios like Superflux and Studio Drift have exemplified this approach, merging art, technology, and critical thinking to create works that challenge our perceptions of reality and provoke discourse on future possibilities.

For instance, the project "United Micro Kingdoms" by Dunne and Raby presents four fictional kingdoms, each representing different social, political, and technological models. This project stimulates discussion on the kind of future society might want to avoid or pursue. Similarly, Superflux's "Mitigation of Shock" envisions a future affected by climate change, presenting a transformed domestic environment adapting to food scarcity. Speculative design has also been employed to envision and test out urban scenarios and policies before they are implemented. For instance, city councils and urban planners use speculative design to simulate the outcomes of urban policies on city life, allowing them to make more informed decisions. In the realm of technology, speculative design aids in assessing the societal and ethical implications of emerging technologies, serving as a sandbox for exploring the potential consequences and ethical dilemmas posed by these innovations.

Speculative design is a critical tool for making sustainable experiences more visible. Its strength lies in its ability to make abstract concepts tangible and emotionally resonant. This is crucial in the context of sustainability, a field often overwhelmed with data and distant projections. For example, project like "Planetary Personhood" by Nonhuman Nonsense is a speculative design initiative proposing Mars as an independent entity with rights, prompting reflection on our interaction with a supposedly lifeless planet. The studio fosters debate on space decolonization, exploring in a creative way the topics of nonhuman relations and ethics. Through its critical approach, speculative design subverts the established colonial legacies embedded in design norms, advocating for a plurality of narratives and visual languages that empower diverse, decolonized futures.

As a design discipline, speculative design encourages interdisciplinary collaboration, bringing together designers, scientists, policymakers, and the public. This collaborative approach ensures that diverse perspectives are included in shaping futures, leading to more equitable and sustainable outcomes. The participatory potential of speculative design empowers communities and democratizes future-making, encouraging a multivoiced and multivisioned approach by fostering a sense of agency and responsibility toward their future.

Design Fiction is a method increasingly applied when speculating futures. While some frameworks consider Design Fiction as a subset of Speculative Design, others perceive them as complementary approaches. Dunne and Raby (2013) note the close alignment between Speculative Design and Design Fiction, often using the terms interchangeably. Design fiction sits at the intersection of design and futures. It was first introduced by science fiction author Bruce Sterling in 2005. Sterling has honed his definition over time, describing Design Fiction as the deliberate use of narrative prototypes to convince us of potential changes (Sterling, 2005).

While Design Fiction may seem similar to conventional science fiction, the former offers a more pragmatic and hands-on approach to experiencing the future. It may forego some of the awe-inspiring elements of science fiction, but it delves deeper into the intricacies of social-technical conflicts (Sterling, 2005). As he wrote in 2005, "Design fiction is the deliberate use of diegetic prototypes to suspend disbelief about change." Breaking down this statement, we could begin by stating that the term 'deliberate use' implies that Design Fiction is executed with a clear intention and objective. The term 'diegetic' is borrowed from performance studies, where film and theatre employ scenarios, props, and sets to bolster a narrative, which also resonates with speculative design.

When integrated into a speculative process, Design Fiction acts as a catalyst for igniting creative thinking, posing questions, and exploring a plethora of conceivable futures (Celi & Formia, 2017). Speculative Design, activated by the "stuff" of Design Fiction, creates a space for discussion, promoting dialogue and facilitating transformation within the frame of design research (Celi & Formia, 2017). It is a catalyst for change, opening up new opportunities and enhancing individuals' capacity to navigate uncertainty. This concept is not only confined to purposeful materials created for design-related goals, it also includes other cultural objects that similarly contribute to shaping future visions (Candy & Dunagan, 2016). It generates social value through design by heightening awareness, fostering collective involvement, and incorporating expertise from non-designers. The speculative design project evolves into a critical medium for scrutinizing the present, formulating tangible tools, and exploring and sharing possibilities. In this manner, speculation can trigger a transformational process by aligning with the six primary characteristics identified by the Design Council (2018). It functions upstream of traditional briefs, engaging in a more undefined framework. It mediates diverse viewpoints through cross-disciplinary dialogue and utilizes participatory design techniques that include users and front-line workers. By comprehending and molding relationships, Design Fiction transcends the delivery of tangible artifacts and strives to instill a distinct critical mindset in everyday life.

ACTIVATING SPECULATIVE PRACTICES

Design fiction, as a practice that investigates the future while embracing uncertainties, is a contemporary manifestation of the speculative practices of the Italian Radicals. To speculate a future, Design fiction projects often use prototypes and media content to illustrate the potential provocations of a future scenario. In a Design Fiction project from Polimi Futures Fiction course, Forget.me.not reflects on the memories and methods of dealing with various types of traumas. Three objects focus on three distinct kinds of memories, gestural and ritualistic motions, stressful and anxiety-related thoughts, and physical trauma, among others. Each product offered a specific use that helped the user in erasing the different types of memory to overcome certain life experiences. The scenario description sets the context in the year 2368 in Eurasia. The constant exposure to social media and the internet has led the civilized world to attribute increasing value to their image. Everyone is the curator of their own digital soul. The obsession with curating the appearance of our lives led to the need to curate life itself. From the outset, memories have always been the closest thing to the identity we possess, they compose our ego. High-tech beauty companies have developed devices capable of communicating with our brain and erasing the memories we wish to get rid of, curating our personality from the core. Curating memories is now part of the routine of many affluent individuals: the market is a growing trend and there are now three products that have come out with the latest upgrade (Figure 2.4).

Another Design Fiction story is that of egstrogen farms. Throughout history and current events, we can find numerous instances of speculative and critical design practices. Today, many exploratory studios are merging art, science, and design to bring critical projects and research to a variety of audiences. The use of anticipatory design-driven tools is diverse and widespread. A multidisciplinary approach is evident, with audiences and users being engaged through various mediums such as gallery and museum exhibitions, Design Fiction videos, provotypes (provoking prototypes), and images and photomontages shared on social media.

In these examples, we see that Design Fiction has a transformative power due to its ability to circulate new visions and potential futures. This power is influenced by the unique style and artistic approach of each designer or artist. The level of engagement it generates is often directly proportional to the strength of its aesthetics and its ability to convey clear messages, thereby increasing people's awareness of certain issues. However, there is a potential bias where Design

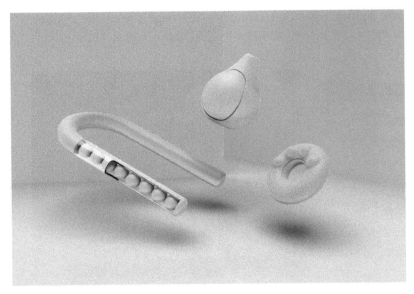

Figure 2.4 Forget.me.not poster and video stills showing the use of prototypes to effectively communicate scenarios.

Source: Polimi Futures Fictions (2019). With permission.

Fiction aims to create a strong initial impact through shock, fear, or extremism, resulting in critical yet dystopian visions that are rooted in the extreme consequences of current problems.

The subjects tackled by these projects intersect with a broad range of values, including ethical, technological, economic, social, and political implications, among others. The issues being addressed span a wide spectrum, from reproductive rights to healthcare and gene editing, and from the future of the workforce to speculative leisure activities. The sectors being studied are determined by the backbone of the research, but are also kept relevant to current debates. This way they aim to stimulate thought and discussion on critical issues that could shape future trajectories.

A case in point is egstrogen farms by Mary Maggic at the MIT Media Lab. This project featured a women-targeted commercial on transgenic chicken eggs, or egstro-eggs, which contain specific amounts of estrogen to address fertility deficiencies. Egstrogen farm is portrayed as a fictional company that genetically modifies hens to produce eggs with high levels of gonadotropins in their whites. These eggs are sold in grocery stores just like any other egg carton. Consuming these eggs results in a higher egg count for women who are egg donors or trying to conceive. Through the catchy slogan "One egg a day is the fertility way," Maggic aims to expose the

Figure 2.5 Video still from the egstrogen farms commercial showing the genetically modified eggs in their packaging.

Source: Courtesy of Mary Maggic.

Part I: Anticipate Better Futures

rhetoric behind bio-consumerism, combining it with imagery that references both the pharmaceutical industry and organic produce.

The initiative took its cue from the 2009 Cultures of Eugenics publication by subRosa, a cyberfeminist art collective. In their hypothesis, they drew parallels between women and chickens, viewing the collection of their eggs as a valuable resource for biotech research. Following the cloning of the sheep Dolly in 1996, the Roslin Institute of the University of Edinburgh collaborated with the now-defunct company Viragen to produce Britney, the inaugural cloned chicken (Figure 2.5).

In the realm of avian transgenic technologies, experts searched to engineer chickens capable of laying eggs infused with specific drugs aimed at combating a variety of diseases, including cancer, as articulated by Dr. Helen Sang, the leading scientist at the Roslin Institute. Pioneering the efforts in creating a transgenic hen, the team put forth a groundbreaking proposition that had not been previously explored, a claim corroborated by Karen Brown from Viragen. The forward-thinking projection undertaken by subRosa hinted at the potential of similar research being applied to the development of a new human eugenic using women's eggs. Her proposal puts forth a rather ironic yet plausible advertisement, where the egg has transcended its symbolic role as the reproductive matrix and now serves as a conduit for medicine, drugs, and designer babies (Figure 2.6).

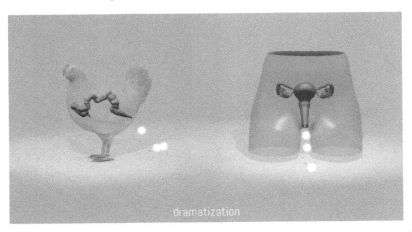

Figure 2.6 Video still from the egstrogen farms commercial suggesting the critical side of the project.

Source: Courtesy of Mary Maggic.

SPECULATING FUTURES: A PRACTITIONER'S PROFILE & PRACTICES

Cherry-Ann Davis is a maker and creator, storyteller, and an independent researcher with a specialization in hybrid ethnography, focusing on Pan African narratives. Her work is deeply rooted in storytelling, experimenting with a variety of formats and mediums, influenced by her native Trinidad and Tobago. She advocates for a curiosity-driven approach that promotes independent research with the capacity to inspire a strategy, integrating foresight. As she incorporates ancestral knowledge, particularly the process of creolization[2], into her work, she amplifies the ancestral wisdom that is often overlooked. She views the cultural and aesthetic evolution of Trinidad and Tobago as a fusion of Indigenous, European, and African influences. Through the integration of music, storytelling, and other formats, she seeks to uncover this knowledge, bridging the gap between the past and the present.

Davis reflects on these traits throughout her work. As illustrated in Figure 2.7, she encapsulates the culture of Trinidad and Tobago using symbolism as a narrative tool. Initially, her focus was on

Figure 2.7 Cherry-Ann Davis' work: a textile, a book, and also a poster.
Source: Courtesy of Cherry-Ann Davis.

design and education, but she soon observed the perpetuation of colonial structures within these domains. This insight redirected the project toward a more profound exploration of design education in colonial spaces, challenging the aesthetics of colonized areas. The final product was a textile, and also a book and poster, all designed to engage the public and underscore the ubiquity of visual communication in various forms of expression.

In this work, and others, Davis demonstrates the importance of valuing personal aesthetics and cultural heritage, noting that mainstream narratives often marginalize certain perspectives and cultural languages. The task, she suggests, is to challenge these biases and recognize the damage caused by restricting makers, creators, and designers from exploring their visual languages. By acknowledging the biases in dominant narratives and embracing a degree of self-centeredness, she aims to amplify marginalized narratives, disrupt traditional norms, and emphasize the importance of engaging diverse audiences and creating accessible formats for effective communication.

Davis encourages practitioners to challenge conventional perceptions of design and underscores the power of visual storytelling in broadening the scope of creative expression. She advocates recognizing diverse methods of making and creating, defying the rigid definitions of design imposed by dominant narratives impoverishing individual perspectives and cultural languages. By embracing a more comprehensive understanding of design, she believes we can make room for multiple stories and ways of visually communicating. By emphasizing the importance of valuing her own methods of creation, she challenges the notion that acceptance must come from external sources. By cultivating self-confidence and sharing her story from her perspective, Davis aims to amplify marginalized narratives and disrupt dominant norms. She highlights the disservice of trying to confine vibrant cultural expressions into narrow categories and encourages embracing experimentation and diversity in both formats and execution.

To develop your futures literacy to *speculate futures* (Figure 2.8), and as we prepare to augment our capacity to generate visions, check out these resources to strengthen your capacity to speculate better futures:

Figure 2.8 Designing sustainable futures literacy: speculate futures.
Source: By authors.

- FUEL4Design – Future Philosophical Pills (http://www.fuel4design.org/index.php/future-philosophical-pills/)
- The Manual of Design Fiction (https://www.nearfuturelaboratory.com/the-manual-of-design-fiction/)
- Climate Fiction - Grist (https://grist.org/climate-fiction/)
- Dreams and Disruptions (www.dreamsanddisruptions.com)
- Co-Creating Fearless Futures: A Feminist Cartographer's Toolkit (https://www.awid.org/sites/default/files/2022-08/Fearles%20Futures%20Toolkit%20ENG.pdf)
- Our Futures: By the People for the People (https://www.nesta.org.uk/report/our-futures-people-people/)
- Metadesigners Network 2022 (https://metadesigners.org/Metadesign-Introduction)

Notes

1 http://www.fuel4design.org
2 The process of creolization as a linguistic theory has been applied to other forms of cultural production by other scholars within the Caribbean and beyond. Davis's approach builds on the work of mainly Edouard Glissant who coined the term, and Stuart Hall who further expounded on the theory to apply it specifically to design.

3

Generating
Visions

Our journey towards designing sustainable futures can come to the aid of the nascent practice of generating visions through generative AI (GenAI). Generating visions serves as a crucial addition to Anticipating Futures because the signals from artificial intelligence (AI) indicate new methods for ideating beyond our biases and visualizing better futures at scale. We will begin by looking to the past, and how technology and creativity have always been intertwined in the production of cultural artifacts. Under the advisement of Jeremy Kirshbaum, we will look into current and future emerging practices of generating visions with AI. We explore the potential of generative AI to scale cocreation, which opens a level of agency and accountability for designing sustainable futures. We will learn from practitioners on the edge of this innovation practice and see how AI (and other emerging technologies) triggers a novel anticipatory competency – augmenting intelligence, and at scale. This requires a shift in method, and mindset, for practitioners to conceive, at an unprecedented scale, visions of plausible, probable, and preferable futures. We will all need to prepare for the impacts of generating visions in order not to miss this unique opportunity.

TECHNOLOGY IN CREATIVITY: LOOKING BACK TO LOOK FORWARD

Artistic imagination has always been intertwined with technology, dating back to ancient civilizations where rudimentary tools such as chisels, brushes, and the potter's wheel facilitated creative expression (Gombrich, 1960). These rudimentary yet profound illustrations marked the beginning of a journey in artistic expression, one that has continuously evolved alongside technological advancements. Agustín Fuentes, in "Creative Spark: How Imagination Made Humans Exceptional," delves into the role of tools in shaping human creativity (Fuentes, 2017). From primitive implements to modern digital technologies, each tool has played a pivotal role in expanding the horizons of human creativity and expression.

The 15th-century introduction of the Gutenberg printing press marked a significant turning point in reading and writing. In music, the transition from basic instruments like drums to complex systems such as the pianoforte (and much later the Midi synthesizer) fundamentally changed musical composition and experience for

DOI: 10.4324/9781003451693-5

generations of listeners (Goodman, 1982). In the visual arts, just as the use of light played a crucial role in the style of Renaissance painting, the Impressionists revolutionized the art world by making their canvases portable. Outside they captured natural light and color in previously unconsidered ways. The emergence of photography and film further transformed the landscape of visual storytelling. Innovations in cinematic techniques, such as Eisenstein's mise-en-scène and the French Nouvelle Vague's use of jump cuts, were driven by technological advancements and economic constraints (i.e., the cost of the film). In architecture and design, the Bauhaus's innovative use of new technologies and manufacturing processes in design and architecture set a new standard for modern design. All these evolutions significantly broadened the cultural influence of creators, because creations are containers of cultural significance.

Even in the digital era, where creations are digital, we see that when technology advances, creativity does as well. Ivan Sutherland's Sketchpad program at MIT in the 1960s revolutionized the way artists and designers interacted with the digital world, heralding the future of computer-aided design (CAD) (Sutherland, 1963). The proliferation of the "mouse" and the advent of the internet accelerated and democratized digital artistry. Renowned British artist David Hockney, celebrated for his vibrant and influential works, created landscapes and life studies with the "Brushes" app on his iPhone. Architect Zaha Hadid further advanced this field by utilizing CAD technologies to create fluid, dynamic architectural forms. Creators like Neri Oxman have used 3D printing to create complex, biologically inspired structures, merging art with science and engineering. Refik Anadol has utilized AI algorithms to transform data into stunning visual experiences, showcasing the potential of AI in redefining artistic boundaries. Artists like Beeple harnessed these platforms to reach global audiences, culminating in the sale of digital artwork titled "Everydays: The First 5000 Days" – as Non-Fungible Tokens (NFTs) – for $69 million at Christie's auction in March 2021, raising still unresolved questions about ownership and value in an AI-fueled world.

The ongoing narrative of technology and art reflects humanity's quest to continually redefine the boundaries of expression and understanding. In the early 20th century, Walter Benjamin, philosopher and art theorist, feared that technological change (specifically photography) might diminish the "aura" and authenticity of traditional art forms (Benjamin, 1968). As advancements continue in machine learning, computational power, processing toolkits, GitHub libraries, and expansive datasets like ImageNet, the potential of GenAI to augment human creativity with machine imagination is enormous. Harkening back to Benjamin, this will spark questions about creativity in our digital era (Elgammal et al., 2017; Bruno 2022) and spur artists like Trevor Paglen, Kate Crawford, and Lynn Hershman Leeson to critically examine issues related to bias in the AI systems (Paglen & Crawford, 2019; Rea, 2021). As we look backward to look forward, we can see that since artistic imagination and technology are symbiotic forces, their vector will only increase in velocity.

Anticipating GenAI's Opportunities to Generate Visions

If artistic imagination and technology are symbiotic forces, then generative AI emerges as a transformative catalyst to unravel the complexity of sustainability's underlying grand challenges, including climate change, social inequities, and economic disparity. A signal of this future kicked off in December 2023, with the COWI consulting group facilitating a conference entitled "Collaborative Intelligence: How can humans and AI join forces to accelerate the green transition?" (/imagineFutures, 2023). Just as a centuries-long trajectory of technology ignited the imagination and skills of creators, creators have an unparalleled opportunity to harness the power of AI to augment their creativity and engage stakeholders with more meaningful cultural artifacts. For those who want to flourish in this AI-enabled landscape can leverage AI to engage the collective imagination by creating engaging narratives, both in textual and visual mediums, that serve to inspire, caution, and guide. They can provide a sensual and cultural experience that serves as both a compass and a mirror – reflecting both the directions we are headed in and the opportunities to recalibrate our course.

In anticipation of how AI might be incorporated into designing sustainable futures, we foresee at least six opportunity spaces to augment design at the time of writing. As illustrated in Figure 3.1,

AI can augment the generation of more engaging visions by crafting immersive narratives, visualizing sustainable infrastructures, conceptualizing circular economies, simulating social equity impacts, forecasting policy, and fostering interactive public engagement. Based on a few signals at the time of our writing, let's speculate these scenarios in more depth (Figure 3.1).

Visualizing Sustainability

The most straightforward use case of generative AI (GenAI) for design will be visualization. Image generation platforms like Midjourney and video generation platforms like Pika have the capability to swiftly produce realistic visualizations of any future

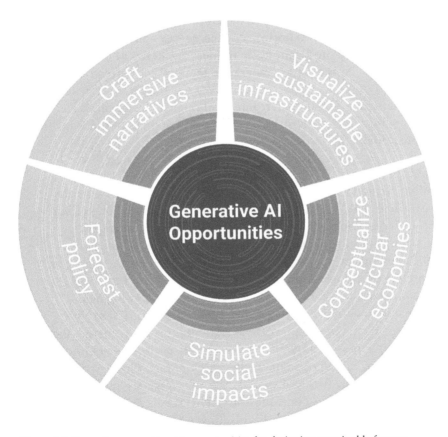

Figure 3.1 Emerging generative AI opportunities for designing sustainable futures.
Source: By authors

scenarios with just a well-formulated prompt (already possible with large language models such as OpenAI's ChatGPT). In a very near future, everyone – not just formally trained creatives – will have the powers that start up Diagram.com offers "... to unleash creativity with ... design tools from the future." As GenAI extends its visual prowess into architecture and urban planning, sustainability will receive an invaluable asset for creating vivid, data-driven visualizations of sustainable infrastructure. It will go beyond schematic designs to present holistic, interactive visual ecosystems where every building, every public space, and even every tree is optimized for sustainability. Designers will input various sustainability criteria – such as energy efficiency, water conservation, and carbon footprint – and AI will propose the optimal settings for any environmental conditions. Digital twins such as the one of Singapore use AI to optimize green energy sources, mobility, food harvesting, and commerce to meet the needs of every citizen. Projects like Autodesk's "Generative Design" tool already leverage GenAI to optimize building designs for various factors, including material efficiency and environmental impact. By adding a compelling narrative visualization, AI will accelerate the transition to sustainable infrastructure.

Cultivating Collective Narratives

When articulating futures, particularly those of environmental sustainability, GenAI will weave intricate data into compelling stories and visual realities that can mobilize communities, galvanize policymakers, and inspire real change. These stories and accompanying visualizations breathe life into the long-term implications of our present-day choices. By leveraging GenAI to synthesize and model extensive datasets – spanning fields from climate science to social demographics – we will produce dynamic narratives that evolve as data and insights emerge. Picture an AI-orchestrated narrative that teleports policymakers into a 2050 scenario where renewable energy reigns, illustrated through intricate visualizations of solar-powered cityscapes and first-person accounts of eco-conscious lifestyles. This scenario is indicative of the emerging signals. Tools like Google's "Environmental Insights Explorer" – part of Google Sustainability toolset – offer a glimpse into this potential by using data analytics to inform sustainable city planning (Google, 2021); generative AI stands poised to elevate this into a narrative art form. The Refik Anadol Studio is building the *Large Nature Model* (DATALAND), the world's first open-source, generative AI model dedicated to trained on "nature's inherent intelligence." Such an immersive, multi-dimensional narrative can serve as a compelling advocacy tool, enabling a deeper emotional and intellectual connection to the urgency of sustainability.

Conceptualizing Circular Economies

In the economic landscape, AI will serve as a powerful tool for simulating and visualizing the interactions and dynamics of circular economies. Here, the AI system will illustrate complex scenarios that demonstrate how various sectors – be it manufacturing, agriculture, or retail – can transition from a linear "take-make-dispose" approach to a more sustainable, circular model. AI will create scenarios showcasing how waste can be minimized through reuse, recycling, and regeneration. For instance, an AI-generated model could vividly illustrate a circular food supply chain where waste from one process becomes input for another, thus creating a loop of sustainability. These dynamic models serve as a policy guide, raise awareness, and influence public perception. AI could significantly expand on this by generating comprehensive, interactive narratives that bring the concept of a circular economy to life for both policymakers and the general public.

Social Equity and Justice Simulations

While environmental considerations often take center stage in discussions of sustainability, social equity remains an equally crucial challenge. GenAI will simulate how sustainability-related actions impact diverse communities. GenAI will create complex models incorporating socio-economic data, cultural factors, and policy variables to generate narratives that illuminate the social justice dimensions of various sustainability initiatives. The AI startup Mnemonic AI provides an example of how generative algorithms can make visioning insights interactive through autogenerated personas. After workshops with real participants, Mnemonic AI can instantly synthesize archetypal user personas reflecting the diversity of needs and perspectives. Design teams can then rapidly envision solution experiences tailored to these AI-generated yet human-inspired characters. This can be applied in a social impact simulation of an urban greening project, exploring questions such as who benefits most and least and what adjustments could make the initiative more equitable. Such simulations would allow policymakers and practitioners to identify and address potential inequities proactively, making the sustainability journey inclusive.

Policy Forecasting

The integration of GenAI into participatory foresight interventions will simulate systems interventions and policy impacts. Platforms that employ natural language generation, like ChatGPT or Claude, will model geopolitical dynamics between nation-states, creating speculative news articles and transcripts of speeches of possible scenarios of international diplomacy. This ability to quickly simulate intricate social interactions will enable designers to work with stakeholders to manage such national disruptions. Imagine using AI on data including policy briefs and news articles to identify early signs of geopolitical changes, modeling dynamics like power balances between nations. Such a future offers data-driven insights into emerging issues that foresight workshops could delve deeper into.

Interactive Stakeholder Engagement

The final frontier for GenAI in envisioning sustainable futures lies in its potential for fostering interactive public engagement. GenAI can create dynamic, user-friendly platforms where individuals can explore various sustainable future scenarios. Unlike static reports or presentations, these platforms offer an interactive experience, inviting users to tweak variables and explore different outcomes. For example, a city resident could interact with an AI-generated model to see how different sustainability policies, from waste management to renewable energy adoption, could impact their daily life in future decades. This level of interactive engagement would educate and also empowers individuals to participate in the sustainability discourse actively. Platforms like Earth 2050 by Kaspersky Lab provide a glimpse of this interactivity by offering a user-engaged platform to predict the future of the planet (Kaspersky Lab, 2021). Imagine adding in digital twins of people – including the designers themselves – that cross the "uncanny valley" (Mori, 1970), then even the sky is not a limit.

Innovation for sustainable futures must be more inclusive, so designers of sustainable futures will need tools to engage stakeholders across all the communities they serve. Conversational AI could support more equitable visioning by adapting to people's diverse communication styles. For example, any natural language assistant can facilitate free-flowing generative sessions through text or voice. Participants will feel acknowledged as the AI responds to each person's unique articulation of their aspirations for the future. If conflict arises, the AI can diplomatically summarize perspectives and helps the group find common ground. While not replacing human facilitators, AI's conversational versatility will remove barriers to participation. For real-time visioning workshops, the conversational moderator Speakeasy.ai uses AI-powered speech recognition to visually map discussions, ensuring no one voice dominates. Participants feel empowered to share creatively as the AI analyzes sentiments in the room, guiding activities to build energy and alignment. For remote or asynchronous visioning of better futures, AI will integrate contributors across time and space into a shared tapestry of insights, enables designers to act as midwives in birthing collective purpose.

Through the lens of generative AI, the potential of co-creating, engaging narratives in interactive experiences at scale and with authentic depth, is exciting. Generative AI guides innovation toward expanding, not constraining possibilities, which makes it an ideal tool for designing sustainable futures.

GENERATING VISIONS WITH AI: URBAN LEXICONS

By leveraging AI and other emerging technologies across various design domains – from urban planning and economics to social equity and public engagement – practitioners are empowered with a dynamic toolkit to envision, narrate, and interact with more sustainable futures. Urban Lexicons (www. urbanlexicons. org) is a design-research methodology and creative practice that explores the emerging practices of generating visions with GenAI. Founded by urbanist Rosanna Vitiello of The Place Bureau (www. theplacebureau.com), and Marcus Willcocks, Senior Research Fellow at Central Saint Martins` Socially Responsive Design and Innovation Unit, Urban Lexicons explores how a city speaks to its inhabitants and how they speak back – with the aim of strengthening the emotional connections to place (Vitiello & Willcocks, 2021).

In a workshop at the Media Architecture Biennale '23 in Toronto, Vitiello and Willcocks collaborated with a group of international designers, researchers, and architects to explore questions like: Can we work with Urban AI to develop empathic cities as well as intelligent cities? If the city could speak to us and reveal a collective mindset, what would it tell us? Inspired by Photovoice method for engagement, which uses photography in communities to facilitate conversation about their environment to tell stories about their needs and aspirations (Wang & Bur, 1997), the team decided to pilot text to image AI as a collaborative design tool for generating urban futures. The workshop started with extremes, exploring the components of architectures of fear as a kickoff point and considering the opposite signs of trust in an urban context. By building a collective experiential vocabulary through gathering images, we created a springboard for discussion. With this visual vocabulary in hand, teams then explored four scenarios that centered on big challenges hitting cities right now where lack of trust was a major driver: safety on public transit, cultural gentrification, homelessness, and transparency of AI. Teams explored various components of the scenarios, including settings, rituals, objects, and characters, by prompting AI to create an immediate and exciting playback of scenes that brought these "cities of trust" to life.

The approach generated incredibly creative concepts like the *Drag Queen Police Station*, the *Euphoric Subway*, and the *Hippie Robots,* all countering challenging scenarios of cultural gentrification in queer neighborhoods, safety on public transport, and AI's slow dominance of cities. As illustrated in Figures 3.3 and 3.4, the visions generated enabled teams to create a scene for a future narrative – working from person-scale, through to building, and up to neighborhood. This story-driven approach helps communicate the future vision to wider audiences. The immediacy of image-making generated by AI supported an incredibly rich discussion, as to what participants do and don't want to see (Figure 3.2).

Vitiello and Willcocks see a huge potential in using AI in this collective way for swift ideation, as she says "It is fun!" precisely

Figure 3.2 Drag queen police station scenes, created in midjourney.
Source: Courtesy of The Place Bureau. With permission.

because participants create critical thinking around the core challenge (see Figure 3.5). With the right starting points and methodology, stakeholders "Consider the components of the world they want to create ... and view the scenes they create as points for discussion rather than finalised solutions." Vitiello and Willcocks advise

> When working with AI, having a high level of definition in text and image input creates really specific prompts, which in turn creates much more definitive images. AI works well when considering atmosphere and emotion, in ways that are harder for more traditional forms of image making for cities to respond to.

The next step of this approach would be to prototype the experiences using AI-generated renderings, short videos, and even AR (Figure 3.3). Piloting such prototypes is a more sustainable and cost-effective approach to working with stakeholders and local people, building trust, and taking small risks together to bring innovative and sustainable urban futures to life (Figure 3.4).

Figure 3.3 Drag queen police station scenes, created in midjourney.
Source: Courtesy of The Place Bureau. With permission.

Figure 3.4 Generating insights, workshop participants.
Source: Courtesy of The place Bureau, Bruce Mau Design. With permission.

Part I: Anticipate Better Futures

This experience with AI to elicit grassroots insights simultaneously uncovered a community identity. It promoted people's connections to their surroundings and used this place meaning to collaboratively design for the future. These learnings on how GenAI can catalyze creative, community-anchored sustainability strategies while capturing diversity and local identity, gives more voice to wider ranges of people, is a strong signal for designing sustainable futures at scale.

ANTICIPATING WHAT'S NEXT: AUGMENTED DESIGN

As AI increasingly intertwines futures with design, and vice versa, every stakeholder's anticipatory capability is augmented. Professionals will soon find themselves at a precipice – the promise of augmented human intelligence, untapped creative dimensions, and approaches to address complex global challenges at scale. This evolving landscape suggests that designers may need to recalibrate their methodologies and mindset to steer these potent technologies toward outcomes that are both innovative and ethical. In this dynamic context, we anticipate a practice we might refer to as "Augmented Design" – a technology-driven scaffold that could guide practitioners through the multiple opportunities of emerging technologies who seek more sustainable futures. With that context in mind, let's delve into what the steps of an anticipated Augmented Design process could be (Figure 3.5).

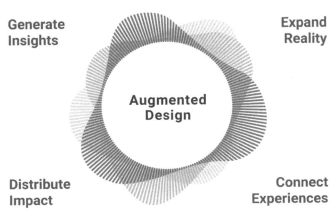

Figure 3.5 Emerging practices of augmented design.
Source: By authors.

Generate Insights

In what might be the foundational phase of an evolving Augmented Design practice, Generate Insights could serve as a critical first step in shaping more sustainable futures. Enabled by the capabilities of generative AI, this phase could transcend mere data accumulation, synthesizing disparate elements into compelling narratives and rich visual landscapes. For example, one might envision a model of an urban environment, fully renewable and sustainable, born from a blend of geographical data, demographic trends, and energy metrics. However, this potential to transform comes with a need for caution; close attention to the quality and diversity of the data is likely essential to circumvent perpetuating societal disparities. This initial phase, then, could serve as a precursor to the next step, Extend Reality, where these conceptual frameworks potentially take on a more tactile, experiential form. The success of such a transition would likely be contingent on the robustness of the foundational intelligence gathered in this first step.

Extend Reality

As the Augmented Design process unfolds, the next likely phase could be Extend Reality. Here, generative AI transcends the limits of traditional design tools, enabling practitioners to construct immersive prototypes that bring previously crafted narratives and visuals to life. With the aid of virtual or augmented reality technologies, such as Unity for real-time 3D development or Microsoft's Azure Mixed Reality services, stakeholders may experience the promise of a sustainable future in an embodied manner. For instance, those narratives about renewable urban landscapes might manifest as a walkable virtual cityscape, complete with interactive elements that demonstrate the function of sustainable technologies. However, it's worth noting that while these experiences can be captivating, they must also be deeply rooted in reality. Therefore, digital twins – precise digital replicas of physical objects and systems – could serve as invaluable tools for ensuring the accuracy of these virtual realities. As stakeholders venture through this second phase, the immersive experiences crafted could offer crucial insights for the next stage, Connect Experiences, where the aim would be to anchor these far-reaching visions in near-future pragmatism.

Connect Experiences

Building upon the immersive prototypes, the next stage – Connect Experiences – aims to bridge the chasm between the speculative and the attainable. Here, Gen AI might play a role in making the leap from experimental prototypes to actionable, near-future experiences. Technologies like IoT platforms and real-time data analytics could facilitate this connection. For example, the data generated from the virtual walkthroughs of sustainable cityscapes could inform real-world urban planning initiatives. However, this connection goes beyond mere data translation; it extends to aligning policies, devices, systems, and even cultural values for a more interconnected experience of sustainability. As this stage progresses, the interconnected experiences pave the way for the final step, Distribute Impact, where the focus would likely shift to equitable and sustainable community practices.

Distribute Impact

In the likely final phase of this evolving process, Distribute Impact, the focus could shift from conceptual and experiential design to the tangible distribution of sustainable practices. Here, generative AI could assist stakeholders in identifying equitable means to incentivize and financially support community practices. Yet, as with previous stages, caution is necessary. The push for equity should be underpinned by transparent governance and decision-making models to ensure the transition to sustainable practices benefits all.

As practitioners navigate through these interconnected stages, each phase builds upon the achievements of the previous and also sets the anticipatory groundwork for what comes next. In this way, an augmented design approach serves as a holistic framework, guiding the design community through the labyrinthine challenges and opportunities of sustainable futures-enabled emerging and ever-evolving technologies.

GENERATING VISIONS: A PRACTITIONER'S POSSIBLE JOURNAL ENTRY

Generating compelling visions requires unleashing imagination at both individual and group levels. Practitioners need to nurture their own creative capacities while also fostering collaborative creativity among diverse stakeholders. Given the accelerating pace of technological and societal change, practitioners need to become comfortable with constantly learning, unlearning, and reimagining possibilities. An agile mindset that welcomes change enables more effective visioning.

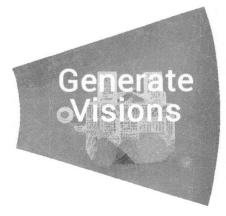

Embracing technology's transformative potential: Practitioners need to stay inspired by emerging innovations and maintain

Figure 3.6 Designing sustainable futures literacy: generate visions.

Source: By authors.

an openness to how technology can expand human potential. An optimistic mindset that gets excited about possibilities enables more inspired visions. Generating meaningful visions requires always viewing technology as a means rather than an end, and keeping the focus on human dignity, creativity, and collective potential. This ethical grounding allows envisioning futures that uplift shared human values.

Knowing that AI is traveling at lightspeed in comparison to a printed book, we are sharing a few signals to develop your futures literacy to *generate visions* (Figure 3.6) of a better future:

- Climate Change AI (www.climatechange.ai)
- Institute for Computational Sustainability (https://computational-sustainability.cis.cornell.edu/)
- Collaborative Intelligence: How can humans and AI join forces to accelerate the green transition? (https://imagine-futures.cowi.com/event-ai-after)
- Can Generative AI & ChatGPT Help Protect Our Planet? (Research Article) (www.earth911.com/eco-tech/can-generative-ai-chatgpt-help-protect-our-planet/)
- An Artificial Intelligence-based Framework to Achieve the Sustainable Development Goals in the Context of Bangladesh (https://arxiv.org/abs/2304.11703)

Part I: Anticipate Better Futures

- Google Sustainability (https://sustainability.google/working-together/tools/)

If AI empowers us to look beyond the limitations of our immediate horizon and explore the broader implications of our actions on both human societies and the planet, we may be able to imagine sustainable futures and design them as well. By processing and visualizing diverse inputs, AI surfaces interconnect and uncover blind spots on the path to converging on more sustainable futures. However, guiding AI's ceaseless imagination requires what Herbert Simon called a uniquely human capacity, design (Simon, 1969). In designing sustainable futures, AI provides the pixels, while humans provide the purpose. As we will explore in Part III, building worlds with co-created prototypes in participatory processes is essential to guiding the multitudinous nature of anticipation toward the shared meaning of a better future.

Part II

Create
Sustainable
Experiences

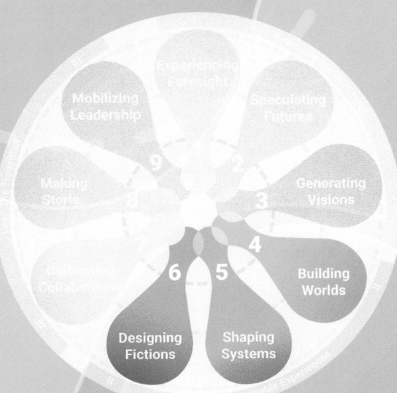

Part II of *Designing Sustainable Futures* emphasizes the pivotal role of Creating Sustainable Experiences in catalyzing societal transformation toward sustainability. As Part I activated our collective imagination, Part II offers the theory and practice to activate our collaborative creativity. Well-designed experiences can serve as conduits that translate systems thinking into purposeful artifacts with more meaning in the worlds they inhabit. If co-created, the shared experience can translate into more motivation for overcoming the challenges of changing the present. Despite the pressing need to create more sustainable experiences, and an increasing number of more sustainable solutions, our present practices remain firmly rooted in our routines. This is precisely where co-creating sustainable experiences is essential because it can augment engagement across all the levers of designing sustainable futures.

Part II opens with Chapter 4: *Building Worlds*. Guided by narrative hacker Jacques Barcia, we explore how the meticulous crafting of plausible worlds expands the horizons of what is possible and sets the stage for participatory visioning. Readers can expect to learn about worldbuilding techniques that imbue fictional worlds with consistency. With a robust foundation, systems plausibly enable the world to function. In Chapter 5: *Shaping Systems*, we will learn from Professor Silvia Barbero how the transdisciplinary nature of systemic design enables practitioners to tackle complex, multidimensional sustainability challenges in STES environments. Readers will know how systems thinking exposes the interworking of worlds, boosting our creative capacity for impactful design. Chapter 6: *Speculating Designs* coalesces worldbuilding and systemic design into provocative objects that make sustainability tangible. This chapter explores how the participatory experience of speculating elevates creativity to spark dialogue about what could be a more sustainable experience. By eliciting emotions from hope to concern, these artifacts become conduits for collective meaning-making, opening the space for the difficult decisions that we need to face today.

Part II aims to activate our collaborative creativity by immersing practitioners in the design of worlds, systems, and the "stuff" of better futures. It posits that if we create more sustainable and

DOI: 10.4324/9781003451693-6

meaningful experiences together, we can more deftly shape the narratives that captivate consciousness and spark change. With an open mind and hopeful hands, we can ask ourselves how these capabilities might empower practitioners to play an active role in building an equitable and sustainable tomorrow?

Let's explore the preferred future scenarios that could emerge if we create sustainable experiences.

Networked Nexus

In a city where every street corner hums with the synergy of digital and handmade, Ana, a local artisan, uses a hybrid marketplace to sell her smart-fabric garments globally. Her workshop overlooks a park with solar walkways, while her daughter attends a VR school, learning about cultures in ways textbooks never could. It's a world where technology and tradition craft a vibrant tapestry of life.

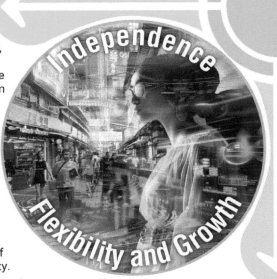

Global
Production

Lila, a freelance designer, thrives in a world where work is unbound by office walls. Her digital platform matches her with global projects, while local coworking spaces offer community and collaboration. Her eco-pod home adapts to her needs, reflecting a society where independence and environmental consciousness go hand in hand, fostering a life of resilience and adaptability.

Steadfast Strands

Individual

Society

Regenerative Weave

In a community where shared solar grids light up homes and local produce fills the markets, Sam contributes with his knowledge of circular economics, learned not in a distant university but right here, in community workshops. His home, built from locally sourced, sustainable materials, stands as a testament to what communities can achieve when they weave together, creating a resilient fabric of society.

Local
Production

Max transforms his apartment balcony into a lush vegetable garden, thanks to skills learned at the local micro-factory. Here, he also crafts biodegradable planters, contributing to the community's zero-waste initiative. Education now means kids learning about permaculture alongside math, preparing them for a future where sustainability is a way of life.

Quiet Evolution

Society

4

Building
Worlds

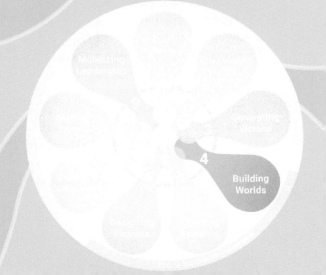

Building
Worlds

Designing sustainable futures is anchored to the worlds we can build; hence, we open Part II with the theory and practices of Building Worlds. From the foresight practice of scenarios to the speculative narratives of science fiction, the narrative spaces of worldbuilding offer platforms for a collective exploration of potential future experiences. To delve into the construction of credible worlds, we will be steered by Jacques Barcia from the Institute For The Future (IFTF). With Jacques as our navigator, we will explore the art and craft of worldbuilding, and reveal new perspectives to create more sustainable worlds. With the aim to elucidate and exemplify frameworks that guide building robust worlds, designers will be empowered to enhance the experiences of future designs. Integrated with the UNESCO capacity for problem-solving, the frameworks can also develop our capacity to unpack sustainability challenges to devise feasible, inclusive, and equitable solution alternatives that foster sustainable development. By integrating worldbuilding into our practices more formally, practitioners can generate more vivid, captivating visions of tomorrow to inspire change.

FROM SCENARIOS TO THE STORIES OF SPECULATIVE FICTION

A shared consensus across almost all examined futures research initiatives is the existence of three fundamental stages: initially, the thorough search for future insights; subsequently, the creation of diverse possibilities; and finally, the development of an outcome, which could take the form of a scenario, strategy, or narrative about potential futures. For this reason, scenarios are located high in the hierarchy of the Expanded Experiential Futures Ladder (Figure 4.1). The term "scenario" has undergone a significant evolution in its meaning and scope. Originally a term from theatre, it denoted the ensemble of stage elements and the setting where the play unfolds. It also served as a placeholder for "outline" or "blueprint" – a guide meant to steer actors toward a performance that mirrors the pre-stage vision of the director, producer, and writer. Scenarios play a pivotal role in designing sustainable futures, helping to translate the setting into a more understandable description of a possible future.

Scenarios as decision-making tools, and later as tools for design, have a diverse history, enduring for over 50 years. As mentioned

DOI: 10.4324/9781003451693-7

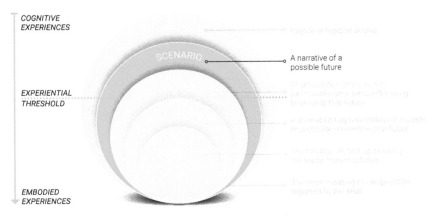

Figure 4.1 The Experiential Futures Ladder, spotlight on the Scenario.
Source: Adapted from Candy and Dunagan (2017). With permission.

in Chapter 1, scenario planning can be traced back to the 1950s, during which Herman Kahn used it to strategize for thermonuclear war, coining the provocative notion of "Thinking About the Unthinkable" (Kahn, 1960, 1962). Peter Schwartz describes scenarios as a tool for helping us to take a long view in a world of great uncertainty. Scenarios are stories about the way the world might turn tomorrow, stories that can help us recognize and adapt to changing aspects of our present environment (Schwartz, 1991).

Given that stories are processed differently from other forms of information, the use of storytelling in the design of sustainable futures has great potential. As Zaidi quotes in her 2019 paper (Zaidi, 2019), a story-

> ...can be a way for humans to feel that we have control over the world. They allow people to see patterns where there is chaos, meaning where there is randomness. Humans are inclined to see narratives where there are none because they can afford meaning to our lives — a form of existential problem solving.
>
> (Delistraty, 2014)

Utilizing narrative techniques enables the exploration of alternative perspectives and the prompting of critical reflection on prevailing norms and beliefs.

The stories of design fiction, specifically science fiction and fantasy, are of most interest to designing sustainable futures as they open a creative connection between foresight and design. The worlds of science fiction reflect the emergent nature of our socio-ecological systems. These worlds imbue a sense of wholeness, acknowledging the never-ending cycles of growth, accumulation, and restructuring inherent in these complex systems (Holling, 2001: 392). However, despite its importance, worldbuilding remains a relatively understudied act of intentional design. Raven and Elahi lament the lack of literature that applies the narrative strategies and logics employed by writers, filmmakers, and cultural scholars to the methodologies employed by futures scholars and practitioners in the creation of their final outputs.

Many cultures across the globe leverage the power of stories to enable the exploration of alternative perspectives. These practices can also prompt critical reflection on prevailing norms and beliefs in and across cultures (Bruner, 2002). For example, the fiction genres of Afrofuturism and Solarpunk reflect have a distinct focus on envisioning a future that is hopeful and empowering for marginalized communities. Afrofuturism can be described as a cultural and political movement within speculative fiction that positions African protagonists at the forefront of the future. This ideology envisions the potential futures of its diaspora. Afrofuturism seeks to populate science fiction with African and Afro-diasporic visions of the future, creating an inclusive narrative that acknowledges and celebrates the richness and diversity of these cultures (Womack, 2013). Solarpunk, first published in Brazil 2013, envisions a future that is powered by renewable energy sources and more sustainable, focusing on a harmonious coexistence with nature (see Chabria & Taneja 2021). These genres are more optimistic responses to the catastrophic predictions prevalent in the sub-genres cyberpunk and steampunk.

Storytelling in science fiction often revolves around the struggles and efforts taken to achieve this better world, providing a unique narrative perspective for the world we desire. By depicting diverse characters and societies, science fiction expands empathy across cultures and surfaces hidden assumptions that influence sustainability (Bussey & Barcia, 2018). Ursula K. Le Guin's *Always*

Coming Home imagines a future California tribe who have rejected consumerism to live in harmony with nature (Le Guin, 1985). Their values challenge Western notions of progress. Speculative fiction broadens perspectives on how multidimensional systems transition toward sustainable futures (Raven & Elahi, 2015). Such compelling stories make complex futures feel accessible (von Stackelberg & McDowell, 2015). They inspire hope that through ingenuity and solidarity, humanity can overcome existential risks like climate change. For instance, Kim Stanley Robinson's *Ministry for the Future* follows advocates using political activism, cryptocurrency hacking, and nonviolent direct action to force climate action (Robinson, 2022). Inspiring narratives kindle optimism around dealing with shared challenges ahead (Suvin, 1979). It is through the intricacies of the worlds we build that such transformative potentials can be realized, inviting audiences to engage with and contemplate new possibilities (Raven & Elahi, 2015: 49).

THE FOUNDATIONS OF WORLDBUILDING

Science fiction, like fantasy, gaming, and even unforeseen genres of speculative fiction, relies heavily on the processes of worldbuilding; worldbuilding refers to the process of constructing an intricate and believable imaginary world that serves as a contextual backdrop for a narrative. It involves the creation of fictional realms characterized by cohesive geographic, social, cultural, and other defining elements. These accurately crafted worlds establish comprehensive contextual frameworks that extend beyond individual stories, offering a deeper comprehension of the underlying systems that govern them. Regardless of the setting, all narratives necessitate some degree of worldbuilding.

Leah Zaidi, a notable futurist and futures studies scholar, deftly describes the foundations of worldbuilding in her Master's Thesis (Zaidi, 2017) as the process of constructing a complete and plausible imaginary world that serves as a context for a story. As illustrated in Figure 4.2, Zaidi breaks down worldbuilding into seven core categories: philosophical, political, economic, environmental, scientific, social, and artistic. These foundations represent the interconnected elements needed to build a plausible future civilization.

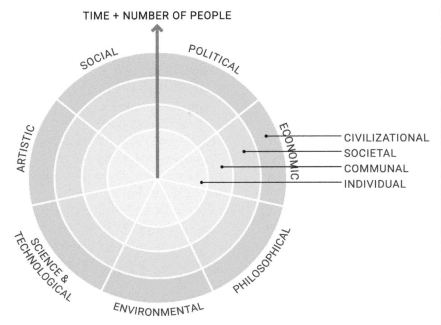

Figure 4.2 Seven foundations of worldbuilding, generational version.
Source: Courtesy of Leah Zaidi.

Because worldbuilding is a complex act of creation across various fields, its transformative potential is seismic. In Zaidi's definition, worldbuilding is the meticulous crafting of an intricate and believable imaginary universe that serves as the setting for a narrative. It involves the creation of fictional realms characterized by cohesive geographic, social, cultural, and other defining elements of her model. She describes worldbuilding as "… the process of constructing a complete and plausible imaginary world that serves as a context for a story. It is the creation of imaginary worlds with coherent geographic, social, cultural, and other features." (Zaidi, 2017). Well-crafted universes establish comprehensive contextual frameworks that extend beyond individual stories, offering a deeper understanding of the underlying systems that govern them.

Frameworks like the Seven Foundations provide scaffolds for co-creating "transtopias" – stories incrementally transitioning between dystopia and utopia that demonstrate step-by-step backcasting methods currently absent in fiction (Zaidi, 2017).

Worldbuilding reveals how altering one part of a complex societal system ripples across other foundations (Holling, 2001). In Pacific Edge, economic localization shapes architecture, urban planning, and transportation systems that enable sustainable lifestyles (Robinson, 1990). Examining these interconnections helps identify root causes and holistic levers of change. Speculating allows radical new social, political, and economic models to be explored on paper before real-world testing (Carroll, 2000). For example, Ernest Callenbach's novel Ecotopia imagined a breakaway sustainable society in the Pacific Northwest (Callenbach, 1975). Science fiction provides a sandbox to safely develop and stress-test systemic innovations (Calvino, 2012).

It is through the intricacies of worldbuilding that such transformative potentials can be realized, inviting audiences to engage with and contemplate new possibilities (Raven & Elahi, 2015). Creating immersive fictional universes, each with its own consistent rules, cultures, histories, and laws, enriches the reader's or viewer's experience by providing a genuine and detailed setting for the narrative. The task of fleshing out alternative future worlds across Zaidi's seven foundations necessitates articulating a shared vision of a sustainable civilization (Glenn, 1972). For instance, Kim Stanley Robinson's novel Pacific Edge imagines sustainable societies powered by solar energy, organizing participatory politics around the community level, pursuing steady-state economies, and embodying an ecological ethos (Robinson, 1990). Envisioning relationships between foundations in this way brings clarity about the integrated systems change required for sustainability (Celi, 2013). Simulation and gaming go even further – turning worldbuilding into an educational tool for active learning about socio-ecological systems (Weines & Borit, 2021). Through participatory simulation design, learners collaboratively create complex scenarios and environments, reflecting real-world situations. This practical approach fosters critical thinking, problem-solving skills, and a comprehensive understanding of complex systems.

Worldbuilding offers powerful tools to ignite our imagination and help us contemplate and rethink our realities toward sustainability (Weines & Borit, 2021). Whether in fiction, media, strategic foresight, or education, worldbuilding is essential due to its ability to engage audiences. By meticulously crafting fictional worlds, creators can instill a sense of authenticity that deeply resonates with content consumers. Integrating practices like speculative fiction broadens the scope for narratives that entertain and educate by provoking new perspectives. They open inclusive and optimistic visions of the future that serve as a reminder of the significant role of creating worlds in shaping our perceptions and aspirations. This process facilitates artistic expression as it simultaneously enriches learning experiences, provides a platform for immersive storytelling, and presents potential directions and consequences.

Cognitive Estrangement and Novum

As we navigate a fictional world, we constantly assess its components, occurrences, and dynamics against our real-world understanding. Beyond the captivating narratives and fantastical landscapes, science fiction provides a unique and profound mechanism for questioning the practices of the present. We recognize something we know – whether it's a city, an institution, or a natural process – yet, within the context of the fictional world, these familiar elements appear with a degree of unfamiliarity. For example, if we encounter a society in a sci-fi story that generates energy in ways vastly different from ours, we draw comparisons and contrasts with our own energy systems. This comparative evaluation leads us into "what if" scenarios about our own world. Our cognitive and imaginative faculties intertwine in this process, leading to a simultaneous recognition of the familiar and the perception of the unfamiliar – we experience Cognitive Estrangement. Conceived by science fiction scholar Darko Suvin (Suvin, 1979), the duality of Cognitive Estrangement is where readers or viewers juxtapose the fictional worlds depicted in science fiction with their own reality. This comparative exercise is not just a literary analysis but a transformative process that reshapes our understanding and perception of our own world.

Consider a fictional world where humans have established a symbiotic relationship with a new species of bioluminescent plants, harnessing their light as a primary energy source. The idea of a city lit by natural, living light may initially seem foreign, yet we can relate it to our own reality, comparing it with our use of electrical lighting. This comparison prompts us to evaluate the potential impacts, benefits, and challenges, such a change might bring about in our own world. This process alters our perception of our world, and the cycle of comparison, alteration, and recomparison continues, fueling Cognitive Estrangement. Cognitive Estrangement is both cognitive, rooted in our understanding of reality, and creative, extending beyond the familiar into the domain of the novel and unexpected. It is a continuous interplay between the known and the unknown, the real and the invented. It's an imaginative framework that allows us to reflect on our reality, enabling us to perceive our world differently and broaden our understanding.

An essential element in Cognitive Estrangement is the concept of Novum. Novum refers to the unique, innovative aspect or phenomenon in a science fiction narrative that distinguishes it from our norm of reality. It's the seed of divergence that fundamentally transforms the universe of the story. It could be a piece of technology, a sociopolitical structure, an alien species, or a natural phenomenon. Using the previous example, the bioluminescent plants serving as a primary energy source could be considered the Novum. This 'cognitive innovation' alters the world, resulting in a ripple effect of changes impacting society, economy, and perhaps even the human psyche.

Science fiction authors craft their stories around one or multiple Novums, envisioning a range of deviations from the norm. They contemplate the implications of the Novum, questioning how its existence might alter society, give rise to new organizations, or affect interpersonal relationships. They consider potential new forms of crimes, governance models, social inequalities, or revolutions that could emerge. Futurists, akin to science fiction authors, latch onto Novums – in their case, these are often emerging technologies or social trends – to explore possible futures. However, their Novums are rooted in reality, often being real-world innovations with the potential to disrupt the status quo. Cognitive Estrangement and Novum are two powerful concepts in science fiction that extend beyond the realm of literature, serving as potent tools for futures thinking and exploring the transformative potential of our own world.

Introducing Cognitive Estrangement and Novum into worldbuilding acts as potent sparks for the design of sustainable experiences. Crafting a robust fictional world requires coherence and consistency, where the setting, no matter how fantastical, adheres to a set of established rules. This consistency extends to institutional motivations, ensuring a clear cause-effect relationship that resonates throughout the world.

THE PRAXIS OF WORLDBUILDING

As inspired by the worldbuilding in Wonderbook (VanderMeer & Zerfoss, 2018), our approach to build robust worlds is circumscribed within the "focal issues" that bring life and meaning to a scenario. As illustrated in Figure 4.3, focal issues provide design-able factors around the core Social, Technological, Economic, Environmental,

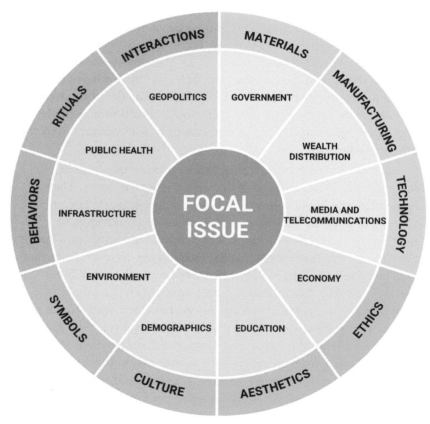

Figure 4.3 Focal issues for the scenario.
Source: Adapted from Fuel4Design. With permission.

Part II: Create Sustainable Experiences

Political (STEEP) model (or expanded PESTLE model, a deviation from the PEST Analysis created by Francis Aguilar (1967) in Scanning the Business Environment, Macmillan; 1st THUS edition), focal issues aim to seed agency in shaping the external uncertainties that broadly affect business, government, and society. Within this framing, worldbuilding integrates strategic foresight and speculative design, so not surprisingly, we begin with signal hunting.

Step 1: Unveil Future Insights with Signals

Signal hunting is where we discover specific and tangible signals related to the Sustainable Development Goals (SDGs). These signals form the basis for understanding and envisioning the future landscape. This research process is crucial for the commencement of worldbuilding; signal hunting has been introduced in Chapters 1 and 2 with the Trends Timeline as a facilitating tool, where these signals are mapped according to a specific timescale, enabling us to illustrate the past events that led to it and the future events that stem from it.

Signal hunting entails moving beyond generic observations and seeking out unique events or phenomena that hold significance for the future. Instead of merely acknowledging broad concepts like climate change, we aim to identify specific instances that offer valuable insights. For instance, an immigrant whose deportation is reversed due to climate change represents a concrete and noteworthy signal that underscores the intersection of migration and environmental factors. By concentrating on such specific signals, we acquire a deeper understanding of the forces shaping the future.

Identifying these signals amidst the vast ocean of information is a challenge that requires a discerning eye and an ability to recognize patterns and emerging phenomena. It is an ongoing practice that necessitates ongoing skill development and a keen awareness of the world around us. By concentrating on specific signals, we can explore their implications and envision alternative futures. Each signal serves as a catalyst for envisioning a different world, one that diverges from the current trajectory. This process enables us to contemplate the potential consequences – both intended and unintended – of these signals and their ripple effects across various spheres of life (Figure 4.4).

Figure 4.4 Futures wheel template.
Source: Adapted from Fuel4Design. With permission

Step 2: Explore Impacts with The Futures Wheel

In the realm of worldbuilding, the Futures Wheel (Figure 4.2) emerges as a potent instrument for understanding the direct and indirect repercussions and implications of specific matters or occurrences. First introduced by Glenn J.C. in 1972 in his work *Futurizing teaching vs. futures courses* the Futures Wheel offers a systematic approach to scrutinize and envisage potential futures.

Start by dissecting the issue or subject at hand and identifying its core elements. These core elements represent potential issues that will mold the futures design project. Clearly define and elaborate on this issue to aid the mapping of potential consequences and scenarios.

Set a timeline for the futures design project. By charting future events within a specific time horizon, you can contextualize and position your exploration.

Part II: Create Sustainable Experiences

Chart the primary or direct effects triggered by the focal issue. Identify the immediate impacts and consequences. Next, contemplate the secondary effects, which are less direct, and finally, explore the tertiary effects, which are indirectly influenced by the core focal issue.

Based on this mapping, pinpoint different potential scenarios that emerge. Each scenario represents a unique vision of the future based on the identified impacts and implications. Assign each scenario a name that mirrors its unique traits and storyline. Naming the scenarios aids in creating a sense of identity and facilitates discussions and analysis.

The resulting branches from the Futures Wheel that become potential scenarios require a thorough exploration to transform into envisioning tools. The first aspect to analyze are the main elements that emerge from the chosen scenario, scrutinizing the key components, events, and dynamics that shape its storyline. For this, the consideration of specific categories assists in the further understanding of the scenario; these could include qualities such as provocation, coherence, consistency, sensory stimulation, and immediacy.

Step 3: Create a Scenario

An essential step is to craft a compelling narrative that links all of the different elements from the scenario. The scenarios act as potent tools for provocation, captivating the audience and persuading them to act in alignment with long-term objectives. By shattering stereotypes and stirring emotions, scenarios cultivate empathy and motivation. Throughout the process of creating scenarios, certain principles should steer your approach; coherence is vital, ensuring internal consistency within the scenario while allowing for adaptations and decontextualization of certain elements. Consistency, on the other hand, concentrates on the plausibility of the scenario within the envisioned future, rather than strict probability. Sensoriality plays a pivotal role in creating impactful scenarios. Images and words should stir emotions and provoke sensory experiences, amplifying meaning through thoughtful combination and presentation. Finally, scenarios should possess immediacy, effectively conveying their message and meaning in a clear and engaging manner. Evocative images and concise language contribute to the scenario's immediate impact and resonance.

The employment of visual aids such as images or sketches also assists in the description and visualization of the scenario, conveying intangible meanings and providing a clearer future direction. The social, cultural, and technological contexts of the worldbuilding also play a significant role in shaping the narrative and outcomes, enabling the creation of immersive narratives and provoking thoughtful responses about a more sustainable and inclusive world.

Constructing Stories of Environmental Asylum: Climate Refuge Narratives

Departing from signal hunting, as a foundational component of worldbuilding and involving the scrutinizing of the present for trends or incidents that could significantly mold our future. We individuate the case for "Environmental Asylum." In 2021, a French court overturned a man's deportation order, citing the severe air pollution in his home country, Bangladesh, as a potential exacerbator of his asthma, which could lead to fatal outcomes (The Guardian, 2021). The Global Ambient Air Quality Database by the World Health Organization reveals that Dhaka, the capital of Bangladesh, is among the world's most polluted cities, with an annual average PM2.5 concentration of 83.3 micrograms per cubic meter, far exceeding the recommended limit of 10 micrograms per cubic meter.

The acknowledgment of this case as a signal – an incident sparking critical "What If" inquiries about the future – carries several implications. This could inspire courts worldwide to rule in favor of climate refugees, and more broadly, individuals displaced due to environmental factors seeking asylum from life-threatening conditions in their home countries. This shift from being perceived as "refugees" to "asylees" could transform public attitudes toward immigrants and establish a legally recognized pathway in international courts.

Once the signal is identified, we proceed by posing "What If" questions. What if by 2032, seeking climate asylum becomes a standard international policy? What would occur if individuals from environmentally endangered or hazardous locations could apply for climate asylum in countries with more stable climates?

These questions could elicit numerous answers, revealing the multiple implications of such a policy. For example, "clean" countries might erect barriers, indicating the emergence of climate nationalism. Another option could be the establishment of a ministry for the future. Cross-country climate mobility might increase, or we could even imagine the creation of an international institution that provides international citizenship due to climate asylum.

For instance, they could suggest the possibility of cities learning to adapt to accommodate more people and the potential creation of new social structures to accommodate climate refugees. However, this thought exercise is not limited to these direct implications only. We advocate for the contemplation of wider impacts on how they might influence the SDGs. For instance, one potential negative impact could be the loss of cultural norms and rituals due to increased mobility. Conversely, a positive effect could be the regrowth of forests in areas from which people are departing.

This signal-hunting exercise demonstrates how a single, tangible event can trigger a multitude of "What If" questions, leading to the generation of multiple forecasts around different parts of the system, thereby aiding in the construction of a future world. The integration of these forecasts broadens the discussion and *constructs* a more detailed, comprehensive vision of the future world, taking into account not merely migration, but also food, energy, geopolitics, and policy.

Reimagining Recife: Worldbuilding a Sustainable Hometown

Following signal hunting, the worldbuilding process may be concretized and envisioned using digitally modified images. For instance, our expert Jacques Barcia conceived a project that provides an alternative vision of his hometown Recife, in Brazil, in collaboration with a Brazilian organization for professional development. The Recife project presents an innovative way of utilizing speculative fiction as a tool to critically examine our existing societal structures and to imagine diverse future scenarios. In the depicted world, a radical shift in wealth distribution has occurred following the extinction of billionaires, leading to a distinct social transformation.

Figure 4.5 Recife project photomontage.
Source: Courtesy of IFTF and SENAI Nacional.

To augment the narrative and aid the audience's understanding of this reimagined reality, the project employs photomontage. This powerful visual tool acts as an instrumental narrative device, effectively communicating the envisioned future and stimulating a critique and thought-provoking dialogue among viewers. By re-envisioning Recife as a green corridor and integrating elements such as advertisement billboards, graffiti, and street signage, the photomontage lends a sense of tangibility to Barcia's design fiction, transforming abstract ideas into tangible visual narratives. Some of the concepts introduced through these tangible elements in the digitally altered image include community farming, an index of Universal Basic Income, a TV show titled "The Last Billionaire," symbolizing a fundamental shift in societal wealth and structure, and embodying the principles of sustainability and communal responsibility (Figure 4.5).

This case engages the viewer through Cognitive Estrangement, prompting them to compare and contrast this speculative reality with the actual world. This enables the audience to reconsider current societal structures, thereby broadening the discourse on the potential implications, issues, and inconsistencies that may emerge in the newly visualized future. It provokes questions about energy production, food cultivation, distribution, and storage in the real world, and how these aspects might evolve in the fictive world. This storytelling method and the Cognitive Estrangement it induces have wider implications for our perception of the real world.

In essence, Barcia's project triggers a unique iterative process where viewers continuously reassess their perspectives of the real and the fictive world, adjusting their perceptions accordingly. This cycle of comparison and adjustment cultivates a deeper understanding of both worlds and fuels the viewer's speculation on what future possibilities might entail. The Recife project presents an imaginative future through worldbuilding by using visual storytelling tools to effectively communicate these possibilities. The project's strength lies in its ability to reimagine realities, challenge existing structures, and engage viewers in a deeper exploration of potential futures.

BUILDING WORLDS: A PRACTITIONER'S POSSIBLE JOURNAL ENTRY

Worldbuilding is inherently multicultural, recognizing and integrating the richness of diverse cultures. To shift from scenario-based planning to worldbuilding, we will need to engage our collective imagination with foresight and holistic storytelling. These elements provide a foundation for our worldbuilding methodology, offering specificity, crafting unique terms, objects, and organizations that inject a distinctive essence into the envisioned world. Constructing future worlds becomes even more crucial when addressing significant global challenge (Figure 4.6).

Figure 4.6 Designing sustainable futures literacy: build worlds.

Source: By authors.

Here are a few resources to further develop your futures literacy for worldbuilding:

- World Building Institute | The Future of Narrative Media (www. worldbuilding.institute)
- Worlds – Other Atlas (www.otheratlas.com)
- Dragonfly: An Exploration of Eco-Fiction (www.dragonfly.eco)
- Weltenbau Wissen List of Worldbuilding Questions (www. weltenbauwissen.com)
- Science Fiction Studies (SFS) (www.depauw.edu/sfs)
- Journal of Media Psychology (www.hogrefe.com)
- Simulation & Gaming (www.journals.sagepub.com/home/SAG)
- SOLARPUNK Planet (www.solarpunkplanet.com)
- Good Anthropocenes (www.goodanthropocenes.net)

Worldbuilders who approach the practice of constructing future worlds with a mindset of openness and curiosity will be ready to embrace the complexity of the systems at play. It is the interplay between worlds and their systems that open a trove of opportunities for more meaningful experiences. The next chapter dives headfirst into this complexity, offering designers an additional layer of depth to mine in the design of more sustainable futures.

5

Shaping Systems

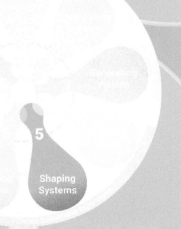

As the worlds we live in – speculative or real – become more complex, the need to see and shape the underlying interconnections is more pressing than ever. Conventional design methodologies often prove inadequate in tackling design challenges that are multidimensional. Systemic Design, a blend of systems thinking and design practices, exposes the underlying structures of our complex world and offers a novel perspective for structuring more sustainable futures. Guided by Professor Silvia Barbero from Politecnico di Torino and founder of the Sys Lab research group, we will dive into the nature of the systems to reveal how we might facilitate the design of sustainable futures. We will share practical tools and examples that illustrate how this approach engages our collective imagination to comprehend the seemingly incomprehensible STESs. Systemic Design is also a mindset, so in this chapter, we aim to further develop the competency of systems thinking: the ability to identify and comprehend relationships; to analyze intricate systems; to understand how systems are embedded within various domains and scales; and to manage uncertainty (Miller, 2018).

THINKING, SEEING (AND SHAPING) SYSTEMS

Design has always been about problem-solving, but the complexities of the 21st century have amplified the challenges we face. Often associated with improving user satisfaction, historically design has missed social, economic, or environmental challenges (Papanek, 1971). This has inadvertently contributed to dilemmas such as climate change, social inequality, biodiversity loss, and economic disparity. Unlike conventional design methodologies that may concentrate primarily on the person, product, or service, thinking in systems' basic assumption is that nothing is isolated; everything is interconnected, and therefore interdependent. System thinking starts by examining the flows of energy, matter, and information within a system, and how this relates to the actors and the features of that territory. These connections tell a more comprehensive story that enables more complex problem-solving. Fundamentally interdisciplinary, this approach is adept at bridging divides between sectors, industries, and disciplines, critical for engaging the collective imagination to create more sustainable experiences.

DOI: 10.4324/9781003451693-8

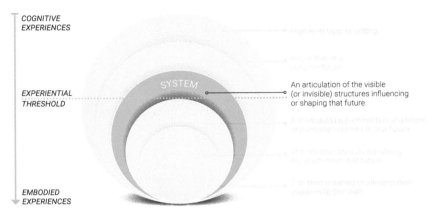

CrossCOGNITIVE
EXPERIENCES

EXPERIENTIAL
THRESHOLD

SYSTEM

An articulation of the visible
(or invisible) structures influencing
or shaping that future

EMBODIED
EXPERIENCES

Figure 5.1 The Experiential Futures Ladder, spotlight on the System.
Source: Adapted from Candy and Dunagan (2017). With permission.

Moreover, as illustrated in the Experiential Futures Ladder, Figure 5.1, systems bridge the experiential threshold by both revealing the intricacies of the scenario and provide design materials for scenes of more sustainable experiences, both essential ingredients for designing sustainable futures.

Systemic design, though a relatively new nomenclature, has roots that trace back to the mid-20th century, a period marked by significant advancements in systems theory and cybernetics. From Ludwig von Bertalanffy's General Systems Theory to Norbert Wiener's foundational work on cybernetics, these early frameworks laid the groundwork for what would become system thinking. Incorporating aspects of complexity theory, one of the core principles of systems thinking is shifting from linear and reactive representations to complex and adaptative representations of the world (Figure 5.2).

Although many contributed to bringing system thinking into mainstream thought, Donella Meadows was a critical catalyst in this paradigm shift. Building on the key message from *The Limits to Growth* to incorporate systemic perspectives into planning and decision-making, Meadows returned in 2008 with *Thinking in Systems* (Meadows, 2008). Encapsulating the essence of systems theory for a wider audience, Meadows explains how systems

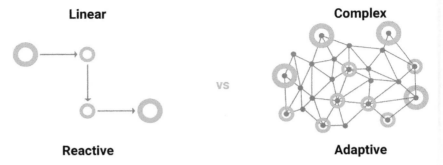

Figure 5.2 Shift from linear and reactive to complex and adaptative representations. *Source*: Courtesy of Sys Lab.

can be understood, managed, and changed, offering a set of practical tools for systemic change. Her insights are particularly valuable for designers aiming to make impactful and sustainable interventions in the complex systems of the modern world. Her approach was applied to solve complex social problems like education and healthcare in David Stroh's *Systems Thinking for Social Change* (Stroh, 2015). Daniel Christian Wahl's *Designing Regenerative Cultures* (Wahl, 2016) outlines how a culture of sustainability that spans all aspects of life, from personal decisions to global policy-making, informs new design practices. In emphasizing the interconnectedness and interdependence of all life forms, he proposes that the power of system thinking is in fostering cultures that are not merely sustainable, but regenerative. By grounding us all through what Capra refers to as the "intricate web of life" (Capra, 1996), systems offer a binding connectivity that engages people towards more sustainable futures.

Sys Lab's contribution to the evolution of Systemic Design is a detailed analysis and systemic solutions that contract the traditional economic models often advocate a linear "take, make, dispose" strategy that is unsustainable in the long haul. The approach promotes the creation of circular systems that minimize waste and repurpose, recycle, or reuse resources, thereby nurturing sustainability (Figure 5.3). This underpins a deeper, designerly understanding of systemic design, based on

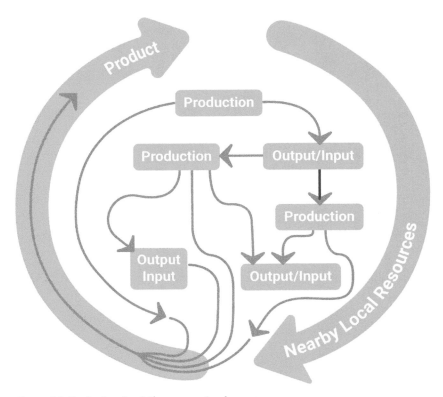

Figure 5.3 Designing the shift to more circular systems.
Source: Courtesy of Sys Lab

an integrated approach, where ecological considerations are balanced with social and economic dimensions, to truly achieve sustainable solutions.

A key tenant of Systemic Design lies in its design roots – it calls on practitioners and stakeholders alike to represent the systems at play in their STES. Visualization, modeling, and prototyping have emerged as essential tools to make the complex nature of systems more tangible. By giving "shape" to complexity with visual representations, everyone can understand the complex systems, and plant the seeds of designing new systems. This classic design practice – problem-solving through problem setting – is a critical feature of Systemic Design that makes it so suitable for creating sustainable experiences. These function as inspirational visions

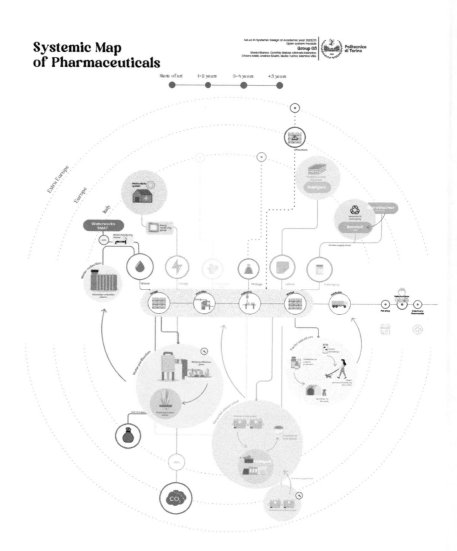

Systemic Map of Pharmaceuticals

Figure 5.4 Holistic diagnosis of pharmaceuticals' production systems.
Source: Courtesy of Sys Lab.

that underscore the urgency and importance of Systemic Design in crafting sustainable futures.

For example, one such technique is the *Holistic Diagnosis (HD)*, a structured method that offers a lens to scrutinize complex systems and their contexts (Battistoni et al., 2019). HD delves into assessment, research, data gathering, visualization, and interpretation. As illustrated in Figure 5.4, an HD of Pharmaceuticals Production Systems incorporates defining the systems scope to visualizing intricate data, culminating in the identification of relationships and revealing potential innovations.

Similarly, *Gigamapping* is an extremely extensive mapping across fields, silos, boundaries, disciplines, and groups with the goal of rendering these relations in support of design dialogues. It inherently triggers boundary critiques on the conception and framing of systems. Because it is able to visually accommodate many types of data representations, illustrations, models, and perspectives (Sevaldson, 2022), it also acts as a canvas for fostering innovation by connecting multiple perspectives (Ryan, 2014). As illustrated in Figure 5.5, The Unsustainable Loop of Sustainability, seeing a visual representation of the systemic complexity of sustainablity triggers thinking about its unsustainablity. (Figure 5.5).

These visualization techniques highlight that Systemic Design is about both problem-setting and planting the seeds for systemic transformation. With the long-term goal to co-create self-sustaining, adaptive systems that are resilient enough to evolve with shifting circumstances, Systemic Design seeks clarity with flexibility, relationships over isolation, autopoiesis rather than allopoiesis, local self-sustaining, and self-generating solutions, and as Don Norman now writes, humanity-centered rather the human-centered approaches that have contributed significantly to the present sustainability challenges (Norman, 2023).

SYSTEMIC DESIGN: SHAPING SUSTAINABLE EXPERIENCES

Visualizing complexity is a small part of Systemic Design's capacity to enable stakeholders to shape the complexity of sustainability. The Sys Lab proposes an approach that integrates methods and tools of systemic design for environmental, social, and economic sustainability and enriches the design vocabulary, while ensuring adaptability in ever-evolving contexts.

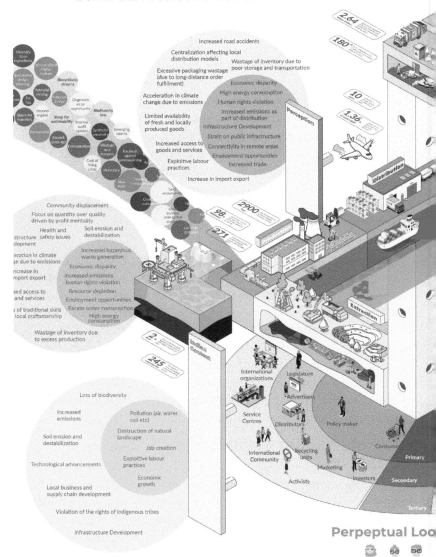

Figure 5.5 Unsustainable-loop-of-sustainability.

Source: adapted from Didmishe, Variar, Moopan, Kale, Nahar, Thappa RSD12: proceedings of relating systems thinking and design 2023, https://rsdsymposium.org/unsustainable-loop-of-sustainability/#pdf-rsd12_paper_176/1/.

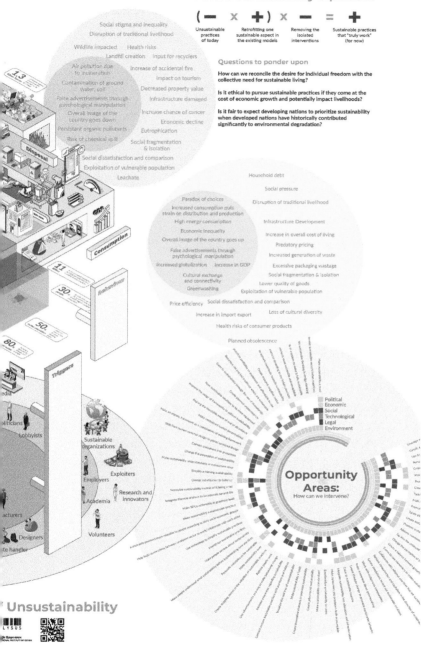

Future sustainability equation?

$$(- \times +) \times - = +$$

| Unsustainable practices of today | Retrofitting one sustainable aspect in the existing models | Removing the isolated interventions | Sustainable practices that "truly work" (for now) |

Questions to ponder upon

How can we reconcile the desire for individual freedom with the collective need for sustainable living?

Is it ethical to pursue sustainable practices if they come at the cost of economic growth and potentially impact livelihoods?

Is it fair to expect developing nations to prioritize sustainability when developed nations have historically contributed significantly to environmental degradation?

Political
Economic
Social
Technological
Legal
Environment

Opportunity Areas:
How can we intervene?

Unsustainability

L Y S U S

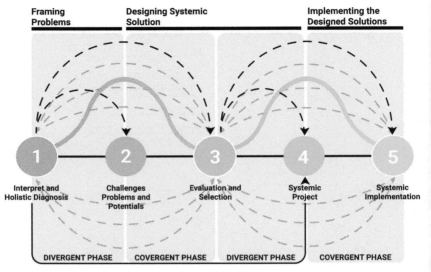

Framing Problems

Designing Systemic Solution

Implementing the Designed Solutions

1
Interpret and Holistic Diagnosis

2
Challenges Problems and Potentials

3
Evaluation and Selection

4
Systemic Project

5
Systemic Implementation

DIVERGENT PHASE COVERGENT PHASE DIVERGENT PHASE COVERGENT PHASE

Figure 5.6 Sys Lab systemic design methodology. Courtesy of Sys lab.
Source: Courtesy of Sys lab.

As illustrated in Figure 5.6, the Sys Lab Systemic Design Methodology is a series of thoughtful and interconnected stages. It starts with framing the problem, a stage where understanding and defining the issue at hand lays the foundation. Then, moves into the realm of designing the solutions, where the focus is on humanity-centered design, seeking to bring community interactions with the systems at the core of any experience. The final stage is the implementation of these solutions, a critical phase where the plans and designs are brought to life, addressing complex challenges within the system through various interventions like policy changes and organizational restructuring. This methodology, while structured, is dynamic and evolves with the needs and complexities of the system it aims to improve, in the following manner:

I) Framing Problems

   1. Interpretation and Holistic Diagnosis (Divergent)

      This initial stage lays the groundwork for the Systemic Design process. A comprehensive HD involves in-depth assessment, research, data gathering, visualization, and interpretation. This multifaceted approach provides

Part II: Create Sustainable Experiences

a panoramic understanding of the situation, laying down a well-defined canvas for the subsequent phases. Resonating strongly with this phase is the Life Cycle Design (LCA) approach because it reveals and defines the boundary of the systems in play – from raw material extraction to disposal or recycling. As a multifaceted strategy, LCA encourages responsible decision-making across sectors by proactively anticipating environmental repercussions. Industries benefit by integrating this approach into their sustainability initiatives, enhancing brand value, and mitigating risks. Governments can frame policies that balance economic, environmental, and social outcomes, thereby showcasing global responsibility. Consumers, armed with transparent information, can make more sustainable choices. By facilitating a broad spectrum of stakeholder dialogue, the LCA approach bridges local, national, and international strategies for sustainable development in a divergent stage, while also incorporating vital opportunities for sustainable solutions in a convergent stage.

2. Challenges – Problems and Potentials (Convergent)

This phase narrows down the focus, converging on the core challenges and their potential solutions. By identifying and understanding these systemic challenges, the stage is set for the formulation of effective strategies. The approach of multilevel system interventions is crucial here. Given the interconnected nature of challenges such as climate change or biodiversity loss, solutions are designed to function at various scales, from individual behaviors to global policy formulation. This ensures the development of strategies with wide-ranging, sustainable impacts.

II) Designing Systemic Experiences

3. Evaluation (Divergent) and Selection

In this stage, potential solutions are brainstormed, critically evaluated, and the most promising ones are selected through a multicriteria analysis. The focus is on drawing from a range of ideas and refining them for implementation. The trend of co-design and participatory processes is particularly relevant in this phase. By involving all stakeholders, sustainable solutions can become more inclusive. This ensures that the systemic designs resonate with a diverse audience, fostering wider acceptance and success.

4. Systemic Project (Convergent)

The focus in this phase is on transforming the selected solutions into actionable projects. These are not mere interventions, but holistic strategies aimed at achieving short-term, medium-term, and sustainable impacts. This phase aligns with the trend of resilience and regenerative design. The focus is on developing solutions that are adaptable, evolvable, and self-renewing. Drawing inspiration from principles such as biomimicry and ecological design, the solutions developed are in harmony with nature, promising longevity, and sustainability.

III) Implementation of Designed Solutions

5. Systemic Implementation (Convergent)

Beyond the ideation and planning stages, this phase actualizes systemic designs by prioritizing the actions based on which will have short/medium/long term and their scale (micro/meso/macro). The prioritization aims to ensure the longevity and sustainability of the implemented designs. The trend of shifting from linear to circular models is crucial here. By advocating for solutions that promote circularity, waste is minimized, resource efficiency is maximized, and sustainable consumption patterns are encouraged. Additionally, the trend of moving from isolated interventions to holistic strategies ensures that the solutions, once implemented, have a ripple effect, influencing and optimizing broader systems. As the conversation on sustainability evolves, the need for systemic approaches becomes increasingly clear.

To enable practitioners to use the Sys Lab Systemic Design methodology, the team created the Systemic Design Toolkit to be an all-encompassing resource for Systemic Design initiatives. One essential tool in the kit is the Social Ecosystem Tool: Mapping the Landscape for Sustainable Experiences (Figure 5.7).

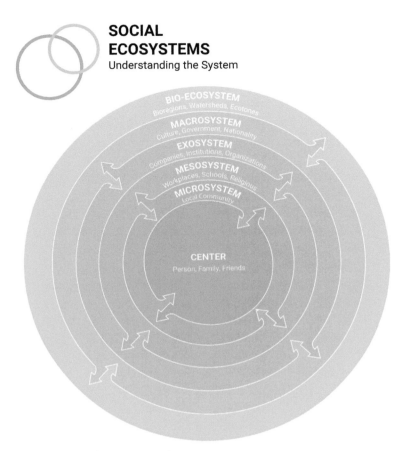

SOCIAL ECOSYSTEMS
Understanding the System

BIO-ECOSYSTEM
Bioregions, Watersheds, Ecotones

MACROSYSTEM
Culture, Government, Nationality

EXOSYSTEM
Companies, Institutions, Organizations

MESOSYSTEM
Workplaces, Schools, Religious

MICROSYSTEM
Local Community

CENTER
Person, Family, Friends

Figure 5.7 Social ecosystem tool.
Source: Adapted from Sys Lab.

The Social Ecosystem Tool is based on Uri Bronfenbrenner's bio-socioecological model of human development and adapted for social systems by Peter Jones and Ael (2022). The tool is essential to navigate the intricate web of stakeholders by providing a panoramic view of the entire social ecosystem. Here lies the essence of the social ecosystem tool, an avant-garde framework that transcends the conventional to craft experiences resonating with sustainability and shared value.

1. *Delineating the Ecosystem* – The first step in this journey is to broaden the scope of the investigation. Traditional stakeholder models may restrict themselves to the immediate,

such as customers or investors, but the social ecosystem tool expands the view. It encourages organizations to listen to the community's subtle signals, the whispers of grassroots movements, and even the silent aspirations of future generations. This holistic approach ensures that designs are not isolated but are a harmonious part of the larger societal stakeholder symphony. Begin with an exhaustive exploration of every potential actor that orbits an organization's sphere. By using techniques such as ethnographic studies, primary dialogues, and social media analytics, the outlines of this ecosystem begin to form. Whether it's a local craftsman contributing to a global brand or an environmentalist influencing public opinion, these diverse entities provide invaluable insights for creating richer experiences.

2. *Prioritizing within the Ecosystem* – Once this extensive list is solidified, the social ecosystem tool assists organizations in assessing the influence and enthusiasm of each stakeholder. Visualizing stakeholders along axes of influence and interest provides a strategic perspective. Those with significant influence but lukewarm interest emerge as prime candidates for alignment, while those overflowing with interest but minimal influence represent untapped sources of innovation. This nuanced understanding customizes the creation of experiences that resonate across the spectrum. However, like all ecosystems, this one is also in a state of constant change. It requires regular revisits to capture emerging voices, shifting alliances, and evolving dynamics. This dynamic recalibration ensures that organizations stay in tune with the changing frequencies of their ecosystem, thereby iterating and refining their offerings for enduring relevance.

3. *Strategizing with the Ecosystem* – Adopting the social ecosystem tool provides organizations a visionary perspective. It cultivates a symbiotic relationship with the wider society, anticipates potential challenges, and fosters resilience in the face of change. This philosophy signals a shift from a directive design approach to one that's participatory, recognizing the collective in shaping sustainable outcomes. By grounding experiences in this rich fabric of stakeholder insights, organizations craft offerings that are not contemporary, but timeless.

The social ecosystem tool advocates for the creation of experiences that are sustainable in essence and also harmoniously aligned with the vast array of societal stakeholders, essential in navigating the journey of more sustainable experiences. In this dynamic context, Systemic Design offers an approach for advocating for policies that are both flexible and aimed at fostering social innovation and sustainable transitions.

An exemplar of Systemic Design`s potential as systemic change catalyst occurred during the COVID-19 pandemic. Launched in the midst of a health and economic crisis, the RETRACE project sought to promote systemic design as a methodology to steer local and regional policies toward a circular economy. It examined how the COVID-19 pandemic influenced the development of the circular economy strategies in the regions, including the Italian region of Piemonte (Figure 5.8), with the intention of developing recovery strategies.

RETRACE's mission was rooted in the conviction that by incorporating the principles of Systemic Design into policy-making, regions can effectively transition to a circular economy. RETRACE's strategy was based on a simple premise: that waste from one process can be repurposed as input for another, creating a closed-loop system that encourages sustainability and minimizes waste.

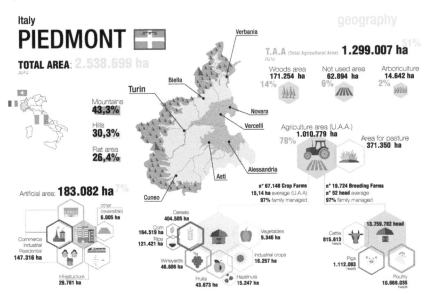

Figure 5.8 Piedmont geographic systemic analysis.
Source: Barbero (2017).

It set out with the ambitious goal of driving circular economy policies across five diverse European regions. Each region, with its unique socioeconomic conditions and industrial priorities, was viewed as a unique canvas, presenting its own set of challenges and opportunities.

To navigate this complex landscape, RETRACE utilized a Systemic Design approach, designing solutions that were innovatively holistic, considering the intricate web of environmental, economic, and social interconnections in each region. From April 2016 to September 2022, the program was marked by a series of interconnected steps that seamlessly integrated systems thinking.

The foundational phase involved creating holistic diagnoses to map the intricate interconnections existing between environmental resources, key industrial sectors, and prevailing socioeconomic conditions in each region. Such comprehensive mapping ensured a deep understanding of the territorial complexities, laying the groundwork for subsequent phases.

Learning from the holistic diagnosis, the team identified over 70 good practices of Circular Economy in the five regions of intervention, promoting the exchange of experiences during nine interregional events involving five regional and national stakeholder groups and numerous policy makers. The practices published in the final report are marked by their innovativeness, potential systemic impact, and adaptability to varied contexts, provided valuable models for regions aiming to transition to a circular economy

Stakeholders, representing a cross-section of society, played a pivotal role throughout RETRACE's journey. By convening regional working groups, the project ensured that the voices of diverse stakeholders – from the public and private sectors to civil society representatives – engaged in the critical activities for change – knowledge-sharing, strategy formulation, and action planning.

The outcomes of the RETRACE project were both tangible and transformative. From comprehensive diagnoses that visually represented regional complexities, the project's deliverables serve as valuable resources for regions worldwide. Action plans, co-created with stakeholders, provided a strategic roadmap for the transition to a circular economy. The results of the RETRACE project were to examine the impact of the pandemic on regional action plans, pinpointing actions that could hasten the transition to a circular economy despite the crisis

Due to the extensive dissemination activities, the outcomes of RETRACE elevated awareness among policymakers about the transformative potential of systemic design. By taking a systems view, it demonstrated that the transition to a circular economy is feasible and sustainable in the long run. However, as with any pioneering initiative, challenges emerged, from data accessibility issues to cultural barriers between the ethos of design thinking and entrenched institutional norms. Yet, despite these challenges, RETRACE stands as an important example of how Systemic Design can integrate social, economic, and environmental systems thinking to create sustainable experiences.

SHAPING SYSTEMS: A PRACTITIONER'S POSSIBLE JOURNAL ENTRY

Systemic Design is both a method and a mindset – a way of seeing, understanding, and acting to address complex challenges of sustainability (Figure 5.9). Practitioners need to be willing, not just able, to descend into a multitiered context, whether that context is a corporation, a region, or a multistakeholder ecosystem. A systemic design mindset is defined by its curious, open, and integrative character, emphasizing collaboration and a human-centric approach. By inviting diverse perspectives, practitioners must foster an inclusive environment to share complex scenarios and adapt frameworks for continuous learning and innovation. By exposing interconnected relationships, and revealing the complexity of sustainability challenges, practitioners can better navigate and shape the participatory processes essential to synthesize diverse perspectives into unified, socially inclusive solutions.

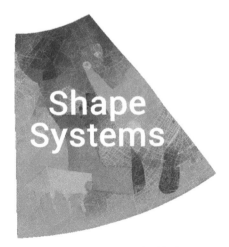

Figure 5.9 Designing sustainable futures literacy: shape systems.
Source: By authors.

A systemic design mindset also requires an adaptive learning mindset, a readiness to iterate and evolve designs in response to different viewpoints that contribute to the development of sustainable systems. A focus on integration, adaptability, and collaboration equips systems designers to develop solutions that are responsive to the needs of various stakeholders and the complexities they face. Emphasizing humility in the face of interdependent values, as is the ability to empathetically integrate the unique experiences of each stakeholder into comprehensive solutions. Navigating uncertainty is also key, allowing systemic designers to explore new possibilities and uncover innovative approaches. Here are a few additional resources to help practitioners strengthen a systemic design mindset

- Systemic Design Toolkit (www.systemicdesigntoolkit.org)
- Design Council Systemic Design Framework (www. designcouncil.org.uk/our-resources/systemic-design-framework/#c8282)
- SYS LAB - About (www.systemicdesignlab.it)
- Systemic Design Association (www.rsdsymposium.org)
- LOOP Circular Economy Ecosystem (www. circulareconomyloop.com)
- Symbiosis in Development (SiD) – Integrated Sustainability Development Framework (https://thinksid.org)
- System Mapping Toolkit (https://miro.com/miroverse/system-mapping-toolkit/

Despite developing a systemic mindset, embracing the interrelationships, interdependencies, and even conflagrations, requires a depth of empathy, patience, and presence that does not come easily to mere mortals. This is when the latent power of the designed object as nexus for human (and natural) interactions is critical. Artifacts from the speculative worlds and their systems open opportunities to focus our exploration of the unknown to contribute to sustainable, resilient, and harmonious futures. In Chapter 6, we will continue our exploration of creating sustainable experiences by examining the dynamics of designed objects to prepare stakeholders to make proactive commitments to create a better future for all.

6

Designing Fictions

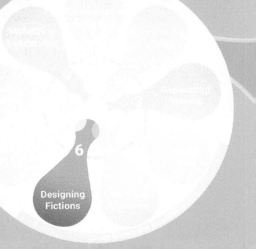

6

Designing
Fictions

When designing sustainable futures, the experiences of these futures need to be as tangible and immediate as possible. After building worlds (Chapter 4) and shaping the systems (Chapter 5), we now speculate about what might be the "stuff" or "things" in that future. This chapter will explore how speculating the design of objects from the future makes engaging with that future more concrete, and more visceral because it is more meaningful. Drawing on the theory and practices of speculative design, we will think and act like the archeologists and anthropologists who unearth the meaning of artifacts for the communities and societies that produced them. We will learn how speculating on the design of artifacts from the future[1] reveals insights into our present biases, norms, and paradigms. These tangible representations or mock-ups of products, services, or just ideas that could exist in the future stimulate discussion and thought about potential futures. Speculating artifacts can turn a "thing from the future" into a bridge between cognitive understanding and embodied experience, between worlds and the underlying systems, and the future and today.

As we will see, designing fictions is an intrinsically participatory exercise. Herein lies its power to motivate stakeholders to mobilize for collective climate change, if the representations of the artifacts are created in a manner that invites a design dialog. The more sketch-like and unfinished the artifact is, the play of co-creating seems more real. Because we must engage people to move toward more sustainable futures, the possibilities engendered by speculating artifacts hold a unique potential for systemic change.

Therefore, our objective in this chapter is to explore how speculating artifacts collaboratively can create a tangible foundation on the path toward a shared understanding of a more sustainable future. Our guide is Victoria Rodriguez Schon, a design researcher who specializes in plural and decolonial futures. Accordingly, this chapter lays the groundwork for developing and honing the

---

1 IFTF refers to such speculative objects as "artifacts from the future" which we will shorten to just "artifacts."

DOI: 10.4324/9781003451693-9

competency of collaboration, in the process of co-creating artifacts from the future.

UNESCO (2017). Learning to Become Sustainable.

Speculative design and design fiction serve as engines of collaborative anticipation, with the former fueling the latter. As boundary objects, designed fictions enable stakeholders to create new meta-narratives of more sustainable futures. These speculative designs afford the design of better futures, offering opportunities to overcome the inherent incommensurability of modern philosophies by bridging the spectrum delinated by modern absolutism and postmodern nihilism. Designing fictions acts as an antidote to these epistemological and ontological conundrums by transforming our innate biases into a bias for the collective good. By establishing more meaningful boundaries, designed fictions shape the contours of a meta-modernism necessary for a better future to emerge from a chaotic present.

DESIGN FICTION: FROM ABSTRACT ARTIFACTS TO EMBODIED EXPERIENCES

As described in Chapter 2, as a contemporary practice of speculative design, design fiction does not narrate stories, it instead designs and situates prototypes within a context that suggests a shift in our reality. Design fiction raises awareness about changes in our behaviors by examining the current state of affairs and proposing alternative realities, and alternative ways of being. Its potency lies in the ability to "suspend disbelief" by introducing to its speculative artifacts with a significant amount of artifice. The theoretical and ethical questions that are raised emerge because of its theatrics. In this context, design fiction is not intended to mislead or dupe the audience, but rather to stage a creative act that contextualizes a conceptual space or scenario.

Design fiction, as a contemporary speculative practice, has become an important element for designing sustainable futures because it engages the near future, exploring a variety of probable, possible, and preferable scenarios. Grist, a nonprofit independent media organization uses climate fiction to tell stories on topics like politics, energy, equity, solutions, and how they intersect with climate. In this field, a speculative approach is used to rethink the conventional aspects of design by making prototypes for potential futures, promoting a critical viewpoint.

However, the success of design fiction in corporate concept videos and promotional advertisements has led to the "…hijacking of its sharpest, funniest critics." (Maughan, 2020). In response, Julian Bleecker, an artist, technologist, and futurist, offered a different take on design fiction in 2009. According to Bleecker, design fiction is a blend of design, science, storytelling, and facts. It serves as a tool to investigate alternative methods of creation and to delve into the tangible outcomes of one's imagination. Design fiction, using its speculative attitude, challenges the typical limitations of commercialization and fosters innovation, exploration, and critical thinking. It merges the traditions of writing, storytelling, and object crafting to create socialized objects that participate in the creative process and stimulate the human imagination (Bleecker, 2009).

Despite some more banal uses of design fictions, speculative artifacts serve as a tool to explore and navigate future scenarios, pushing the boundaries of what is possible and challenging our assumptions about the present. The resulting openings are pathways toward more tangible, actionable, and thought-provoking future scenarios. This intentional approach produces prototypes that exist within an altered reality, merging art with purpose, in the pursuit of multiple potential futures rather than uniformity (Bleecker, 2009). This approach enriches how we envision and interact with potential futures while creating an environment conducive to creative insights, robust discussions, and transformative actions.

Since design fiction opens innovative trajectories for stakeholders to imagine situations and the *stuff* of more sustainable experiences, it acts as an epistemological anchor in the Experiential Futures ladder (Figure 6.1). When scenarios serve up dynamic spaces for collective aspirations, and systems indicate the potential linkages to the tangible world, speculating on the design of scenes and their stuff becomes catalysts in a new futures narrative.

Despite the plethora of scientific evidence, we have witnessed over the years that it is a necessary, but not a sufficient condition, for motivating sustainable action, particularly for climate change (2022). By materializing science-based signals and speculative concepts into tangible objects, artifacts from a future scenario act as experiential portals that transport audiences into envisioned future worlds. Design fiction artifacts, with their speculative approach and attitude,

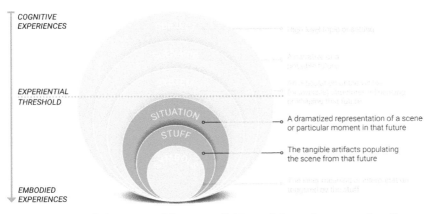

COGNITIVE
EXPERIENCES

EXPERIENTIAL
THRESHOLD

SITUATION ———○ A dramatized representation of a scene
or particular moment in that future

STUFF ———○ The tangible artifacts populating
the scene from that future

EMBODIED
EXPERIENCES

Figure 6.1 Expanded experiential futures scaffold, spotlight on the scene and stuff.
Source: Adapted from Candy and Dunagan (2017). With permission.

act as prompts that encourage us to think about the various futures that could unfold; by focusing on a specific object, we are nudged to imagine the surrounding objects, our relationship with them, and the wider context in which they might exist. Because they elicit visceral reactions that spark deeper contemplations – artifacts from the future are pivotal because they enable people to transcend theoretical discussions and engage concretely with sustainable possibilities. For instance, an artifact from a sustainable city future, such as a "smart garbage-can," prompts people to consider how might they feel talking to their garbage daily. The emotions and reflections elicited by artifacts open doorways to reexamine assumptions, beliefs, and priorities related to sustainability. By making sustainability experiential through artifacts, people can connect with preferred futures at a deeper, more personal level and become invested in bringing that vision to fruition through positive change.

THE SOCIAL CONSTRUCTION OF ARTIFACTS

In speculative design, the creation of artifacts from future scenarios provides a critical lens for uncovering and interrogating present-day cultural norms, cognitive biases, and systemic issues. This approach, deeply rooted in social constructionism, suggests that our understanding of reality is shaped by the collective social processes and interactions we engage in (Berger & Luckmann, 1966). Social constructionism, as a foundational theory in this context, posits

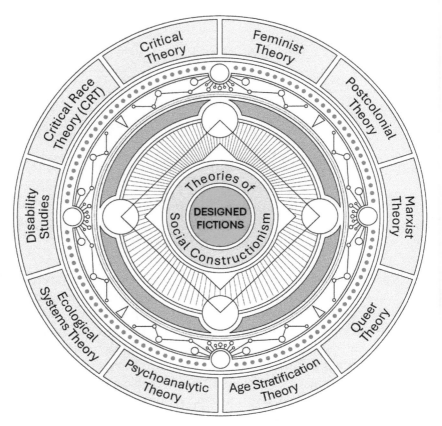

Figure 6.2 A Designed Fiction acts as boundary object of the theories of social constructionism.

Source: By authors, inspired by Michael Reddy's Toolmaker Paradigm (Reddy 1979).

that our social realities are constructed through language, symbols, and interactions, thus making it an apt theoretical foundation for speculative design that aims to reveal and challenge existing societal structures. As contemporary scholars like Gergen (2009) argue, Social Constructionism is essential for understanding how future-speculative artifacts can reflect and challenge existing societal norms and biases.

With Social Constructionism at the center, Figure 6.2 illustrates the multitude of perspectives available for examining the speculative design of artifacts in ways that can reveal insights on our collective *mis*-understandings. Critical Theory, as initially formulated by Horkheimer (1937), coalesced the work of several generations of philosophers and social theorists in the Western European Marxist tradition known as the Frankfurt School. The Frankfurt School held that theories are historical, subjective, and a part of society, rather than merely propositions which can be verified empirically, This shift to critiquing societal structures and addressing power dynamics and inequalities was further elaborated by Adorno (1947), and Foucault (1966). Contemporary applications of Critical Theory, including postcolonists such as Edward Said (1977) and Bhabha (1994), offer insights into the lasting impacts of colonialism on design. Particularly in speculative design, these theoretical approaches encourage the questioning of dominant paradigms and the exploration of alternative social and political structures through artifacts. For example, speculative designers who reexamine Eurocentric narratives seek to ensure that any artifacts from a speculative future represent a wide spectrum of cultural and historical experiences and challenge colonial legacies.

Feminist theory has profoundly shaped speculative design, advocating for creations that interrogate and reimagine gender constructs. While Butler's work (1990) delves into the realms of gender and queer theory (Anzaldúa, 1987), suggesting fluidity and performativity beyond binary norms, Haraway's (1985) philosophy infuses feminist thought into our relationship with technology and non-human agency. Such theoretical frameworks encourage speculative artifacts that challenge traditional gender roles by engaging with broader questions of inclusivity. Following in the tradition of thinkers like Simone de Beauvoir (1949), contemporary speculative design often echoes themes found in the writings of Haraway, as well as Braidotti (2013), whose work further explores posthumanism within feminist contexts.

Psychoanalytic Theory, interpreted through a modern lens by scholars like Mitchell (2000), focuses on the role of unconscious desires and motivations in shaping societal norms. In speculative design, this perspective aids in uncovering the deeper psychological dimensions of societal issues, providing a nuanced understanding of human behavior as it relates to design. Lastly, Ecological Systems Theory, as updated by contemporary environmental thinkers, emphasizes the interplay between environmental and societal systems. This theory, echoing Bronfenbrenner's (1979) original concept, is crucial in speculative design for advocating environmentally sustainable and socially just future artifacts.

To enrich this analysis, we incorporate elements of design justice. Design justice, as proposed by Costanza-Chock (2020), focuses on the equitable distribution of design's benefits and burdens, the participation of marginalized communities in design processes, and the recognition of design as a sociopolitical act. Similarly, Arturo Escobar's concepts in *Designs for the Pluriverse* (2018) and designing autonomously (2019) contribute vital insights into creating designs that respect a multitude of worldviews and promote autonomous design practices. Furthermore, the work of the Decolonising Design Group (2018) complements this framework by interrogating how colonial legacies influence contemporary design practices. Sasha Costanza-Chock's *Design Justice* (2020), describes community-led design practices to break systemic biases that "build the worlds we need." Together, these theories encourage a critical examination of how we envision future artifacts and underscore the importance of diversity and inclusivity in design.

The application of these theories to the design of future artifacts (rather than scenarios themselves) facilitates a deeper understanding of present societal conditions. For instance, the "Aguahoja" project by the MIT Media Lab's Mediated Matter group, led by Neri Oxman, exemplifies this. It uses biodegradable materials to construct architectural structures, challenging the norms of western industrialized building practices and promoting sustainability, a crucial aspect in many Global South contexts. Another relevant example is the Chindogu projects by Kenji Kawakami, which involves the creation of absurd and impractical gadgets that ironically comment on consumerism and technological advancement, reflecting deep-seated cultural and economic critiques relevant to both Global North and South contexts.

To embed social justice more deeply, speculative design must actively engage with diverse communities, to ensure that the co-creation of future artifacts is inclusive and reflective of a broad range of cultural perspectives. This approach provides a platform for underrepresented voices to challenge the dominance of Western-centric futures. Together, these contemporary interpretations of classical theories offer a rich and nuanced framework for participatory speculative design. By situating social constructionism at the core, the framework underscores the constructed nature of our societal perceptions, while the surrounding theories provide additional critical perspectives. This approach ensures that the speculative design of artifacts is a comprehensive process that reveals by actively challenging collective biases, cultural norms, and systemic injustices, thereby enriching design as a powerful tool for societal reflection and transformative change.

THE ARTS AND CRAFTS OF DESIGNING FICTIONS

The trigger at the root of the theories is simply how well the artifacts provoke a range of feelings – excitement, disgust, confusion, fear, or joy – in order to achieve their actual purpose of sparking conversations and contemplations about the future. An emotional resonance is essential to trigger deeper engagement and discussions. It's important to clarify that the creation of these artifacts is not an end in itself. Rather, their purpose is to. While they might seem extravagant or even farfetched, they seamlessly integrate into their respective scenarios, triggering a range of emotions. While artifacts are the medium, the meaning is the message. By triggering personal and communal experiences, they can contribute to a more comprehensive and critical dialogue. Let's examine the arts and crafts of speculating artifacts that invite participants to experience all five senses of a more sustainable world.

The Thing from the Future: Gaming to Create Artifacts

To delve deeper into speculating artifacts, we introduce "The Thing from the Future," developed by the Situation Lab. This game acts as a fast-paced exercise in conceptualizing potential elements of our future world. The game consists of cards, each carrying distinct prompts divided into three categories: a "future" world, a thing, and a thematic "concept." Players use these suggested prompts to quickly create a future artifact (the "thing"). Using the example shown below, a player will come up with a saying related to taxes in a divided future. A player might suggest "we'll all be paying for our choices" or "audit yourself before the system does" (Figure 6.3).

In a recent workshop with a group of change practitioners, a provocative prompt was used to design a policy from the future: *In a more sustainable future, there is a law protecting natural resources. How would you anticipate it to be written?*

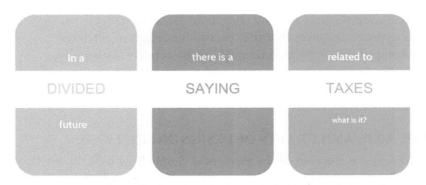

Figure 6.3 Prompt from *The thing from the future* (2nd ed.). Game design and contents by Stuart Candy and Jeff Watson, situation lab, 2018. Reproduced with permission.

Source: Game design and contents by Stuart Candy and Jeff Watson, situation lab, 2018.

- **Grassroots Future Interpretation:** The team initiated their process by linking the term "grassroots" with notions such as "bottom-up," "commons," and "cooperatives." This viewpoint underscored community-led, decentralized structures.

- **Law Perspective:** The concept of "law" was connected with modern technological trends like smart contracts, Web 3.0, and blockchain. The emphasis was on emerging technologies that could support and enforce laws in the future.

- **Resources Perspective:** Rather than financial or human resources, the team focused on tangible materials. They drew inspiration from the maker movements, which advocate DIY production, and deliberated on access to recycling and regenerative infrastructures.

- **Law Formulation:** Transitioning from ideation to synthesis of their thoughts, they examined how global agreements or laws are structured (e.g., the Paris Agreement) and contemplated naming their proposed law the "Immutable Value Act of 2050." The fundamental premise of this act would be to ensure that at a grassroots level, the value of material resources is preserved and can't be manipulated at higher systemic levels. Essentially, the value is "immutable."

- **Rewards and Resource Distribution:** To encourage the preservation and responsible use of materials, the team explored ideas similar to universal basic income. Their concept of "universal basic materials" proposed that every individual, at a grassroots level, receives a predetermined volume of materials (they suggested three cubic meters) that they are responsible for recycling and repurposing.

Futures Artifact Design Brief

The Futures Artifact Design Brief, based on IFTF's *Artifact from the Future*, is a template that facilitates making abstract sustainable futures tangible by guiding users to envision and depict objects from envisioned worlds. Users start by describing a sustainable future scenario through three words in five categories: inhabitants, mood, actions, innovations, and objects. Selecting one word from each column and combining them into a sentence sparks a narrative. For example, the sentence "In this future, animals self-select the humans they heal" tells a story about how healthcare can bridge the perceived gap between people and the planet, revealing an opportunity to literally close this bifurcated thinking inhibiting climate change (Figure 6.4).

Users then expand on the details evoked by this sentence, concretely describing the people, settings, and interactions. This creates a design brief for a generative artificial intelligence to illustrate the artifact – an image encapsulating this future scene of a young child and animal enveloped by a Symbiotic Blanket.

The Futures Artifact Design Brief aims to bridge the concrete and the abstract, empowering users to visualize sustainability futures that make them relatable, experiential, and actionable. In tandem with the Experiential Futures Scaffold, here's how it can work:

1. Start with a Scene Selection: Revisit the world-building activities you engaged in earlier. Select one specific scene from the future world you envisioned, which can range from a routine moment, like breakfast, to special events like graduation ceremonies. The definition of this scene lays the foundation for everything that follows.

2. Characters and Stakeholders: Elaborate on who is present in the scene. Examples can include a scientist, a grandparent, a child, etc.; this will assist in envisioning the objects and technologies

Artifact Name: Symbiotic Blanket

Artifact Description: In this future, animals self-select the humans they heal. The Symbiotic Blanket amplifies the neurological synchronicity between patent and animal, producing significant health benefits for both.

Why is the artifact meaningful?

A bridge between humans and animals for better health of both

At home or in community health centers, where health is understood to be holistic and interdependent with nature

Where is the artifact located?

Children in need of neurological stimulation of immune system and/or physiological treatments

Who are the primary user/s of the artifact?

Brain implants in both human and animal community via the Symbiotic Blanket, triggering hormonal secretions through the nervous system of both

The resulting neurochemicals throughout the nervous system bring a sensation of calmness and over multiple treatment, health and well-being

How does the artifact function?

How does it feel to interact with the artifact?

Figure 6.4 Futures artifact design brief. Adapted from IFTF foresight essentials toolkit. *Source*: Adapted from IFTF foresight essentials toolkit.

they might use or interact with. While your key stakeholders might not be directly present in the scene, determine their interactions with it, are they influenced by this scene? How would they react or experience it?

3. Capture the Emotions & Values: What is the emotional tone of the scene? Is it hopeful, somber, or exhilarating? Reflect on the

values and emotions that drive this scene. This can be drawn from previous discussions or brainstorming sessions.

4. List Actions & Interactions: Document what's happening in the scene. Are there any specific actions or interactions between characters or with objects?

5. Identify Objects & Assets: This is where commonplace objects can become artifacts from the future. List tangible items present. This could range from household items to futuristic technologies. Consider assets like campaign posters, tools, or even pieces of art.

6. Go Beyond Sustainability: Connect the artifact or the scene with sustainability principles. Choose a relevant Sustainable Development Goal (SDG) for your project. Determine how your artifact or scene contributes to or interacts with this goal. How does my artifact respond to the needs related to the SDGs?

7. Name & Define the Artifact: Assign a title and purpose to your primary artifact, and briefly describe its function.

8. Illustrate or Describe Your Artifact: Use the space provided in the tool to sketch or detail your artifact. It is encouraged to be creative here. Collage images, sketches, or even digital mock-ups can be used to give a tangible feel. Make the description as detailed as possible. This will also give it a powerful reality aspect. Think deeply about tangible entities that might exist in the chosen scene. This can include objects, products, ads, etc. We suggest the use of various resources, such as art supplies or digital tools, to manifest this object.

Futures Artifact Design Brief aims to increase the ability of individuals to visualize and then converse about various scenarios. The combination of structured brainstorming and guided design ensures that the resulting artifacts are both imaginative and grounded in reality. These artifacts then serve as tangible representations of potential futures, rendering abstract ideas accessible and promoting deeper involvement. Together, the game and template function as catalysts, converting imaginative ideas into effective instruments for future exploration and strategizing.

Syntharian Lunch Menu: A Glimpse into a Compassionate Future

Our recognition of societal norms, values, and technological progression evolves, often finding its most compelling manifestation in the sphere of speculative fiction and design. This domain pushes the envelope, prompting us to contemplate the "what ifs" and "maybes" of tomorrow. As created by Jacque Barcia (our expert on worldbuilding), the Syntharian Lunch Menu turns a mundane meal into a vibrant portrayal of potential futures.

Imagine entering a room with meticulously arranged lunch menus, suggesting a meal crafted for a world profoundly aware of its ethical obligations toward all sentient beings (Figure 6.5). This is not merely a progression beyond vegetarianism or veganism; it was a monumental stride into a future where no life form – animal or plant – exploited for our gastronomic pleasures.

The menu read:

- Spicy Synth Stroganoff: A tantalizing dish made from naturally fermented air protein, accompanied by a cultured mustard enzyme sauce.
- Glycodo: This was a perfect imitation of a white carb risotto, enriched with mineral flakes and a sumptuous glycoprotein broth.
- Desserts: Though unspecified, it promised a sweet experience that wouldn't hurt any life form.
- Beverages: The offerings were unique – Janist water and molecular whiskey. The former intriguingly hints at Jainism, a religion that emphasizes non-violence to all life forms, hinting at a drink that imbibes this principle.

However, astute observers would notice some playful hints pointing to the fictional nature of this menu. A seal declared the menu to be certified by "PETAL (People for the Ethical Treatment of All Life)" for the year 2032, implying an organized entity committed to ensuring the ethical treatment of all life forms, albeit in a future yet to come.

The efficacy of this speculative design exercise was demonstrated when a student posted the menu on Instagram. The ensuing

INSTITUTE FOR THE FUTURE

SYNTHERIAN MENU

LUNCH

Spicy Synth Stroganoff: *naturally fermented air protein served in a sauce of cultured mustard enzymes and nature-identical white carb grains.*

Glycotto: *nature-identical white carb 'risotto' served in glycoprotein broth and mineral flakes*

DESSERT

Mocha Vat Mousse: *origin-simulated roasted cocoa cells, synth coffee syrup and egg-white protein créme chantilly.*

DRINKS

Jainist water.

Molecular whiskey.

Figure 6.5 Syntharian lunch menu.
Source: Courtesy of IFTF.

wave of comments unveiled genuine curiosity, bewilderment, and fascination. Many were in awe, pondering about the "Syntharian diet," a term previously unknown. It beautifully underscored the exercise's objective: making abstract future concepts concrete and sparking discussions about them.

What does such a menu reveal about the world of tomorrow? It portrays a society that respects all life, emphasizing sustainability, technological advancements in food production, and a culture deeply rooted in empathy and responsibility. The menu is not merely a list of dishes but a relic of a world where ethics and technology intertwine to create a harmonious existence. Through such vivid examples, the participants engaged with, questioned, and discussed the myriad possibilities the future might offer.

Toilet Surveillance: The Intricacies of Privacy in the Future

The domain of speculative design often ventures into uncharted territories, aiming to promote dialogue about potential futures. A fascinating instance of this is nestled within the humble setting of a restroom at Institute for The Future in Palo Alto, California, USA. Those visiting the Institute for The Future's restrooms were greeted with a sign: the toilet was under the watchful eye of the City of Alameda and the State of California (Figure 6.6). This surveillance, as the notice elaborated, gave the city, state, and any associated third parties the permission to scrutinize the user's biological waste. Going a step further, the information extracted from this waste could potentially be combined with facial recognition or other identification technologies, enabling authorities to contact the user about any discoveries from their "contribution."

This speculative intervention prompts reflection: What would it be like to inhabit a world where a trip to the restroom divulges intimate information about one's physical or mental wellbeing? Such a scenario brings up a host of societal, ethical, and technological concerns, ranging from data privacy and personal agency to the ramifications of state-led surveillance. Some of the questions that might arise could ponder the worth of such intimate data. If it's valuable to the authorities, why shouldn't individuals monetize it? In theory, such a system could allow people to "deposit" data and receive payment in return.

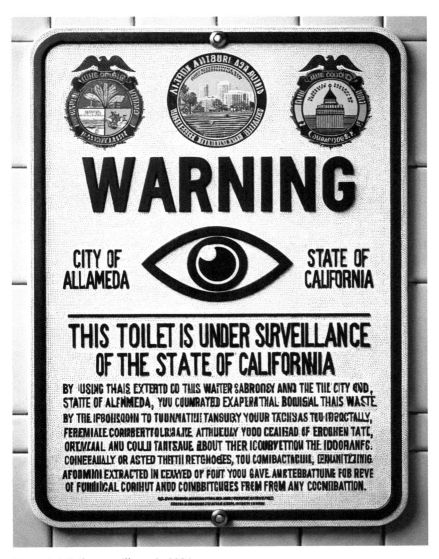

Figure 6.6 Toilet surveillance in 2034.

Source: adapted from IFTF, authors augmented by Midjourney Courtesy of IFTF.

However, those paying close attention would notice subtle clues pointing to the fictitious nature of the initiative. The date on the sign was set for January 2034, hinting at a futuristic scenario not yet in existence. To further engage restroom users in this speculative setting, other imaginary tools were introduced: an "anonymizing spray" that one could use to erase or anonymize the data before flushing. This added layer amplified the depth of the scenario by revealing the intricacies of personal data management in an increasingly digital age.

The artifact at the Institute for The Future achieves something remarkable. By simply placing a sign in a restroom, it triggers profound reflection about the possible paths our society could take in relation to surveillance, privacy, data ownership, and personal freedom. Even if such a reality is not present today, the sign pushes us to contemplate its implications – and how we might navigate or shape such a future.

Interspecies Matrimony: When Nature and Technology Hold Human Rights

In our course Designing Sustainable Futures, a group explored the practice of creating artifacts based on future scenes and systems, aided by employing a world-building artifact template that incorporates sustainability and the SDGs. The result ventures into a captivating and, occasionally, perplexing scenario. In this speculative future, non-human entities encompassing both the natural environment and technological progress are granted human rights. This assertion redefines societal standards and fundamentally reveals the biases embedded in traditional relationships, legal frameworks, and cultural customs.

The core insight of this world is non-human rights. To enable this, nature is endowed with sensors that make AI actually intelligent by information to legitimately express emotions, give consent, and even engage in legal procedures. The imaginative, yet logical conclusion, is interspecies marriage as a means to safeguarding the rights of the non-human domain, thereby cultivating deep bonds between disparate entities. A result of this fiction was an invitation for an interspecies wedding, celebrating the union between a human bride and her groom, an oak tree named James (Figure 6.7).

The invitation carries details in both human language via DNA language. This fictional design symbolizes the union of biology and sensor technologies in a world is named the Plantiverse, set within the lush Amazon rainforest.

The Wedding of

Estella & James the Oak Tree

Save the Date

14 August 2028 / 3pm
Amazon Rain Forest

Figure 6.7 Estelle and James' wedding announcement. Participant's work from the Designing Sustainable Futures course.

Source: Course participants.

The team continued to design this fiction by bestowing James with a birth certificate detailing his DNA and origins, the scenario

Figure 6.8 Estelle and James' marriage certificate. Participant's work from the Designing Sustainable Futures course.

Source: Course participants.

grants him undeniable legitimacy, leading to a marriage certificate (Figure 6.8). This artifact reinforces the idea of interspecies unions and introduces a unique qualifier: a "certified carbon-free" seal. Here, couples can only manifest their marriage if they can present evidence of a healthy carbon footprint.

These artifacts act as a meaningful contemplation of the evolving paradigms of relationships, rights, and responsibilities in an urgent sustainable future. The vision, while undeniably speculative, incites profound self-examination: How could the fusion of nature and technology redefine societal standards? How might bestowing rights upon non-human entities affect human interactions and obligations? And perhaps, most importantly, are we ready to embrace a world where humans, nature, and technology intertwine in the most personal and profound of ways? The answers remain elusive, but the questions are crucial for charting our course towards a better future.

DESIGNING FICTIONS: A PRACTITIONER'S POSSIBLE JOURNAL ENTRY

Designing fictions for sustainable futures involves crafting immersive experiences through artifacts like mock advertisements for futuristic products, blending fiction with reality through vivid details to emotionally transport individuals into envisioned worlds. It extends to sparking imaginative conversations via thought-provoking objects, encouraging open-ended discussions on possible futures and preparing for a spectrum of interpretations. The Futures Literacy of Speculating Artifacts also encourages

Figure 6.9 Designing sustainable futures literacy: design fictions.

Source: By authors

designers to anticipate diverse reactions to artifacts, such as sustainable food packaging, using feedback to deepen understanding of future scenarios. Emphasizing inclusivity, it involves creating artifacts like architectural models that consider potential unintended consequences, fostering narratives that support ethical, inclusive futures for everyone. Moreover, fostering deeper meaning involves looking beyond the immediate aesthetics of futuristic gadgets to uncover the stories, systems, and societal structures they signify, thereby revealing profound insights into sustainable futures

Many tools exist to augment the designing artifacts. With generative AI, many more will become available (see appendix for more details). Here are a few more resources to include in your toolbox:

- IFTF: Artifacts from the Future (https://legacy.iftf.org/what-we-do/artifacts-from-the-future/)

- The 2023 Work Kit of Design Fiction (https://shop.nearfuturelaboratory.com/products/the-work-kit-of-design-fiction-2023-mj-edition)
- TBD Catalog (www.tbdcatalog.com)
- SpeculativeEdu - Speculative Design – Educational Resource Toolkit (www.speculativeedu.eu)

Using any tool effectively is dependent on cultivating an atmosphere where participants can expand their thinking beyond the present, and create innovative ideas about potential futures. In particular, speculating artifacts often triggers complex and uncomfortable topics, so creating "safe spaces" for difficult conversations can be initiated and navigated without fear is essential before starting any workshop or organizational meeting. Additionally, anyone who contributes to a futures intervention brings their subjective perspective. Becoming aware and even mitigating personal biases that may unconsciously be projected onto artifacts is vital to guiding artifacts to make abstract sustainability futures experientially tangible, relatable, and actionable.

Part III explores how to create spaces – physical and mental – conducive to designing sustainable futures by participatory design, storymaking, and leadership. Without a view on how to engage leadership – personal, organizational, and communal – even the best futures will only remain good ideas and not contribute to transitioning people in the planet to more sustainable practices.

Part III
Lead The Transition

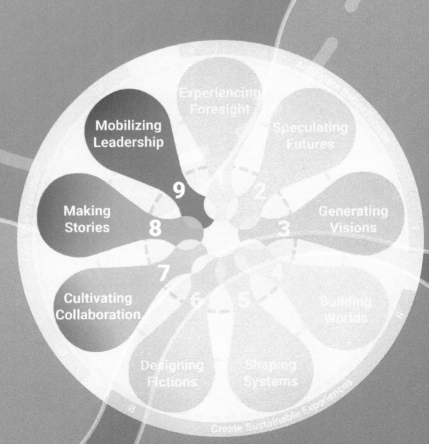

Experiencing
Foresight

Speculating
Futures

Mobilizing
Leadership

Making
Stories

9

1

2

Generating
Visions

8

3

7

Cultivating
Collaboration

6

5

4

Building
Worlds

Designing
Fictions

Shaping
Systems

Create Sustainable Experiences

Part III: Lead the Transition shifts our focus to tools for engaging communities, stakeholders, and leadership to prepare for co-creating sustainable futures. Although all aspects of designing sustainable futures include members of the communities seeking a better world, Part III explicitly focuses on the key to any change – people. Leading the Transition builds on Part I equipping practitioners to anticipate the future using experiential foresight, and Part II insights for creating experiences to make sustainability tangible. Part III offers perspectives and practices for guiding the social coordination needed to lead the transition toward more just, resilient, and ideally, regenerative systems.

As Part I is framed by imagination, and Part II creation, Part III is framed by participation. As Tanja Schindler, Vice-Chair of the Association of Professional Futurists (APF) and Foresight Advisor to the EU Commission explains, "Participatory Futures champions a simple yet revolutionary idea: involve a broad number of voices in crafting futures narratives that can serve as a starting point for holistic scenarios. Rather than leaving future-making to a chosen few, like policymakers, corporate strategists, or even seasoned futurists, Participatory Futures seeks to democratize the process by involving as many people as possible, making futures-building a collective endeavor" (Schindler 2023).

Within this paradigm, we begin Part III in **Chapter 7**: Cultivating Collaboration by examining how participatory design serves as a conduit for collectively navigating the complex, sometimes conflicting dynamics within communities while weaving diverse perspectives into a shared vision. Guided by Professor Anna Meroni, we will see how community participation spotlights participatory design's power to cultivate inclusive spaces where citizens become co-creators, jointly reshaping systems to holistically benefit society. Chapter 8: Engaging Stakeholders delves into the recent research on an emerging practice called "storymaking." Led by Professor Tommaso Buganza, co-founder of the research lab IDeaLs, we will explore how blending diverse experiences and viewpoints into a unified narrative can ignite commitment and action. Chapter 9: Mobilizing Leadership rounds out the conversation by examining how to guide people toward collective action with impact. Guided by co-author Joseph Press, we will explore recent neuroscience

DOI: 10.4324/9781003451693-10

insights that underscore leadership's collective activity as manifest in shared meaning-making. To exploit this space, we will explore what practitioners can do to think *futureback*.

Part III aims to bring us through anticipating and creating to collective leading towards more sustainable futures. With more collaborative dreaming, doing, and dedication, we can increase our readiness for manifesting equitable, resilient, and thriving tomorrows. By recognizing the agency, we each have to design narratives, create artifacts, map systems, convene communities, tell stories, and practice leadership, and we can transform organizations, industries, cities, and societies toward more sustainable futures.

Let's explore the preferred future scenarios that could emerge if we can all lead the transition.

Communal

Networked Nexus

We pledge to unite communities and technology across the globe, crafting smart cities and universal connectivity. We champion digital literacy and global citizenship, fostering shared prosperity while safeguarding privacy. Join us in harmonizing community values with global innovation, where every connection strengthens our collective future.

Global
Production

Our commitment is to independence intertwined with global connectedness. We empower individuals with technology and advocate for gig work guided by fair policies, for autonomy in a global economy. Join us in forging resilient, self-determined paths, where each person's strength contributes to a tapestry of collective resilience.

Steadfast Strands

Individual

Regenerative Weave

We vow to intertwine local communities with circular economies and cooperative models. Through shared resources and community initiatives, we aim to build a society that values collective resilience. We invite every member to weave their strength into this fabric, crafting a future where local ingenuity fosters communal experiences.

Local Production

We commit to a future where local production enables individual well-being. By transforming open spaces into hubs of self-sufficiency, sustainable choices reign. By encouraging green entrepreneurialism, we cultivate fields for mindful living. Join our revolution, where individuals contribute to the collective well-being.

Quiet Evolution

7

Cultivating
Collaboration

Mobilizing Leadership

Cultivating Collaboration

7

We open Part III: Lead the Transition with a chapter on Cultivating Collaboration. With a recognition that communities are melting pots of diverse agendas, needs, and perspectives, the urgency for participatory design in creating more sustainable futures is clear. Professor Anna Meroni, founder of the Desis Lab, will guide us through the realms of participatory practices and the dynamics of navigating the complexities of cultivating community. We will examine how ethnography-based practices that circumscribe the design object can turn the traditional double diamond into a lens for deeper comprehension of the interconnections between social, environmental, and economic dimensions. We will explore the Collaborative Design Framework and its tools that infuse designing sustainable futures with inclusivity and commitment. We will share stories about how *co-design*, an integral aspect of participation, propels users from being a mere subject of examination to becoming a collaborative partner, resonating across the echo chambers of research and innovation.

Practicing participatory design can open a holistic view that replaces compartmentalized approaches with a more nuanced discussion of the opportunities and potential trade-offs. The learning objectives of this chapter will focus on developing the ability to understand and reflect on the norms and values that underlie one's actions, and to negotiate sustainability values, principles, goals, and targets, in a context of conflicts of interests and trade-offs, uncertain knowledge, and contradictions. While democracy and design may be familiar concepts, we will see how a participatory-centric perspective enables practitioners to chart a course toward a more equitable, resilient, and thriving future.

THE COLLABORATIVE DESIGN FRAMEWORK

Within the broad spectrum of options in Participatory Futures, participatory design stands out as a potent catalyst for convergence and change. This fusion draws upon participatory democracy, co-design techniques, and a variety of ethnographic tools. These multifaceted tools navigate the complex tapestry of community dynamics, weaving strands of inclusivity. Through this intricate weaving, an inclusive uniformity emerges, one that envisions a future that resonates with the aspirations of the communities we serve. Collaborative practices have become essential to all facets

DOI: 10.4324/9781003451693-11

of design, influencing various stages of the design process, from inception to evaluation, and extending from labs to real-world applications.

Inspired and informed by the work of Professor Meroni and the Desis Lab, the Collaborative Design Framework underpins the participatory design activity within a Designing Sustainable Futures process. Building on the trend toward collaboration, particularly evident in Service Design, it is rooted in an interactive approach that involves a diverse range of stakeholders beyond designers. To facilitate interactive processes among the multiple entities, it promotes a more collective approach to design (Meroni & Sangiorgi, 2011) by incorporating the many collaborative methods and tools of service design.

Starting with the widely used double diamond design process, the Collaborative Design Framework embeds collaborative experiences across the entire process, starting with the initial "discovery" phase to the final "deliver" phase, as illustrated in Figure 7.1.

The "discovery" phase is characterized by swift ethnographic field surveys, which work in conjunction with other research methodologies to shape insights into the problem. This form of "designerly" ethnography involves engaging with users or stakeholders, promoting a dialogue that fosters empathy and

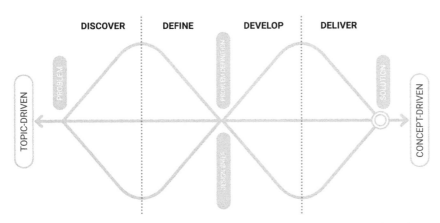

Figure 7.1 The double diamond scheme elaborated with two polarities about the subject matter of design

Source: Adapted from Meroni et al. (2018).

curiosity. This phase can encompass a multitude of participants and generate a wide array of input.

The "definition" phase is concerned with interpreting the possibilities that were identified during the discovery phase. This often requires collaboration with experts and stakeholders to establish the project brief. Divergent positions are progressively synthesized, paving the way for innovation. The participation of experts and decision-makers ensures a solid design brief, occasionally with the assistance of digital technology for data interpretation and decision-making.

The "develop" phase is centered on the creation and iteration of solutions. This phase, inherently collaborative, employs a variety of approaches and methods. The process starts with an orientation and explores numerous options. Emphasis is placed on cooperative dialogue, encouraging a diversity of perspectives without immediate resolution.

The "deliver" phase concludes the project, requiring collaboration among stakeholders to bring the design to fruition. Collaboration evolves into co-production, where collective efforts shape the solution. Project decision-makers play a crucial role, and collaborative testing and prototyping are essential.

Professor Meroni and her colleagues view these iterative processes as a mirror of the collective interactions of framing problems and exploring possible solutions. This linear yet cyclical progression can be condensed into a two-pole axis (Figure 7.2). "Topic-driven"

Figure 7.2 Design subject matter polarities.
Source: Adapted from Meroni et al. (2018).

activities, positioned on one side, involve investigating the problem or situation that the project seeks to address. On the opposite side, "concept-driven" activities pertain to the orientation established by the problem-solving brief, highlighting a solution-oriented approach.

Collaboration within the design process is not solely contingent on its phase; the manner of collaborative engagement profoundly matters. The practice of co-design, which involves a diverse group of individuals collectively exploring and defining problems while also developing and evaluating solutions, relies heavily on successful interaction, expression, and sharing of experiences (Steen, 2013). The way a designer interacts influences participants' awareness of the process, their contributions, relationships, critical thinking abilities, and their willingness to step outside their comfort zones. A harmonious mix of "perceptive" (sensory) and "conceptive" (imaginative) abilities is required for promoting effective interaction. The manner of guidance in a co-design initiative is likewise crucial. The guidance style can fluctuate between "active listening" and "thought-provoking," each serving different purposes and contexts.

The "active listening" approach fosters an open flow of thoughts and empathy among participants. It involves understanding others' perspectives, even when they seem conflicting. It goes beyond empathy, reaching to grasp participants' viewpoints toward shared solutions.

On the other hand, the "thought-provoking" style steers participants' thoughts toward critical elements or opportunities within a topic. This method aligns with a designer's role of bringing ideas and insights to discussions. While valuable, this style requires vigilance and careful monitoring to prevent persuasion from stifling imaginative thinking.

In this scenario, the designer's role is akin to a "design expert" who provides critical analysis and reflections, producing tangible proposals based on the values and visions of design culture (Manzini, 2016). The chosen style of guidance influences the depth of engagement with the subject matter. While "active listening" promotes empathy and diverse perspectives, "thought-provoking" triggers critical reflections, both of which are essential for a comprehensive and effective collaborative design process.

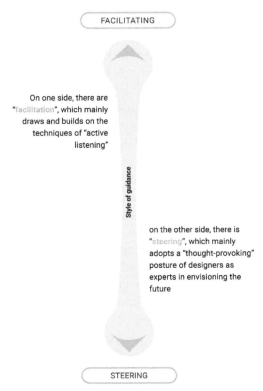

On one side, there are "facilitation", which mainly draws and builds on the techniques of "active listening"

on the other side, there is "steering", which mainly adopts a "thought-provoking" posture of designers as experts in envisioning the future

Figure 7.3 Style of guidance polarities.
Source: Adapted from Meroni et al. (2018).

By comparing these two guidance styles, an axis is formed to demonstrate different strategies for managing co-design activities (Figure 7.3). At one end, we have "designerly facilitation," which is grounded in "active listening" techniques. At the other end, we encounter "designerly steering," which embodies the "thought-provoking" approach of visionary designers.

Collaboration emerges as the backbone of this creative endeavor, driving design toward tangible and enduring visions. The act of collaborative engagement enhances the design process by cultivating a setting conducive to comprehensive dialogues and transformative actions. Viewed through this collaborative lens, design transcends its conventional limits, engaging stakeholders in a thorough and inclusive journey from problem identification to solution development.

The catalyst of collaboration is the concept of *boundary objects*. At the nexus of participatory design, boundary objects are tangible manifestations of the subject matter of design, such as images, sketches, prototypes, and models, utilized to align designers and users in co-designing processes (Star, 1989; Ehn, 2008; Johnson et al., 2017). These objects surpass various community-specific interpretations, aligning diverse stakeholders toward collaborative work. Within the sphere of co-design for more sustainable futures,

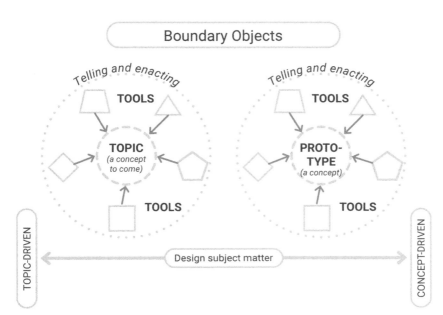

Figure 7.4 The synergies of prototypes, tools, and boundary objects.
Source: Adapted from Meroni et al. (2018).

the role of boundary objects becomes crucial. These entities foster cooperative interactions among disparate communities, each distinguished by unique languages, cultures, and viewpoints. Through this process, they cultivate a shared understanding, bridging the divide between designers and users, and improving the quality of co-created solutions. Essentially, boundary objects are not merely tools but potent facilitators, enabling the realization of superior sustainable futures through enhanced collaboration and the creation of a common vision (Figure 7.4).

In the context of participatory design, the amalgamation of prototypes, tools, and boundary objects works in synergy to propel the development of sustainable futures. These complex boundary objects function as conduits, merging prototypes and tools to aid co-design processes. Prototypes, primarily within the "concept-driven" quadrant, bring service and scenario concepts to life, encapsulating core interactions and complexities (as discussed in Chapter 6). Tools are ubiquitous, empowering participants to delve into design possibilities and refine concepts across all quadrants. These boundary objects, embodying the essence of prototypes and tools, bridge diverse communities, harmonizing languages, perspectives, and cultures. This fusion fosters dialogue, envisioning, and transformative reflections, culminating in the shared creation of sustainable futures. This approach underscores the role of multifaceted artifacts, encompassing prototypes, tools, and boundary objects, as catalysts for co-design efforts, steering the world toward a more sustainable and harmonious future.

Integrating the polarities and the objects that bind them is the Collaborative Framework. As proposed by Meroni et al. (2018), the Collaborative Framework is designed to steer the identification, creation, and execution of collaborative processes that involve a multitude of participants at different stages, with varying objectives, and in diverse formats. The framework is a product of the Design Matter and the Style of Guidance axes, which when interwoven, give birth to the Collaborative Design Framework. This framework presents four unique collaborative approaches within an all-encompassing design process which serve three primary functions within the context of this book: (1) they contextualize the analysis of case studies from our research; (2) delve into the implications of each quadrant in terms of approach, aim, technique, and outcome; and (3) suggest tools and methods for each quadrant.

Together, these elements for the four quadrants of the Collaborative Framework, as illustrated and outlined as follows (Figure 7.5):

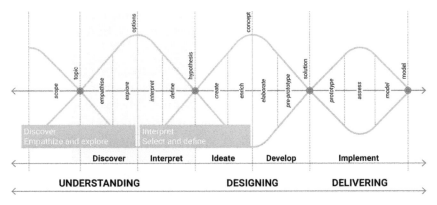

Figure 7.5 The collaborative framework.
Source: Adapted from Meroni et al. (2018).

Part III: Lead the Transition

- In the "Topic-Driven" and "Facilitating" quadrants, co-design initiatives focus on discovering and exploring options. Collaboration involves considering stakeholders' needs and experiences to integrate their knowledge.
- In the "Topic-Driven" and "Steering" quadrants, co-design initiatives target imagining and considering options beyond the world as it is. Collaboration stimulates stakeholders to envision alternative options that challenge norms.
- In the "Concept-Driven" and "Facilitating" quadrants, co-design initiatives aim at expanding and consolidating options. Collaboration involves assessing existing options and enhancing their feasibility.
- In the "Concept-Driven" and "Steering" quadrants, co-design initiatives focus on creating, envisioning, and developing options. Collaboration generates new or refined options through a creative, thought-provoking process that challenges established principles.

PRAXIS OF COMMUNITY-CENTERED DESIGN

The Collaborative Design Framework aims to provide practical insights to aid designers in handling ongoing, intricate, and uncertain processes. These situations require designers to comprehend local subtleties, understand the context of the project, and impart service design skills to others for sustained continuity. This collaborative approach, referred to as Community-Centered Design, promotes a service design mindset that is common in modern creative communities. It underscores the establishment of a collaborative environment to facilitate effective implementation. How can we propel action in this collaborative environment to instigate change? How can we align this collaborative framework with the engaging activity of worldbuilding and the creation of artifacts?

One fundamental participatory design tool is a *stakeholder map*. This visual representation identifies and illustrates the various individuals and groups, known as stakeholders, who have a vested interest in a specific project or challenge. This tool is invaluable in the design process for several reasons. First, it assists in identifying the key players who will be involved throughout the project. Second, it offers insights into the dynamics of power and influence that could impact design decisions. Third, it ensures that all concerned parties are considered and involved, thereby facilitating comprehensive planning and decision-making. Last of all, it aids in understanding the different perspectives and relationships that stakeholders have with the project (Dam & Siang, 2022).

Stakeholders are entities, be they individuals or groups, that can either influence or be influenced by a project. These stakeholders can range from senior leadership within your organization to end-users and even to people minimally affected by the project. The array also includes those who are integral to the communication, reporting, and activity processes during the project's lifecycle (Dam & Siang, 2022). Stakeholder mapping can act as a catalyst for challenging conversations about roles and the distribution of power among stakeholders. This tool is particularly useful in service design and management fields, enabling designers to mediate dialogue among diverse stakeholders and elevate quieter voices to be heard by those wielding more power (Giordano et al., 2018).

Traditional stakeholder mapping often takes a top-down approach focused on classifying stakeholders based on their power and interest relative to the organization's strategic objectives. It is an analytical process done unilaterally by a management strategy team. In contrast, the participatory method explained leverages stakeholder mapping as a collaborative visualization tool for mutual learning between both internal and external stakeholders. It aims to democratize the process by providing a platform for marginalized voices and fostering a shared understanding of the systemic relationships and perspectives at play. The goal is laying the groundwork for human-centered solutions through genuine multistakeholder collaboration.

Manzini et al. (2009) approach of utilizing design tools such as stakeholder maps to facilitate strategic dialogues among diverse groups is noteworthy, especially when these groups have distinct cultures and visions pertaining to specific challenges. These tools establish a democratic platform, enabling even the less influential actors to contribute to the process, thus promoting equal participation in design decisions. The creation of a stakeholder map involves a series of steps: identifying potential stakeholders, visually representing them on the map, and analyzing their interrelationships (Stickdorn & Schneider, 2010). This tool, at times, referred to as "actor network mapping," provides a comprehensive view of the network of involved components, serving as an effective visualization technique for understanding the service and identifying potential challenges (Morelli & Tollestrup, 2007).

In the context of co-design workshops, the stakeholder map assists in articulating diverse perspectives and fosters mutual understanding among participants from different organizations (Hyvärinen et al., 2014; Giordano et al., 2018). As Manzini (2015) suggests, the map can also function as a "conversation prompt," aiding in the clarification of complex relationships and stimulating open discussions, which is particularly beneficial for public employees in comprehending a citizen-centric design approach. Through stakeholder mapping, design teams, particularly those operating in public institutions, can gain a clearer understanding of their focus and how to better position themselves and other stakeholders. This process illuminates the dynamics of power and position, serving as a precursor to other beneficial tools such as motivation matrices.

The Desis Lab's collaborative stakeholder mapping approach aligns with the "Topic-Driven" and "Facilitating" quadrants located at the bottom-left of the Collaborative Design Framework, detailed previously. It emphasizes the discovery and exploration of options by taking into account stakeholders' needs and incorporating their knowledge into the mapping process. This is in contrast to the traditional corporate-centric stakeholder analysis which is categorized under the "Concept-Driven" and "Steering" quadrants located at the top-right.

The co-creation of a stakeholder map allows stakeholders across the ecosystems to visualize the intricate relationships between individuals and groups involved in a project. The result is indispensable for comprehending the complexities and interdependencies of power dynamics and collaboration, ensuring that all relevant parties are considered in the decision-making process (Dam & Siang, 2022; Giordano et al., 2018) (Figure 7.6).

Figure 7.6 Stakeholder map example.
Source: By authors.

Below is a guide that proposes a step-by-step process for creating an effective stakeholder map, two key references were used to create this guide: Stickdorn and Schneider's "This is Service Design Thinking" (2010) and Dam and Siang's "Stakeholder mapping: The complete guide to stakeholder maps" (2022).

1. **Define project focus:** Articulate the core objectives and scope of your project. This foundational understanding serves as the compass for your stakeholder mapping exercise. Knowing your focus helps in targeting relevant stakeholders for the design project.

2. **Initial brainstorming session:** Engage in a five-minute brainstorming session where members of the team independently identify potential stakeholders (this could be done using post-it notes). Remember to consider individuals and groups that might be affected either internally or externally by the project.

3. **Compile and categorize stakeholders:** Collate the post-it notes and begin to categorize them into groups. Stakeholders could range from users to management, and to external bodies. Create a list of these different types of stakeholders.

4. **Prioritize and rank stakeholders:** Plot the stakeholders on a preliminary map based on their level of influence and interest. Classify them into categories such as their level of influence on the project, and their emotional and social engagement. This will allow a deeper, more holistic understanding of stakeholder dynamics.

5. **Develop a map legend:** Create a legend that defines the meaning of symbols or circled material on your stakeholder map. For instance, circles could signify the level of importance, influence, or contact each stakeholder has in relation to the project.

6. **Visualize relationships:** Map out the relationships between stakeholders. Use lines, arrows, or other symbols to indicate the nature and direction of the relationships. This could include value exchanges like trust, money, or information.

7. **Engage and communicate:** Develop a communication strategy for engaging with stakeholders based on the categories you've identified. For example, you could conduct interviews or send out surveys to gather more detailed insights.

8. **Review and update:** Continuously update the stakeholder map as your project evolves. New stakeholders may emerge, and relationships might change. This ensures that your stakeholder map remains a relevant and useful tool throughout the life cycle of the project.

Farmer's Food Box

A hands-on collaboration took place at a Farmer's Market within the broader "Idea Sharing Stall" (Figure 7.7). Although the interventions were conducted locally, the vision was broad, aiming for implications and insights across Italy.

The farmer's food box was structured in the following manner:

- **Objective:** The design process was structured to delve deeper than merely gather initial thoughts. The facilitators guided attendees through a sequence of questions that mimicked

Figure 7.7 Farmer's food box as boundary object on the ideas sharing stall.
Source: Courtesy of Meroni et al. (2018).

a typical user's experience with the product. This was intended to gain more precise insights about what should be included in the food box, its dimensions, affordability, and how it would be distributed.

- **Who took part:** Engagement wasn't limited to any select group; it was open to anyone who found themselves at the Farmer's Market during the event days. The setting of the market likely meant that most participants had a pre-existing interest in quality food, local produce, or sustainability.

- **Interaction dynamics:** The presence of design experts and representatives from the Slow Food movement ensured that the casual conversations were directed and meaningful. They led the activity, yet their role was intentionally minimized to allow participants to fill out a visually engaging questionnaire largely on their own.

- **Guidance style:** Rather than a heavy-handed facilitation style, the approach was one of minimal intervention. Participants were sometimes left to their own devices to complete a questionnaire that captured their user experience journey.

- **Design subject matter:** The whole exercise was concept-driven, based on a rudimentary idea set forth by the designers. This wasn't about brainstorming from scratch; it was about refining and validating an existing concept.

- **Double diamond stage type:** The activity was situated near the end of the "Double Diamond" model, which means it was close to being a field-tested pre-prototype. This was an initial real-world test meant to either affirm or challenge the project's underlying assumptions.

- **Duration and depth:** The event was conducted over two Saturday mornings, each session lasting about four hours. Interactions were brief but could extend if participants showed a willingness to engage in a deeper conversation about the overarching project.

- **Process description:** The design activity was straightforward but well-structured. Upon approaching the stall, whether in response to verbal engagement or lured by the signage, participants were informed about the food box concept. They were then asked to fill out the questionnaire, either independently or with guidance from the facilitator. This simple process was iteratively improved in the second session, based on learning from the first.

- **Boundary objects:** Prototypes and tools were created to facilitate the activity. A physical model of the proposed food box was displayed, not as a realistic representation, but as a provocative object that captured the essence of what the service hoped to deliver. Alongside this was a questionnaire designed to guide the participant through a simplified yet revealing user journey.

- **Final output:** The ultimate product was a diverse farmer food box, focused primarily on fruits and vegetables. There was a system planned for distribution at local collection points, chosen for their convenience to the consumer. While the final prototype did not perfectly align with all the feedback collected – due to the unavoidable constraints of cost and logistics – it did incorporate key insights gathered during the co-design activity.

Feeding Milan

The compelling journey of "Feeding Milan – Energies for Change" (*Nutrire Milano – Energie per il cambiamento*) serves as a vivid example of the power of design-led social innovation in instigating transformative shifts within the food and agriculture sector. This case study showcases a unique intersection of various stakeholders – farmers, researchers, local institutions, and the general public – all harmoniously working together to tackle systemic challenges. We selected this case for its encapsulation of the intricacies and richness of a multiyear, multistakeholder initiative aimed at sustainable transformation, providing valuable insights into the dynamics of collaborative design and community engagement.

The project is meticulously detailed in the book "Massive Codesign. A Proposal for a Collaborative Design Framework" by Meroni, Selloni, and Rossi. The project ran between 2010 and 2013 and was financially supported by local institutions and collaboratively developed by Slow Food Italia, Politecnico di Milano's Department of Design and its Polimi Desis Lab, and the Università di Scienze Gastronomiche. The project was more than just an academic endeavor; it was a community-led initiative. Its goal was to establish a local "foodshed," connecting local food production in peri-urban areas with urban consumers, in an effort to make the local food supply chain more sustainable and equitable. At the heart of the project was the methodology of co-design. Various stakeholders, including farmers and citizens, were engaged in the design process through activities such as "idea sharing stalls" at farmers' markets and consultations designed to gather input for the platform. This inclusive approach was not merely symbolic; it was fundamental to the project's objective of constructing a cooperative and multifunctional platform. Such activities led to the design of innovative services like a local distribution system and a "farmer's food box" pre-prototype that we will delve into in the subsequent section.

The project's outcomes extended far beyond the initial prototypes and services. The project activated underutilized resources in agriculture, bolstered existing best practices, and resulted in the creation of new services. Sub-projects throughout the four-year period encompassed a diverse range of pilot initiatives, from local bread chains to zero-mile tourism. Remarkably, the project also sparked a cultural shift, raising community awareness toward local and sustainable food, an impact that continued to reverberate even after the project's conclusion. The case of Feeding Milan serves as a powerful testament to the potential of design to act as a catalyst for social innovation. It reimagines the role of designers as community organizers and facilitators, coordinating complex dialogues and collaborations among diverse stakeholders.

CULTIVATING COLLABORATION: A PRACTITIONER'S POSSIBLE JOURNAL ENTRY

Professor Meroni and the Polimi Desis Lab's initiatives in Milan and for the European Commission serve as a testament to the power of cultivating collaboration by embedding participatory methodologies throughout the design of sustainable futures. Integrating ethnographic insights, and engaging stakeholders in co-designing futures, can establish a comprehensive pathway for realizing sustainable and impactful results. From food networks to research agendas for European governance, practitioners can utilize these principles to navigate the complexities and opportunities inherent in their field. Moreover, anchoring interventions to Sustainable Development Goals (SDGs) combines innovation and collaboration for greater impact.

For practitioners and community stakeholders to authentically facilitate and navigate a participatory process, blurring the lines between ethnography and co-design is essential. By combining ethnography-based tools and co-design, practitioners can leverage participatory techniques to navigate complex community dynamics and encourage more inclusive and comprehensive action plans, converging diverse voices toward a shared sustainable goal.

Professor Meroni advocates the notion that participation molds the future rather than merely observes it, and understanding the present context can seamlessly transfer to envisioning the future. Boundary objects are the portkeys to this capacity. When visual artifacts or prototypes are in the collaborative process, practitioners are more empowered to promote dialogue and co-creation among diverse stakeholders. Recognizing one's biases is a crucial element in interpreting boundary objects. Since participation is at the heart

Figure 7.8 Designing sustainable futures literacy: cultivate collaboration.

Source: By authors.

of designing futures, acknowledging biases assists in ensuring a genuinely participatory approach, imbued with respectful and empathic values that allow the recognition of power imbalances and disparities. A heightened awareness of bias leads to a more inclusive journey for designing sustainable futures because all voices can be adequately represented, heard, and considered. To increase your future literacy to *cultivate collaboration* (Figure 7.8), check out these sources of insight and inspiration:

- DESIS Network (www.desisnetwork.org)
- Participatory City (www.participatorycity.org)
- Reimaginary – Re-imagining possibilities for just and ecological societies (www.reimaginary.com)
- Participatory Futures (www.nesta.org.uk/project/participatory-futures/)
- Environmental Inequality (www.sesync.org/resources/participatory-futures-planning-lesson-reducing-environmental-inequality)

The cultivation of collaboration is dependent on something shared. Like the role of boundary objects as a nexus for co-design, in the next chapter we will learn how making stories together enables stakeholders to become co-authors of collective tales. Such collective narratives foster solidarity by kindling the collective imagination, contributing to the alignment of stakeholders in the design of more sustainable futures.

8
Making
Stories

Making
Stories 8

As we venture into the next dimension of designing sustainable futures, we shift our attention to the intricate blend of art and science of stakeholder engagement. Building on the foundations of participatory design in Chapter 7, this chapter delves into an emerging practice called "storymaking," an approach to weave collective narratives that cultivate a sense of shared responsibility – vital in the design of sustainable futures. The crafting of a shared narrative has always held a pivotal role in human interaction (Bruner, 1990) and even history (Harari, 2015). In this era of swift technological progress and societal evolution, stories remain the most likely tool to engage stakeholders for systemic change.

However, the traditional methods of storytelling are no longer suffice in the digital era (Press et al., 2021). To understand how to utilize narratives to engage stakeholders in change, we will be guided by Professor Tomasso Buganza, co-founder of the Innovation and Design as Leadership (IDeaLs) research lab at the Politecnico di Milano Management & Engineering School. Central to storymaking is the conviction that stakeholders are not merely passive audience but active contributors to the narrative. This approach acknowledges that the most impactful narratives are those that resonate on a personal level, that connect with individual ambitions, apprehensions, and aspirations. By involving stakeholders in the process of making shared stories, organizations can navigate the complexities of the contemporary world, increasing the likelihood that initiatives are heard and also championed.

Grounded in the theories and practices of sensemaking, innovation of meaning, and neuroscience of leadership, the preliminary insights from the IDeaLs action research underscore the power of co-creating stories for greater engagement. We will share the preliminary findings of a storymaking experiment that indicates that organizations which thoroughly integrate stakeholder engagement strategies that outperform in sustainability metrics and also experience enhanced innovation, trust, and overall resilience. We will also learn from a storymaking practitioner how she crafts collective narratives for developing and honing our critical thinking skills. She shares her reflections on how to challenge norms, practices, and viewpoints; to introspect on our own values,

DOI: 10.4324/9781003451693-12

perceptions, and actions; and to stake a claim in the discourse on sustainability, all the capabilities of future literacies.

STORIES FOR ENGAGEMENT

Since the dawn of civilization, stories have served as humanity's guiding compass. As elucidated by Yuval Noah Harari in "Sapiens," the defining characteristic of Homo Sapiens was their capacity to believe in shared myths, all disseminated through captivating stories. This propensity for shared narrative facilitated cooperation on an unprecedented scale, giving rise to tribes, cities, and empires (Harari, 2015). Indeed, the innate human trait of storytelling allowed individuals to convey ideas, create meaning, establish collective identity, and envision alternative futures (Figure 8.1).

Jerome Bruner, in his influential work "Acts of Meaning" (1990), posits that narrative construction is a fundamental cognitive process, essential for both individual understanding and communal identity formation. He argues that individuals use stories to interpret their experiences and construct their identities, engaging in "narrative

Figure 8.1 GenAI cave drawings illustrate our transition to a more sustainable world.
Source: Created in midjourney by authors.

thinking" which goes beyond mere logical processing to imbue life events with meaning and coherence. Extending this concept to groups and communities, Bruner suggests that shared narratives play a pivotal role in shaping collective memory, cultural norms, and values. These communal stories are instrumental in transmitting cultural heritage, guiding group behavior, and fostering a sense of belonging. Bruner's exploration into the narrative construction thus provides a comprehensive lens to understand how humans, both individually and collectively, perceive and navigate their world, underscoring the intricate interplay between personal experiences and cultural contexts in shaping human cognition and behavior.

One seminal example that illustrates the power of future-focused storytelling is John D. Liu's 2001 documentary "Green Gold." Liu, a Chinese American researcher and filmmaker, adeptly intertwines the stories of Ethiopian farmers in the Rift Valley, battling soil erosion through innovative agroforestry techniques. His emphasis on community knowledge and participation, as showcased in the efforts of Tigray elder Abrha Weatsbha, highlights the potential of local ingenuity in ecological restoration by deploying narrative as a catalyst for lasting change. The film's impact, substantiated by a 2020 World Development Perspectives study, reveals significant improvements in vegetation, soil, water retention, and livelihoods, confirmed by both community testimonials and satellite data. These outcomes underscore the transformational power of Liu's storytelling, which transcends mere documentation to inspire and sustain grassroots action in environmental stewardship. "Green Gold" thus emerges as a paragon of how narrative creation can effectively weave future-oriented visions with participatory approaches, galvanizing communities toward enduring ecological and social resilience.

Despite the potential to accelerate the sustainability transformation with stories, people generally still find it difficult to understand how they can practically act and what type of impact they can have. Contributing to this challenge is the skepticism that emerged from greenwashing, as in the case of Shell and other Oil & Gas companies that exaggerated their renewable energy investments through high-profile ad campaigns that mislead the public and investors (Hickman, 2010). A central reason is the complexity, scale, and severity of the associated challenges, which can lead to overwhelm, anxiety, rejection, or avoidance of the topic (Veland et al., 2018; Markowitz et al., 2018; O'Neill et al., 2013). Sustainability calls for major changes in the way business is done, which can be discouraging for employees being confronted with barriers to these changes. Making the topic closer and personal and associating it with positive emotions, especially hope and empathy, is an important path to inspire and motivate engagement (Nabi et al., 2018). It is important to create a space for people to match these unsettling facts and novel action strategies into their existing mental models so that they can engage with this information (Lakoff, 2010). Finally, there is a need for reflection spaces to create positive narratives that accommodate the personal possibilities for action depending on one's professional role, personal life, and the perception of these challenges that is highly influenced by personal experience, beliefs and perception, ideological polarization, gender, age, nationality, social identity, and psychological traits (Weber, 2016; Knez, 2013; Leiserowitz, 2006).

Infusing a new perspective into the potency of stories for designing sustainable futures comes from change management theory and practice. Karl Weick's theory on sensemaking views organizational change as an ongoing social process in which individuals and groups iteratively develop shared understandings and meanings (Weick, 1995). This co-constructive perspective acknowledged that implementing change involves collectively making sense of circumstances through narratives, symbols, and dialogues. Similarly, dialogic organization development (OD) emphasizes generative, multiperspective stakeholder dialogues and co-creation (Bushe & Marshak, 2015). Companies such as IKEA have organized "sustainability summits" that bring together employees, suppliers, NGOs, and other stakeholders to explore system innovations such as renewable materials. Large group interventions like Future Search conferences, Appreciative Inquiry summits, and Open Space also use structured stakeholder dialogues for real-time learning, vision creation, and community problem-solving on sustainability issues (Weisbord & Janoff, 2010; Watkins et al., 2011; Owen, 2008). Denmark's citizen climate assemblies demonstrate dialogic OD on a societal scale, with representative citizens deliberating solutions like transitioning to green energy (Carson et al., 2022). Similarly, the Presencing Institute's social field theory and "U process" use visual reflection for situations like sustainability innovation (Scharmer & Kaufer, 2013) to collectively connect the dots on complex sustainability issues and reimagine future solutions. The empirical evidence from these and other interventions indicates that participatory storytelling initiatives strive to restore people's agency in driving sustainability change (Paschen & Ison, 2014), indicating an important pathway to greater engagement for leading the transition to more sustainable practices.

In reflecting on the potentials and pitfalls of narrative forms of engagement, from ancient civilizations to their contemporary applications, we acknowledge it as a process of continuous evolution and learning. Stories should incite action, not just awareness, and be inclusive, representing the multitude of stakeholders involved in the process (BSR, 2019). Instead of being passive recipients of stories, there is a growing shift toward active participation in the narrative process and co-creation as a means of engagement for change. While no model is completely able to align all stakeholders toward driving transformation at scale, advances in real-time collective intelligence, interactive visualization, systems modeling, and experiential simulation offer new potential to come closer to that objective. Combining these capabilities with processes of change appears highly promising for leading change toward sustainability solutions. In addition, incorporating experiential principles from foresight and design can reveal new avenues in representing the intricate interconnections of stakeholder realities in a sustainable future.

THE PRAXIS OF STORYMAKING

Rooted in the foundations of stories and driven by the megatrend of storytelling, the IDeaLs research lab at the Politecnico di Milano set out in 2021 to experiment with an approach of participatory storytelling where multiple authors collaborate to co-create, reshape, and redefine narratives. Named "storymaking," this design-driven approach democratizes the storytelling process by co-creating narratives with comprehensive, inclusive, and representative diverse perspectives. With this intent intrinsically woven into the fabric of storymaking, the team created an action research exercise in co-creating narratives that deeply resonate with each participant's unique experiences and ambitions. The research conducted by IDeaLs delves into the depths of storymaking, exploring its critical role in transitioning from traditional, passive storytelling to an active, cooperative narrative approach. Central to the IDeaLs perspective is the belief that innovation is the catalyst for a holistic approach to organizational transformation.

Storymaking seeks to apply participatory story-based processes to stimulate engagement and dialogue on sustainability topics, which are gaining interest (Corner & Clarke, 2016; Nanson, 2021; Gersie, 2015; Rotmann, 2017). Narratives can connect novel facts to one's frame by appealing to values, emotions, concerns, pre-existing cultural narratives, and metanarratives about the world (Corner & Clarke, 2016). It has been shown that stories can be a carrier for imagination of different futures (Morel, 2017; Hopkins, 2019), for developing a sense of efficacy (Perkowitz et al., 2014) and ecological identity (Thomashow, 1996). A study where students wrote their personal life stories in relation to climate change showed how this exercise impacted their self-perception and the types of goals they set for themselves in relation to environmental challenges (Carlin, 2010).

Involving more than 50 participants from five diverse organizations, the storymaking action research experiments sought to engage participants' narratives from overarching, abstract concepts about transformation to specific, actionable initiatives aimed at actualizing the envisioned change. The scientific aim was to investigate the shift from the long-standing practice of passive storytelling to a dynamic, cooperative approach. Rather than a top-down distribution of pre-determined narratives, stakeholders as co-authors might increase the likelihood of richer, multidimensional, and shared narratives. In this manner, the experiments would reveal new insights on how co-creation could engage stakeholders in the transition toward more sustainable futures.

As detailed in the book *Storymaking: How Organizations Can Engage People to Make Innovation Happen* (Buganza et al., 2021), the method proposed involved a variety of stakeholders as active co-creators of transformative narratives. The IDeaLs research team prototyped and tested a "narrative toolkit" to facilitate the co-creation of stories. As illustrated in Figure 8.2, this toolkit assists participants in the storymaking process, guiding them in shaping their narratives, identifying characters, establishing the narrative landscape, and articulating conflicts and resolutions.

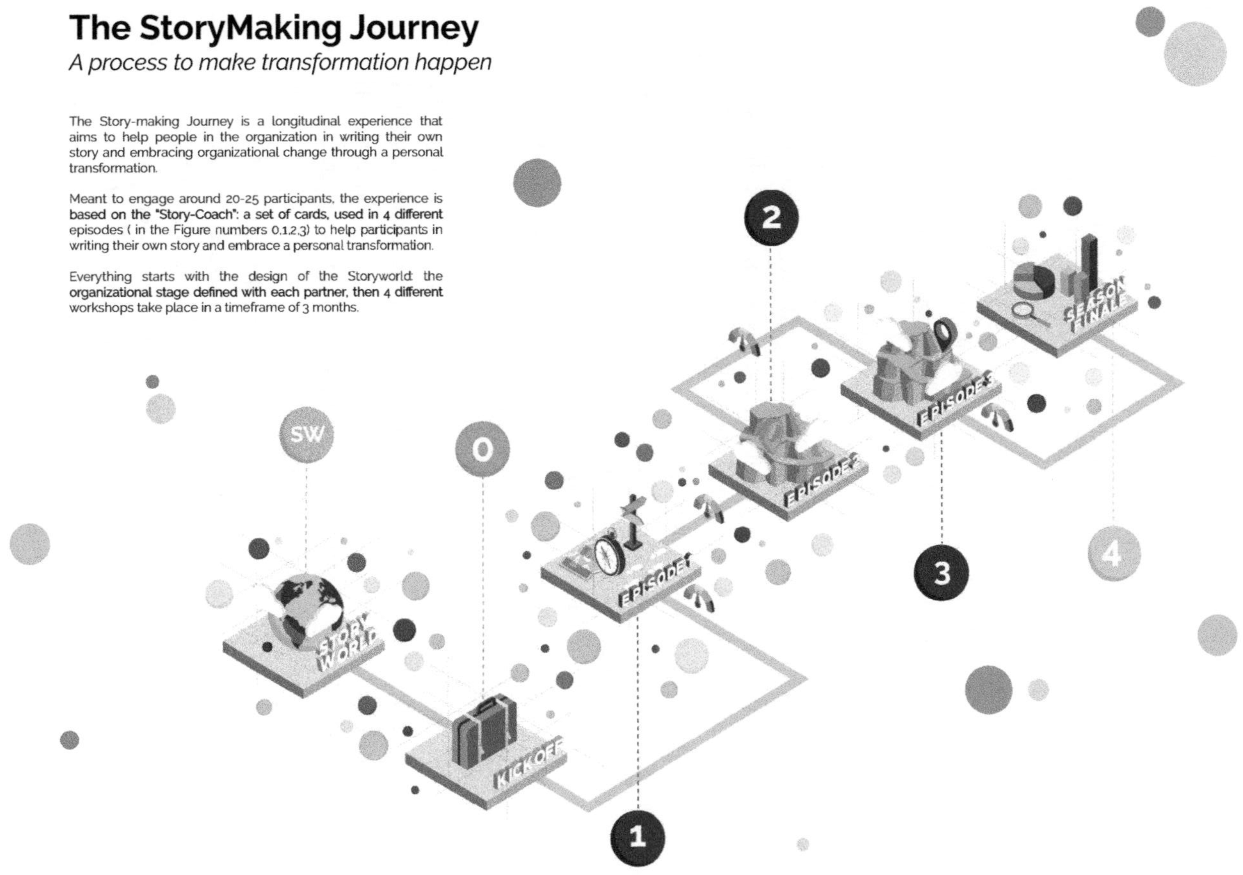

The StoryMaking Journey
A process to make transformation happen

The Story-making Journey is a longitudinal experience that aims to help people in the organization in writing their own story and embracing organizational change through a personal transformation.

Meant to engage around 20-25 participants, the experience is based on the "Story-Coach": a set of cards, used in 4 different episodes (in the Figure numbers 0,1,2,3) to help participants in writing their own story and embrace a personal transformation.

Everything starts with the design of the Storyworld: the organizational stage defined with each partner, then 4 different workshops take place in a timeframe of 3 months.

Figure 8.2 IDeaLs storymaking journey.

Source: Courtesy of Storymaking and Organizational Transformation.

The narrative toolkit typically consists of prompting cards and other materials that direct individuals and groups in constructing their stories. These cards may contain questions, prompts, or themes that encourage participants to delve deeper into their narratives, ensuring they consider various aspects and viewpoints. The toolkit functions as both a guide and a catalyst, sparking discussions, reflections, and collaborative story creation.

The imperative steps in conducting storymaking workshops to steer organizational change are outlined. Initially, the shared context known as the "storyworld" is introduced, setting the stage for participants' personal narratives. Subsequently, individuals create personal transformation stories that align with the change initiative. Concrete action commitments are established after each story episode to maintain ongoing engagement. Regular critical reflection then allows for continuous adaptation and learning.

1. Defining the Shared "Storyworld" Context

    In storytelling, the "storyworld" sets up the shared context that defines the fundamental elements of the envisioned future (Buganza et al., 2021). This sets the stage for participants to construct their personal narratives. The core components of the storyworld are as follows:

- **The Brief:** A succinct statement of the challenge or change that participants are asked to engage with through their stories.
- **The Pillars:** Three or four principles or values that should guide the stories, representing the desired future.
- **Leave Behind:** Three or four practices or mindsets that need to be changed, i.e., what stories should be avoided being reinforced.

    For instance, if the change initiative involved transitioning to regenerative cities, the Brief might ask: "How can we transform our city into a thriving, ethical, and ecologically regenerative future?" The Pillars might emphasize principles like circularity, bio-localization, and social equity. The Leave Behind could identify three practices to avoid: automobile-centrism, extraction of rural resources, and economic inequality. The storyworld anchors participants in the shared context while allowing creative freedom to author unique personal narratives. Following this, participants start crafting their stories within this common framework.

2. Crafting Personal Transformation Stories

The goal is to empower diverse stakeholders to become active protagonists in change narratives. Participants author stories envisioning their personal transformation necessary to enable the desired future outlined in the storyworld. A card-based toolkit

The Storymaking Journey
A process to make transformation happen

SW STORYWORLD

Defined by the company's leadership team, the Storyworld is the organizational direction, the frame within the organizational transformation will happen through participants' personal stories and commitments.

Authors
Leadership Team

O KICK-OFF

The Storyworld is introduced to participants, who are invited to start reflecting on what they need to embrace it. They start by defining the personal direction and the skills, capabilities and tools needed for the journey.

Participants	Duration
ca. 6/group	2h

1 EPISODE 1

Participants reflect about all the elements they may need to embrace their personal transformation journey and foresee possible obstacles or hurdles they may face. Besides, they define a first commitment they aim to complete in the first term to get closer to their personal direction. Finally, the first Episode is written and shared in a small circle.

Participants	Duration
20-25	4h

Figure 8.3 Storymaking journey 1/2.
Source: Courtesy of IDeaLs.

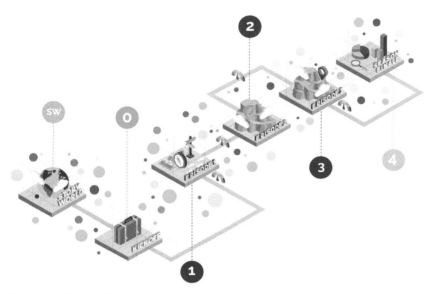

Figure 8.4 Storymaking coach card set.
Source: Courtesy of IDeaLs.

called the "story-coach" (Figure 8.3) provides story elements to incorporate such as motivation, challenges, companions, and mentors (Figure 8.4).

As an illustrative example, in the narrative of an urban transition to a more sustainable city, individuals from various sectors would create a variety of stories visualizing their personal renewal. A policymaker might center their narrative around the construction of systems that foster grassroots community innovation. An urban farmer could emphasize the initiation of a cooperative food distribution platform. Each narrative lends a unique significance to the transformation. After the initial drafting of their stories, participants engage in small group discussions. They then extract and distill three guiding principles from their narratives to start shaping a shared vision. This collective sensemaking continues across multiple story episodes.

3. Committing to Action

Following each story workshop, participants pledge to take short-term actions that will concretely progress their long-term vision for transformation. For instance, the policymaker might pledge to introduce a policy on community currencies to facilitate grassroots exchange innovations. The urban farmer might approach restaurant owners about utilizing their digital platform. These minor actions gradually make the desired future a tangible reality. In the subsequent workshop, participants critically evaluate the lessons learned from their actions and revise their

2 EPISODE 2

Participants start with a retrospective self-reflection about the outcome of the commitment taken. They critically reflect on what they learned and the challenges faced. Besides, if needed, they can update their own direction. Finally, they took a new commitment, write the Episode and shared it in a small circle.

Participants
ca. 6/group

Duration
2h

3 EPISODE 3

Participants start with a retrospective self-reflection about the outcome of the commitment taken. They critically reflect on what they learned and the challenges faced. Besides, if needed, they can update their own direction. Finally, they took a new commitment, write the Episode and shared it in a small circle.

Participants
ca. 6/group

Duration
2h

SEASON FINALE

The results of the experience are presented to the participants and leadership team. Participants and the leadership team critically reflect on what they learned and the impact of the journey both on themselves as individuals and on the organization.

Participants
20-25

Duration
3h

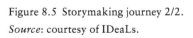

Figure 8.5 Storymaking journey 2/2.
Source: courtesy of IDeaLs.

transformation narratives accordingly. This consistent cycle of commitment and reflection maintains engagement and roots narratives in experiential reality (Figure 8.5).

4. Critical Reflection and Adaptation

Critical reflection allows for collective questioning of assumptions and expectations in light of the change initiative's unfolding reality. As participants gain insights from their commitments and group discussions, they revise their personal narratives and principles. What emerged in practice? What barriers and opportunities arose? How might the storyworld further unfold? This reflective practice fosters a capacity for ongoing regeneration and transformation. The narratives remain dynamic, evolving as participants' comprehension of the required change deepens. For instance, the city transition example might reveal deficiencies in the established principles such as equity or conflicts between pillars, indicating a need to reframe the storyworld. Through consistent critical reflection and rewriting, the narratives maintain a meaningful alignment with the intricate dynamics of sustainability in practice.

The narrative toolkit offers a structured yet adaptable framework, enabling participants, even those unfamiliar with storytelling, to effectively participate in the storymaking process. It breaks down the complex task of narrative creation into manageable segments, ensuring the resulting stories are comprehensive, coherent, and in line with the goals of the storymaking initiative. The storymaking journey fosters stakeholder agency, creativity, and critical consciousness essential for sustainability transformations. There is a pressing need for further research and practice to activate participatory storymaking on a societal scale, especially amidst turbulent times. However, the emphasis of storymaking on collective story work, rather than story consumption, provides grounds for hope. As the African proverb states: "Until lions have their own historians, the hunter will always be glorified." Through inclusive storymaking, sustainability practitioners can empower the "lions" to narrate their own regenerative futures.

Storymaking at Philips

Philips is a leading health technology company with a strong heritage in environmental and social responsibility. In 2021,

Philips reinforced their leadership as a purpose-driven company by adopting a fully integrated approach to doing business responsibly and sustainably and making ambitious environmental, social, and governance (ESG) commitments for 2025. Delivering on these ambitions requires transforming how Philips operates, necessitating new ways to team up with partners and customers to drive the change, and embedding ESG into the company's decision-making tools, processes, reporting, and culture. Most importantly, the role of employees in driving these changes is crucial as they are the ones practically integrating new practices, processes, and mindsets in the company's operations.

In many contexts, including Philips, questions from employees regularly arrive: "How can I contribute in my daily job to sustainability?", "Which concrete actions can I take?", "How can I have more impact?" This opened a space to experiment with the IDeaLs storymaking approach and Philips' intent to enhance employees' sense of purpose and contribution to the company's ESG goals. It had already been piloted as an action-research intervention in Philips in 2020 (Press et al., 2021). The method proved to help people articulate their personal transformation path, meaningfully understand the strategy, and concretely enact this strategy and connect to colleagues.

Designers who took part in these sessions and who were involved in sustainable innovation saw the potential of the IDeaLs method for empowering employees around the ESG strategy. They connected IDeaLs to the team responsible for engagement of the worldwide Philips community around sustainability. A new program of learning and development opportunities had just been created, the Sustainability Ambassador Program, open to employees wanting to further develop their leadership and knowledge in sustainability. The storymaking experience of IDeaLs was integrated into this curriculum and opened for volunteer enrollment for the sustainability ambassadors.

Episode 1: The Storyworld

The storyworld was built by members of Philips Group Sustainability (the horizontal function coordinating sustainability efforts across the company), with the support of Philips designers and IDeaLs facilitators. The goal was to translate the high-level strategic ESG objectives into a storyworld concrete enough for the participants to picture how they could move toward this strategic direction. The storyworld brief highlighted the importance of having a sense of purpose in daily work, the necessary transformation both as individuals and as a company required to achieve the ESG goals, and the challenges met in embedding this purpose into daily work. The key pillars sustaining the storyworld included the company's commitment to focusing on sustainable development goals and on an integrated approach to make a positive impact; empowerment of employees through tools, information, and connections to team up and deliver on the commitments; an entrepreneur mindset to drive purpose and change through small or big actions; embedding commitments and practices in existing systems to sustain the change in the Philips' way of working. These pillars highlighted the existing basis that supports sustainability activities in Philips and encouraged it to leverage and enrich it.

In this storyworld, the elements to question or leave behind during the transformation were the practice of maximizing shareholder value as the single dimension for integral value creation, the idea that sustainability and ESG commitments are the responsibility of leadership and centralized functions only, and the danger for information to stay in silos and for pilots to be prevented from scaling up across the company. These foundations were designed to encourage investigating new business models and challenging business priorities, to elicit a collective sense of responsibility and efficacy, and to stimulate horizontal collaboration and exchange of sustainability knowledge and activities. Approximately 20 sustainability ambassadors joined the storymaking sessions that spread between October and November 2020. The participant group was a heterogeneous mix of employees from Europe and Asia working in varied roles such as finance, supply chain, engineering, innovation, and design, with various degrees of professional involvement in sustainability.

The journey comprised a kick-off, three storymaking sessions, and a finale, prepared and facilitated by the IDeaLs team. In the kick-off, a senior sustainability manager introduced the storyworld brief to participants to foster commitment. After the first storymaking episode, a list of concrete collective actions identified by participants emerged, outlined by the research team as:

- **Us as a community:** Many participants' reflections focused on how to keep nurturing and keeping alive their group also outside of the storymaking experience. They recognized the need to first define a shared interpretation of the vision about sustainability in Philips to create a common vocabulary and language about the topic. This would allow them to find synergies among their stories and align themselves according to shared concrete objectives.

- **Us as leaders:** At the same time, participants were aware that change is possible by taking action on setting examples, increasing visibility about strategic initiatives, and contributing to the general orchestration. Several were ready to take ownership of some initiatives, also involving others to lead together. Their action should serve as a way to empower people, promoting intrapreneurship and a sense of responsibility. Finally, some insights delved into the consideration that others in the network needed to be engaged to spark action. In this regard, effective onboarding was identified as a crucial aspect of the process.

- **Us as change catalysts:** The third vertical focused on the activities that could further push change across different networks of people. First, the creation and dissemination of knowledge emerged frequently as a crucial topic: sharing different approaches between ambassadors, fostering more education about Philips sustainability, or positively contaminating their work team. Then, an interesting reflection revolved around how to make the change toward sustainability more tangible. With this regard, shared inspirational dashboards about sustainability activities, initiatives such as circular walk-ins, and other kinds of meetings could serve to take more concrete steps toward change.

Storymaking in Subsequent Episodes

In the episodes following Episode 1, participants were encouraged to enrich these initial reasonings in their stories to make them clearer and concrete. Their short-term commitments evolved and were captured by the research team as:

- **Driving engagement:** Participants wanted to enable others in the team to activate themselves. They know that collaboration is essential to drive the topic and want to inspire others and facilitate cross-functional team creation.
- **Reach out to others:** They aimed at involving others to help them in pursuing their commitment, for example by getting guidance and ideas from colleagues involved in sustainability and from external experts.
- **Explore/ongoing learning:** Participants intended to nurture their transformation with internal and external knowledge.
- **Pursuing new initiatives:** They planned on proactively launching new projects and including the ESG angle in existing ones.
- **Block time to act:** Participants highlighted the need to prioritize activities related to sustainability in their agenda.

Final Episode

In the final episode, the IDeaLs team presented the results of the stories' analysis and facilitated a dialogue with the participants about their experiences and commitments. A recurrent topic was the subtle task of actively involving others. This is a common enabler as a large part of the commitments involved connecting and teaming up with others, either to inspire, activate, or learn from. In the third episode, the "reaching out for others" became the most important commitment, illustrating this bottleneck. While working on their commitments, participants observed that colleagues have different willingness, time, and possibilities to participate. An important learning was realizing the criticality of understanding how to approach these different stakeholders, for instance using a gradual approach, clear objectives, concrete actions, or persuasive proofpoints.

The participants' main learnings reflected the storyworld pillars and explored their granularity, especially on the approaches and benefits of teaming up and initiating integrated actions. The storymaking experience brought the participants to the next level of reflection on how they can activate sustainability in their work. The process was important in resolving the sustainability ambassadors' initial tension between their ambition to act sustainability and the difficulty to drive environmental and social change in the current economy. By crafting their transformation path, and by iterating on their commitments over the episodes, they were able to understand how their ambition can be translated into actions which, even if they are small, do contribute to the change they aspire for.

MAKING STORIES: A PRACTITIONER'S PROFILE & PRACTICES

Elise Talgorn is a design strategist, narratologist, and artist interested in new methods that catalyze collaborative ecosystems driving meaningful innovation and sustainable development. She develops participatory processes rooted in systems thinking and storymaking. These processes are designed to engage multidisciplinary stakeholders in comprehending intricate, multifaceted problems, co-creating disruptive visions and transformative strategies, and fostering a sense of empathy for both humanity and the Planet. She worked at Philips for 12 years and supported the IDeaLs storymaking process for the sustainability ambassadors.

Figure 8.6 Designing sustainable futures literacy: make stories.

Source: By authors.

She sees storymaking as an important tool to enable sustainability practitioners to articulate and tell their sustainability stories to themselves and others. Storytelling skills are key for innovators who want to promote action, material, and social change within organizations and for general audiences (Corner & Clarke, 2016). Sustainability stories can bridge the gap between knowledge and action by giving meaning to complex information, articulating and managing difficult emotions, and triggering solidarity and collective actions (Moser, 2016; Malena-Chan, 2019). Her experience was that storymaking enabled the ambassadors to craft for themselves their transformation story, which made it easy to further shape it into a communication piece. It could be interesting to include at the end of the IDeaLs storymaking process an exercise where participants are guided to write in an engaging format their story of change that they could use for further communication and sharing.

During the episodes, Elise observed the participants' intense concentration while writing their story – it was almost difficult to make them stop. As a storytelling practitioner, she observed a similar attitude in all the story creation workshops she facilitated with various crowds – innovation and business professionals, artists, students, and children (Talgorn et al., 2022, Talgorn et al., 2023). Through writing, people enter their inner world. Their deep focus and observable desire to stay engaged in writing show how much they need this introspective and reflective break away from a world of over-stimulation and over-information. Several participants mentioned that the storymaking process reminded them of the importance of imagination, creativity, and curiosity. This is particularly relevant to the field of sustainability where there is a call to give more attention to the affective dimension for climate change engagement and to develop soft approaches to trigger environmental action (Leiserowitz, 2006). This angle is critical but too often not prioritized. In the case of storymaking, because introspection is guided and targeted to a professional objective, it gives legitimacy to this type of contemplative and creative moment.

Elise sees storymaking as a very relevant tool to engage communities around environmental and social strategies, because it connects the transformation of the individuals to that of the company, and also to a global transition. In previous research on participatory ecological storymaking, she identifies three paths for sustainability engagement stimulated by the story creation: self-expression, collective expression, and expression of the voice of the Planet Talgorn et al. (2023). Storymaking directly activates the first two channels through the introspective and collaborative format, connecting the individual participants' practical and emotional transformation to a reflection on the multiple facets of cooperation that is a major enabler of sustainable development. A connection to the third channel is made through the storyworld that positions the company strategy into the Planetary needs. Storymaking helps people make sense of their role in the midst of the current socio-environmental challenges and potentially shapes their individual and collective sense of efficacy and socio-ecological identity. To further develop your futures literacy to *make stories* (Figure 8.6), check out the following:

- IDEALS (www.ideals.co)
- StoriesToSaveTheWorld (StoriesToSaveTheWorld_f3cmn4j.pdf (futerra-assets.s3.amazonaws.com)
- The Moth (www.themoth.org)
- StoryCenter (www.storycenter.org)
- Story Arts (www.storyarts.org)

When a collaborative community has co-created a common story, mobilizing members for the transition to a more sustainable future should emerge naturally. In the next chapter, we will learn key principles and practices of "Futureback Leadership" – the why, what, how, and who of transformational change. Mobilizing leadership is all about cultivating a collective understanding of sustainability goals with creativity, shared purpose, and preparedness for complexity. This collective approach positions leadership itself as a conduit for engaging stakeholders in designing sustainable futures.

9
Mobilizing Leadership

Part III concludes with Mobilizing Leadership – not leaders, but on the act of creating leadership itself. Grasping this distinction is essential to tackling the complexity associated with designing sustainable futures, particularly since the traditional models of leadership no longer suffice. In today's world, where stakeholders hail from diverse backgrounds with varying interests and priorities, while all inundated with change, finding a more profound and impactful method of mobilizing leadership is paramount. In our current age of technological solutions to sustainability problems, plus awareness of social justice and cultural sensitivities, co-creating leadership is the most likely differentiator in rallying stakeholders for change.

To understand how to scaffold leadership and leverage it for our great transition, we will be guided by Joseph Press, co-author and co-founder of the IDeaLs research lab. We will share the key insights from the action research conducted by IDeaLs and recent neuroscience insights to propose a method and mindset to mobilize people in the design of sustainable futures.

This chapter lays the stage for acquiring and refining our self-awareness competency – the ability to reflect on one's own role within the local community and the global society; to continually assess and further inspire one's actions; and to manage one's emotions and desires. A more sustainable future necessitates leadership at the individual, organizational, and community levels. We aim to broaden our capacity to engage people across these different dimensions of designing sustainable futures. We will also share insights on how to lead a shift from static systems to regenerative cultures where sustainability is realized through decentralized authority and collective responsibility.

NEUROSCIENCE OF NEW LEADERSHIP MODELS

Securing a sustainable future demands a significant transformation in leadership. Despite efforts like the B-Corp and the UN Global Compact to encourage thousands of companies worldwide to commit to sustainability practices, most corporate sustainability is still centered around reducing negatives such as emissions, rather than innovating systems that generate positive impact (Battilana et al., 2022; Schaltegger et al., 2019). This is in spite of the numerous opportunities to expedite sustainability initiatives, such

DOI: 10.4324/9781003451693-13

as incorporating sustainability into corporate cultures, strategies, and business models beyond isolated projects (Battilana et al., 2022), and conducting open innovation competitions to address systemic social and environmental challenges. The primary obstacle, especially in the corporate sector, is a reluctance to reconsider business models and economic systems based on ever-increasing growth targets or strategic outcomes that "do less bad" (Battilana et al., 2022; Bolton & Landells, 2022).

Leadership commitment at executive levels, as demonstrated by CEOs like Unilever's Paul Polman and Winston (2021), was crucial for embedding sustainability into business practices (Baumgartner & Rauter, 2017; Metcalf & Benn, 2012). However, as Polman's struggle indicates (Smit & Watson, 2023), leadership models that rely on institutional power, hierarchical status, or individual authority figures will continue to fail to inspire the wide-ranging engagement necessary for sustainability (Burns et al., 2022). Furthermore, the engagement of diverse stakeholders, including supply chain partners and activist groups, has been pivotal in driving systemic sustainability changes (Geels, 2019; Senge et al., 2008). Clearly, coordinated efforts from a diverse range of stakeholders across organizations, communities, and all societal levels are required to address shared challenges such as climate change and inequality (Cloutier et al., 2021; Metcalf & Benn, 2012).

This evidence and the urgency for a new paradigm of leadership is clear in considering the effort to engage in collective action to tackle sustainability challenges and design preferable futures. The imperative to shift from merely mitigating negative impacts to actively fostering positive, systemic change in corporate sustainability marks a significant challenge to traditional business models focused on linear growth (Bolton & Landells, 2022). This transition, essential for achieving true sustainability, requires navigating the complexities of modern business environments characterized by volatility, uncertainty, complexity, and ambiguity (VUCA).. Traditional prediction-based leadership strategies, often constrained by cognitive biases and linear planning, are inadequate for this task (Tetlock & Gardner, 2015; Schoemaker et al., 2018). Contemporary leadership needs to adopt more adaptive, collaborative, and visionary approaches, informed by advances in neuroscience that offer insights into decision-making and innovation in uncertain contexts.

Leadership, in a more holistic sense than what traditionally we refer to as "leaders," involves the co-creation of meaning in a community of practice. Here, leadership emerges as a result of the creation of a common direction, the alignment of actions, and the building of commitment. Initially proposed by Drath and Palus (1994) has been pivotal in redefining leadership paradigms, particularly through its emphasis on leadership as a creative, communal process of making shared meaning.

The perspective that knowledge and leadership are constructed through social interactions within cultural contexts resonates with Social Constructivism, particularly the child developmental theories of Lev Vygotsky (Vygotsky, 1978). Communities of Practice also reinforces meaning-making as inherently social and communal activities (Wenger, 1998). These perspectives reinforce the view that leadership emerges in the dynamic interaction within groups, as the collective construction and interpretation of values, visions, and narratives, takes shape.

This view on leadership is metaphorically akin to a neural network, where multiple minds come together to forge new paths of understanding and action (Drath & Palus, 1994). In fact, recent findings in neuroscience, particularly the concept of neural entrainment, provide compelling support for this model. Studies reveal that during collective activities, individuals' brain patterns synchronize, creating a "social synapse" that facilitates shared understanding and collaborative action (Furr et al., 2018). This phenomenon of neural entrainment exemplifies the neurological basis of the communal aspects of leadership posited by Drath and Palus, demonstrating how collective engagement can lead to more effective decision-making and problem-solving. Further research aligns with these insights, emphasizing the importance of emotional intelligence, empathy, inclusion, and psychological safety in modern leadership practices. By engaging community members in participatory processes, the evidence of leadership reimagined as a journey toward common goals and deeply resonant with a community's collective aspirations increases the likelihood of ensuring solutions are sustainable and equitable (McCauley, 2019).

Emerging neuroscience research underscores leadership as inherently collective, underpinned by shared neural processes facilitated by human ultra-sociality. Our brains synchronize during social interactions, a phenomenon evidenced by functional magnetic resonance imaging (fMRI) studies showing neural coupling in communication, where comprehension enhances speaker-listener alignment (Falk & Bassett, 2017). This neural entrainment, or the "social synapse," is amplified by ritualistic activities like music, chanting, and dancing, fostering group cohesion (Wlodarski & Dunbar, 2021; Cozolino, 2006). Such activities, alongside storytelling, elicit similar neural activations across participants, promoting empathy and group bonding at a neurological level (Stephens et al., 2010; Trost et al., 2015), essential for leadership.

Effective leadership depends on this synchronization for rapport, cooperation, and collective sensemaking, leading to shared mental models, narratives, and emotional climates that guide group behavior (Yun et al., 2012; Battiston et al., 2020; Boyd, 2009; Menges & Kilduff, 2015). Cultivating narrative, empathy, and trust through rituals and storytelling, activities that activate the social synapse, are imperative for aligning team mental models and shared leadership (Boyatzis et al., 2014; Wlodarski & Dunbar, 2021). Leaders should foster an environment promoting open communication and collective purpose, highlighting a multi-scale leadership model that integrates individual neurocognition with group and collective dynamics.

These insights propose a multi-scale model of leadership that spans individual neurocognition, group synchronization, and collective meaning, where:

– Individual neurocognition enhances leader capabilities such as social intelligence, emotion regulation, and systems thinking.
– Group synchronization encourages shared resonance and understanding between leaders and followers.
– Collective meaning-making emerges as leadership that enables coherence, direction, and commitment.

By shifting the focus of leadership from the influence of individual leaders to collaborative meaning-making, we can foster a sense of empowerment and sustained commitment (Ford et al., 2021). Viewing leadership as a distributed and emergent process offers a brain-based model for collective leadership. This model is essential for addressing complex challenges. Neuroscience provides a fresh meta-perspective on leadership that includes hierarchical, distributed, and collective processes. Reframing leadership as biologically distributed reorients theory and practice toward catalyzing leadership emergence across resonating brains to meet complex challenges.

IDEALS: SCAFFOLDING SHARED MEANING

Building upon these concepts, the IDeaLs research team proposed a multi-dimensional approach to structure leadership as a collective and creative process of shared meaning-making. The IDeaLs transformation scaffold (Figure 9.1) is a literal and metaphorical space to nurture the transition to a more sustainable world by inspiring innovation, infusing design with dialogue, and reinvigorating leadership with community engagement. A scaffold is a temporary, three-dimensional structure that provides stability and access to support workers and materials in building projects. Metaphorically, the IDeaLs scaffold represents a 3D framework that guides collective action and change within organizations, highlighting a structured yet adaptable approach to navigating complexities and fostering transformation. As a scaffold, it aims to create a space for practitioners to actively cultivate and scale engagement for leading (personally, organizational and

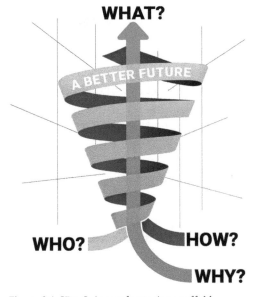

Figure 9.1 IDeaLs' transformation scaffold.

Source: Office Shock: Creating Better Futures for Working and Living.

communal) positive environmental and social change (Press et al., 2023). The scaffold is catalyzed by an intent to change, that is circumscribed by three key dimensions:

1. Intent to change (Why?): This signifies the fundamental commitment to transition from an unsustainable status quo to a regenerative future state. For example, a corporation might commit to dramatically reduce its carbon emissions to contribute to climate stability, or a municipal government might strive to eradicate waste and pollution by implementing a circular economy. Having a compelling vision and purpose to achieve these goals is crucial.

2. A better future (What?): This dimension encapsulates the experiences, offerings, and culture that will facilitate the sustainable vision. For a company aiming for net zero emissions, this might include renewable energy sources, energy-efficient operations, carbon offset initiatives, and a conservation-minded culture. For a circular city, it could include robust recycling and composting facilities, partnerships with businesses to repurpose materials, community repair events, and educational programs. The desired future is shaped by key success indicators such as carbon reduction or waste diversion rates that signal progress.

3. Gameful cooperation (How?): This focuses on the means of actively and creatively engaging all stakeholders in co-creating a sustainable future. Methods such as participatory community design processes (Manzini, 2015), collective storytelling about alternative scenarios (Wahl, 2016), and future-back visioning workshops (Inayatullah, 2008) facilitate gameful cooperation. This dimension necessitates a willingness to embrace new voices and viewpoints (Scharmer & Kaufer, 2013).

4. Leaders with agility (Who?): The individuals who will lead and orchestrate the sustainability transition need to demonstrate adaptability, full-spectrum thinking, and the capacity to work across boundaries. Leadership emerges as the conditions for communities to effect change themselves are cultivated. Leaders provide resources, link efforts, and ensure the vision remains aligned with the intention.

Progressing up the scaffold as all three dimensions increase in influence and impact requires flexive intent – maintaining a clear direction while remaining flexible about the path as circumstances evolve. It emphasizes the role of co-creation in allowing individuals to contribute their meanings, fostering creativity and enabling a shared language essential for transformation. This process is non-linear and dynamic, involving continuous cycles of design-driven dialogue across the elaborated axes of an innovative direction, alignment by design, and committed leadership (Drath & Palus, 1994; Press et al., 2021). Designing sustainable futures requires orchestrating with clarity across the three dimensions of intent, future experiences, and community engagement. By engaging simultaneously in innovation, design, and leadership, the scaffold enables organizations to navigate complex changes, ensuring a holistic and sustainable transformation.

The IDeaLs Scaffold assists organizations transitioning to more sustainable practices in achieving their sustainability objectives (Loorbach et al., 2017). It enables them to:

1. Establish a bold vision for change based on ecological imperatives (Why?)
2. Imagine regenerative futures that meet human needs within planetary boundaries (What?)
3. Foster open, creative participation toward those visions through gameful cooperation (How?)
4. Develop leaders adept at reorienting systems and mindsets as conditions shift (Who?)

By providing an adaptive structure on who to climb toward transformative innovation, the IDeaLs scaffold enables organizations to engage people in shaping an ecologically thriving future.

Revisting A2I - A "Network Entrepreneurship" Story – Leadership as "Network Entrepreneurship"

Designing Sustainable Futures began with Bangladesh's remarkable transformation story, which illustrates that imagining the future, creating meaningful experiences, and preparing leadership is a valid and potent approach to designing sustainable futures. Through BRAC, Sir Fazle Hasan Abed's future for education, healthcare, and microfinance, particularly for women and girls, set the groundwork for sustainable growth in Bangladesh. Anir Chowdhury furthered this vision through the Aspire to Innovate (A2I) program, transforming citizen experiences by digitizing government processes that streamlined public services, significantly enhancing access across the country. Shakil Ahmed's role in transforming the education sector by incorporating futures thinking opened the possibility to advocate for a curriculum that fully addresses the multifaceted nature of climate change (Sabbab & Ahmed, 2024).

Their collective actions demonstrate the multidimensional scaffolding of designing sustainable futures at a societal scale. Moreover, all three exemplify the practices of "network entrepreneurship" in achieving the large-scale social impact of their work. Network entrepreneurs focus on trust-based relationships and collaborative efforts rather than top-down leadership, which resonates with how Abed's BRAC, Anir's A2I program, and Shakil's educational reforms emphasized community involvement, digital collaboration, and educational innovation. Their leadership model exemplifies the notion that effective systemic change arises from empowering others, fostering distributed leadership, and aligning diverse resources toward a shared mission. By reflecting on the principles and practices of network entrepreneurship, their leadership showcases how humility, mission focus, and collaborative networks are pivotal in designing sustainable futures.

FUTUREBACK LEADERSHIP: BRINGING THE FUTURE INTO THE PRESENT

As these changemakers and their stories indicate, a more holistic view of leadership is a necessary condition to trigger and scaffold the transition toward more sustainable futures. Because leadership must be mobilized across distributed networks, individuals must see themselves as part of a larger whole. Herein lies the challenge – neurologically we are dominated by biases that bind us to more narrow perspectives of ourselves and others. Research on how our brains process thoughts about the future has shown that the brain uses the same neural pathways to envision future events as it does to recall past ones. Our brain draws on memories to simulate potential future scenarios (Schacter et al., 2012). Imagination and prediction are thus closely intertwined. If our brains are naturally inclined to assume that the future will resemble the past, how can we perceive disruptive change?

Just as envisioning the future opens significant opportunities for collective action, it also expands an individual's cognitive awareness and ability to adapt to new situations. The future can become the catalyst needed to break free from our restricted perceptions and biases and open up perspectives from the individual, organizational, and community levels. To see the future as a realm of potentialities rather than inevitabilities, we need more of a growth mindset (Dweck, 2008). Far horizon thinking helps to counterbalance the brain's tendency to extrapolate linearly.

By leading from the future rather than the present, practitioners can design better futures out of collective meaning-making. Practitioners who lead futureback are able to coordinate with greater clarity rather than trying to control an inherently organic process. Leading futureback has three primary elements: a method, a mindset, and an intention.

Leading Futureback

We are hard-wired to think present-forward – It's what got us here, for both the good and the bad. Thinking futureback aims to enhance your ability to envision, experience, and enact the change you wish to see. As illustrated in Figure 9.2, thinking futureback starts from imagining multiple scenarios and then projecting them back as preferred future. Institute for The Future recommends focusing foresight on a horizon 10+ years in the future, where uncertainty opens a space for possibilities. By thinking futureback we can transcend outdated perceptions of individual importance by integrating experiential foresight, speculative design, and engaging others for change.

In the book *Office Shock*, practitioners are asked three simple questions to chart a pathway to a more sustainable future:

1. *What Future?* This is exploring Horizon 3, the edges of our aspirations for more purpose and prosperity
2. *What's Next?* This is experiencing Horizon 2, where everything we touch and feel is meaningful
3. *What Now?* This is enhancing Horizon 2, with decisions and actions that turn the present into a glimpse of the future

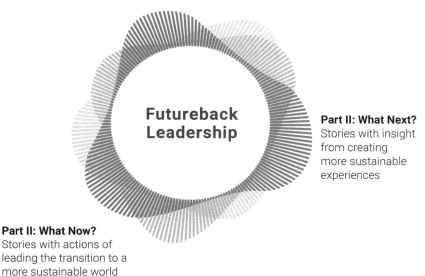

Part I: What Future?
Stories with foresight from experiencing a more sustainable future

Futureback Leadership

Part II: What Next?
Stories with insight from creating more sustainable experiences

Part II: What Now?
Stories with actions of leading the transition to a more sustainable world

Figure 9.2 Futureback leadership.

Thinking futureback starts counterintuitively in reverse – by defining a purposeful vision for the future, then working backward to determine steps to bring the future into the present.

By fusing foresight, narrative, and brain science, leading futureback (see appendix 2 for more details) fosters organizational cultures that promote possibility thinking, empowering individuals to navigate disruption and collaboratively build new futures.

Full-Spectrum Mindset

IFTF futurist Bob Johansen writes: "The future will get even more perplexing over the next decade, and we are not ready." This volatility activates the brain's threat response, favoring caution over creativity (Ghadiri et al., 2020). The cognitive shortcut in these situations is to categorize them. As Johansen continues,

> Categories lead us toward certainty but away from clarity, and categorical thinking moves us away from understanding the bigger picture...Full-spectrum thinking is the ability to seek

patterns and clarity outside, across, beyond, or maybe even without any boxes or categories while resisting false certainty and simplistic binary choices.

(Johansen, 2020)

Full-spectrum thinking encourages a thorough evaluation of all opportunities, seeking interconnections and transcending traditional boundaries or polarities, to ensure the constraints of language and bias do not cloud our clarity.

Practitioners who have a full-spectrum mindset leverage neuroscience to thinking across spectra: They seek a state of homeostasis, a sense of stability in the midst of life's inherent dichotomies. This balance is vital for creating better futures in both working and living environments. To effectively navigate this spectrum, it's essential to move beyond ingrained biases and categorical thinking that often keep individuals anchored at one extreme or the other. Such a shift requires breaking free from the comfort of binary choices and embracing a mindset that seeks patterns and clarity across a broad range of possibilities. Furthermore, this approach acknowledges the discomfort arising from perceived dichotomies, which can lead to challenging conversations. Futureback practitioners foster psychologically safe cultures that endorse exploration of unknown territories. This mitigates reactive risk aversion and propels purpose-driven action, essential for designing sustainable futures.

These experiences are crucial as they trigger neuroplasticity, the brain's ability to adapt and rewire itself. This neuroplastic process is fundamental to changing mindsets and perceptions, enabling individuals to adapt and learn from new experiences and perspectives.

Applying a full-spectrum mindset to four of the spectra elaborated in *Office Shock* (Johansen et al., 2023), Figure 9.3 illustrates 4 spectrums of choice to design sustainable futures in more tangible and specific ways, specifically:

–   Spectrum of purpose: With this mindset, companies can strategically plan for a future where their core objectives are intertwined with global sustainability goals. For example, a tech

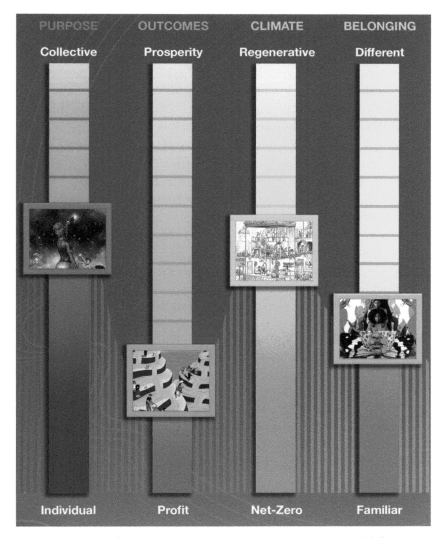

Figure 9.3 Thinking full spectrum about purpose, outcomes, impacts, and belonging.
Source: Office Shock: Creating Better Futures for Working and Living.

company could aim to develop affordable clean energy solutions, transforming its business model while also contributing significantly to global energy challenges. This approach anchors the company's growth in solutions that benefit both the business and the planet.

- Spectrum of outcomes: By focusing on long-term, sustainable outcomes, businesses can initiate projects like developing biodegradable materials or zero-emission transportation solutions. These projects, while profitable, also set a precedent for industry-wide shifts toward environmentally conscious practices, showcasing how commercial success can be achieved without compromising ecological integrity.
- Spectrum of climate impact: Organizations can champion innovative climate actions, such as investing in urban green spaces that double as community hubs, or developing closed-loop manufacturing systems. These initiatives reduce environmental footprints and also serve as blueprints for industry practices that prioritize ecological restoration as part of their operational DNA.
- Spectrum of belonging: In this future-focused approach, companies actively build teams comprising diverse cultural and professional backgrounds, directly influencing the development of products and services that cater to a broader range of global needs. This approach goes beyond mere token diversity, fostering an environment where varied perspectives are integral to addressing complex global issues.

Leading futureback with a full-spectrum mindset enables practitioners to move beyond conventional boundaries, crafting futures where business strategies are inherently aligned with environmental stewardship, social responsibility, and true inclusivity.

Flexive Intent

Underpinning all these is the principle of flexive intent. Leaders with a futureback mindset are distinguished by their unwavering dedication to their purpose and principles. Yet they navigate the path to their vision with adaptability, articulating their overarching goals while recognizing that strategies may evolve based on emerging realities and insights. The future is recognized as a possibility space, not a prediction. Clarity of purpose and principles is maintained, while flexible and revisable as conditions change. Providing clarity of intent and direction offers just enough scaffolding for people to design solutions that are tailored to local realities, distributing authority along the way to foster empowerment and enduring commitment to a more sustainable world.

Elaborating on each dimension of the IDeaLs transformation scaffold across different spectra to illustrate how practitioners can futureback with flexive intent:

- Intent to change (Why) – shared purpose: Flexive intent within the "Why" dimension guides a transformation toward shared purposes that are both sustainable and beneficial for the broader community. For instance, a media company may initially set out to create content that promotes environmental awareness. After feedback that audiences are also expecting actionable solutions, the company can pivot to producing a series on practical sustainability in everyday life, thus aligning its content strategy more closely with the audience's desire for practical engagement.

- A better future for (What) – prosperous outcomes: In the "What" dimension, flexive intent is about shaping outcomes that drive prosperity by contributing to the larger good. Consider a financial institution that plans to invest heavily in clean energy projects. When stakeholders express concern about the neglect of social enterprises, the institution modifies its investment portfolio to include microloans for businesses in developing countries, thereby expanding its impact on global prosperity while maintaining a commitment to sustainability.

- Gameful cooperation (How) – less climate impact: Within the "How" dimension, flexive intent embodies the spirit of playful and collaborative innovation in the journey to a future with less climate crises. Imagine a large corporation's initial plan is to gamify its carbon footprint reduction efforts, encouraging individual departments to compete for the lowest emissions. However, they find that this competitive spirit leads to siloed initiatives rather than company-wide collaboration. In response, the corporation adjusts its strategy to a cooperative game model where departments earn collective rewards by sharing best practices and achieving combined emission reduction targets.

–   Leaders with agility (Who) – more belonging: In the "Who" dimension, leaders apply flexive intent by adapting their approach to foster a sense of belonging. A tech startup might initially focus on recruiting top talent from prestigious universities. After recognizing the need for a more diverse workforce, the startup adjusts its recruitment strategy to include candidates from a variety of educational and cultural backgrounds, promoting a more inclusive company culture that values diverse perspectives and experiences.

Collectively, these elements shape the futureback leadership, a forward-thinking approach that is both visionary and adaptable, ensuring organizations and the communities they serve are prepared for sustainable success in a constantly evolving landscape.

The Sekem Story – An Indication of Futureback Leadership

Resonating with Bangladesh's journey is Sekem, Egypt. Founded in 1977, Sekem has served as a pioneering example of sustainable community development in Egypt. The organization was the brainchild of Dr. Ibrahim Abouleish, a forward-thinking leader who returned to Egypt from Austria with the goal of holistically addressing a range of interconnected challenges, from poverty to environmental degradation.

Sekem was founded on barren desert land, 60 km northeast of Cairo, and its name, inspired by hieroglyphs, translates to "vitality from the sun." At Sekem, Abouleish promoted a futureback approach, working backward from a desired future state to establish strategy and goals. This foresight methodology was embedded throughout the organization, from its governance model to its education programs aimed at helping young people design their futures (Smith, 2018). He championed a multidimensional methodology that integrated economic, social, cultural, and ecological factors. He stressed the importance of designing comprehensive solutions, rather than isolated initiatives. Elements of his leadership reflect thinking and acting futureback, including:

–   What Future – Imagine: The Sekem community imagined overturning the degradation of their land to create a thriving sustainable oasis. They envisioned reversing desertification, empowering young people through education, revitalizing cultural heritage, and enabling both personal and collective advancement. They also envisioned transformative futures at a systems level, with their community as part of global cooperation and regeneration. They shared this vision to align hopes within the community and illuminate a path forward.

- What Next – Design: The community designed integrated solutions that improved lives, culture, economics, and ecosystems. Their agricultural methods regenerated soils while sustainably enhancing prosperity. Holistic medical services blended modern and traditional practices. Education transmitted cultural knowledge while developing youth capacities. This human-centered design approach shaped win–win solutions that improved the environmental, social, and economic fabrics underlying sustainability. The solutions aimed to be inclusive and promote community ownership.

- What Now – Leadership: The Sekem community demonstrated networked entrepreneurialism by bringing together a diverse group of stakeholders, supporting talent, and maintaining commitment over several decades to instigate systemic change. The community members prioritized fostering a sense of shared identity and ownership to catalyze participation. They underscored the importance of youth leadership and exemplified the concept of lifelong learning. This future-focused leadership played an instrumental role in coordinating decisions and actions over time among partners. This method of envisioning, designing, and leading transformation has rejuvenated thousands of hectares and impacted tens of thousands of lives to date.

In the decades since its founding, Sekem has made considerable strides in sustainable development by capitalizing on innovation, design, and leadership. However, recent years have presented challenges ranging from political turbulence to climate change. Abouleish passed away in 2017, entrusting the future of his vision to the succeeding generation. Sekem continues to modify its community-centric model with a flexive intent to navigate current realities while maintaining a future-oriented vision and momentum. While further research is needed, their journey and that of others offer valuable lessons for those who seek to design sustainable futures (Sekem, 2021).

WORK IN PROGRESS! DEVELOPING FUTURES LITERACY TO MOBILIZE LEADERSHIP

The story of *Work in Progress!* illustrates how developing Futures Literacy (FL) mobilizes leadership for more sustainable futures. An essential part of the Dutch Ministry of Foreign Affairs program LEAD (Local Employment for Development in Africa), *Work in Progress!* was designed to contribute to the overall objective of generating sustainable entrepreneurship among youth in prioritized African countries (for more details, see the 10.2023 report "LEAD phase II: Synthesis Study of Mid-Term Evaluation").[1]

A critical dependency of the program was "stubborn optimism" among young people to imagine a better future in the region (Figueres & Rivett-Carnac, 2020). To address this need, LEAD partner Oxfam Novib and local partner Poise Nigeria collaborated with the UNESCO chair on FL at Hanze University of Applied Sciences. FL was proposed as a way to develop the capability to imagine multiple futures and thereby see the present anew. With this ability, program participants would be less path-dependent on the existing obstacles, and therefore able to make better-informed decisions in the present. This would potentially increase the program's impact on the broader goals of poverty reduction and economic justice and even demonstrate the transformative potential of FL in designing a more equitable world.

The partners of *Work in Progress!* focused on establishing the FL Hub in Lagos, Nigeria (Figure 9.3). Their collaboration was crucial in adapting FL to the African context, thereby ensuring that the program's initiatives were culturally relevant and effectively implemented (Figure 9.4).

By retelling this story through the lens of the IDeaLs' scaffold, we can see hints of how the team consciously (and intuitively) cultivated a collaboration that planted the seeds of more sustainable futures:

Why? *A Future with Better Socio-Economic Conditions*

While the genesis of the program was addressing the surge of migration toward Europe, its purpose was much greater than

Figure 9.4 Final day of the FL training week in Lagos in May 2022.
Source: Courtesy of Ramila Khafaji Zadeh.

just this goal. A future with better socio-economic conditions in the migrants' home countries, that fostered economic justice, required equipping youth with market-ready skills to cultivate small and medium-sized enterprises with resilient and sustainable business models. Not only would this necessitate influencing societal attitudes toward employment, but moreover, entrepreneurship. In this future, FL is the critical mindset that creates the desire to acquire the skills of creating new economic opportunities.

What? *The First FL Innovation Hub in Africa*

The FL Hub teaches futures literacies and also aims to embed the mindset within the fabric of the community by providing a place for participants to envision and work toward creating their own sustainable futures. Recognizing the importance of community support and involvement, the Hub organizes events that aim to broaden the conversation around FL beyond the immediate participants (Figure 9.5). These events serve as platforms for sharing insights, fostering dialogue, and building networks among various stakeholders, including local businesses, educators, and community leaders. A significant aspect of the Hub's activities involves conducting research on how anticipation and futures

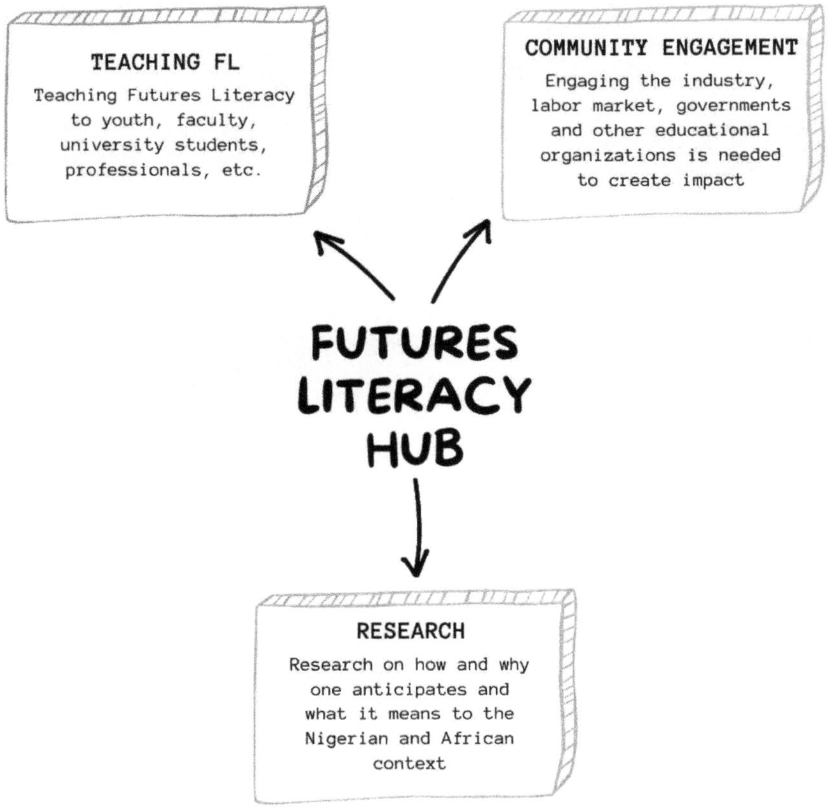

Figure 9.5 Futures literacy hub framework.

thinking can be contextualized and applied in the African setting. This research is critical for tailoring the FL curriculum to the local context and for contributing to the global body of knowledge on FL. The Hub provides ongoing mentorship and support to participants, helping them to apply FL principles in their personal and professional lives. This support network is vital for sustaining the impact of the training and for encouraging continuous engagement with futures thinking and demonstrates the transformative power of FL in fostering resilience, adaptability, and proactive engagement with the challenges and opportunities of the future.

How? *Collaborative Experiences*

Foundational to introducing participants to the concepts of futures thinking and literacy are interactive workshops and seminars. Facilitators employ a variety of methods, including storytelling, scenario planning, and role-playing, to encourage participants to think critically and creatively about the future. However, despite interaction was embedded throughout the experiences, the challenge of fostering FL in these contexts was significant. For many young participants, the concept of imagining multiple plausible futures was alien. The cultural and systemic focus on immediate problem-solving made it difficult for individuals to consider and value the act of envisioning the future. Through the interactive workshops, training programs, and participatory design labs, participants had the opportunity to apply their learning in designing projects or initiatives that address community needs while incorporating futures thinking. One poignant story of a young Nigerian participant who, after attending an FL session, expressed surprise and empowerment at being asked to imagine her own future – a question rarely posed in her previous educational or work experiences. This moment highlights the transformative potential of FL to challenge and expand young people's perceptions of their own agency and the range of possibilities open to them.

Who? *An Alliance of Partners*

Essential to the program was curating an alliance of partners. In addition to Oxfam, Poise focused on advancing employability skills training in the management of the Bits Schools, Ekobits and Edobits. She Leads Africa acted as the accelerator partner due to their focus on women-founded startups, the Enterprise Development Centre (EDC) provided business development support for social enterprises, and VC4A ensured that startups improve their operations and have access to business networks, knowledge, and finance via their online Startup Academy. Mentor-driven capital (MDC) was established to create connections with startup incubators and accelerators. Butterfly Works improved the curricula and supports hubs to improve their services for start-ups and small enterprises.

Hanze University of Applied Sciences rounded out the alliance by providing the basic foundations of FL. This work will be enhanced to fully implement FL in curricula and foster the mindset of FL within students and staff of partner organizations and participating universities.

MOBILIZING LEADERSHIP: A PRACTITIONER'S PROFILE & PRACTICES

Ramila Khafaji Zadeh's contributions to the collaboration with Poise Nigeria have been marked by specific, impactful actions and unique experiences that showcase her innovative approach to integrating FL into youth empowerment programs. Her collaboration has been pivotal in tailoring FL concepts to the Nigerian context, resulting in meaningful and sustainable impacts. Her sensitivities and actions offer many insights on how to role-model mobilize contextual adaptation and empowerment in mobilizing leadership for sustainable futures:

Strategic curriculum integration: A critical contribution was the strategic integration of FL into Poise Nigeria's existing curricula. Recognizing the need for a program that resonates with the local youth, she worked closely with educators and facilitators to weave futures thinking into soft skills and employability training. This effort ensured that participants could envision various future scenarios and also develop the skills necessary to navigate their paths toward these futures.

Facilitator training and mentorship: Understanding the importance of local

Figure 9.6 Designing sustainable futures literacy: mobilize leadership.
Source: By authors.

ownership and sustainability, Ramila led a series of intensive training sessions for Poise Nigeria's staff. These sessions were designed to equip local facilitators with the knowledge and skills to deliver FL workshops effectively. Ramila's mentorship extended beyond training; she provided ongoing support, ensuring that facilitators could adapt the curriculum to meet the evolving needs of their participants. This approach helped build a robust team of local advocates for FL, ensuring the project's long-term impact.

Community engagement and outreach: Ramila's work also extended to community engagement and outreach. She recognized early on that the success of the FL program depended on buy-in from a broader community network, including families, local businesses, and community leaders. By organizing community forums and participatory workshops, Ramila and her team created spaces for dialogue and collaboration, fostering a community-wide understanding of the value of FL.

Designing engaging experiences: Building on the awareness of design thinking, Ramila introduced interactive and participatory methods that encouraged deep engagement with the material. Techniques such as scenario planning, role-playing, and strategic storytelling were employed to make the concept of FL tangible and accessible. These workshops went beyond mere learning experiences to become transformative processes that enabled participants to see themselves as active creators of their futures.

Openness to feedback for continuous improvement: Ramila instituted a rigorous feedback mechanism to capture the experiences of both participants and facilitators. This feedback loop was crucial for continuous improvement, allowing the team to refine and adapt the program in real time. Ramila's openness to learning and adaptation ensured that the FL initiative remained responsive to the needs and aspirations of Nigerian youth.

Sharing meaningful gifts: By actively exchanging gifts, Ramila demonstrates her own appreciation of the cultural and social dynamics at play and her commitment to employing innovative, culturally sensitive methods to enhance the impact of FL. In this manner she was able to contribute to a more engaging and participatory environment, breaking down barriers and encouraging open, heartfelt communication. Not only did this practice convey appreciation, but it also symbolized the potential and possibilities that FL could unlock for individuals and their communities because it served as a tangible representation of the value placed on each participant's contribution and potential. It enriched the learning experience by illustrating how small, thoughtful actions in the present can contribute to building a desired future.

In summary, Ramila's practices in mobilizing leadership exemplify how futures can be effectively localized and embedded within communities of change. In close partnership with the Alliance, by focusing on empowerment, local capacity building, and innovative pedagogical approaches, Ramila has contributed to a scalable model of FL that can be adapted to diverse contexts around the world to encourage everyone to design sustainable futures. By anchoring aspirations for a better future in the fertile ground of local culture and ecosystems, Ramila demonstrates how mobilizing leadership can lead to shared prosperity. As we face a decisive decade, the more practitioners with this FL, who are aware and able to mobilize leadership, the more leadership we will have for the transition to more sustainable practices. Check out these resources for further inspiration (Figure 9.6).

- Work in Progress Oxfam Novib (https://www.oxfamnovib. nl/donors-partners/about-oxfam/projects-and-programs/ workinprogress)
- She Leads Africa (www.sheleadsafrica.org)
- Poise Nigeria – Poise Nigeria Limited (www.poisenigeria.org)
- Transformation Design Design Council (www.designcouncil.org. uk)
- Center for Creative Leadership Development Results That Matter (www.ccl.org)
- NUS Leadership Development Programme (www.nus.edu.sg)

- Transformative Journey: UNESCO-UNEVOC TVET Leadership Programme 2023 (www.unevoc.unesco.org)
- Leadership Development Course (www.school-education. ec.europa.eu)

Note

1   https://www.government.nl/binaries/government/documenten/reports/2023/10/26/
    local-employment-for-african-development-lead-phase-ii-synthesis-study-of-mid-term-
    evaluation-reports/Synthesis+Study+Local+Employment+for+African+Development+
    Program+Phase+II.pdf

Designing Your Sustainable Future

Afterword: Designing Your Sustainable Future

Designing sustainable futures is complex and challenging. We believe that by integrating futures, design, and leadership we are paving a path for a more engaging approach to mobilizing stakeholders across the communities that seek a better future.

Good news is that there are many of us, and that with technology we can connect the many stars out there. An exciting example is the Aotearoa Futures Network (Aotearoa Futures Network Map). Using a mapping platform called Kumu (Figure 10.1), creator Victoria Mulligan describes this as a first step in exploring the futures ecosystem in New Zealand. By visualizing the relationships and interactions among futures practitioners, the platform aims to "maximise the potential for collaboration and alignment across sectors, and accelerate collective action toward a more just, equal and sustainable Aotearoa for future generations."

When people and practitioners connect, coordinate, and collaborate within and across communities, it empowers us to do more together than is possible alone. To prepare ourselves for such cooperation, we conclude *Designing Sustainable Futures* with an approach to shape how we would stand up to the future, and how we will show up in the present.

Our role as facilitators, or curators of designing sustainable futures, can benefit from some shaping. In our experience, sketching a sustainable futures initiative is important for both stakeholders and practitioners. Ultimately, our awareness, agility, and resilience will be key in contributing to long-term change with meaningful and measurable impact. To launch us all on this important path, let's explore a design brief, personal astrolabe, and manifesto that can accompany us along a mission-critical journey.

DOI: 10.4324/9781003451693-14

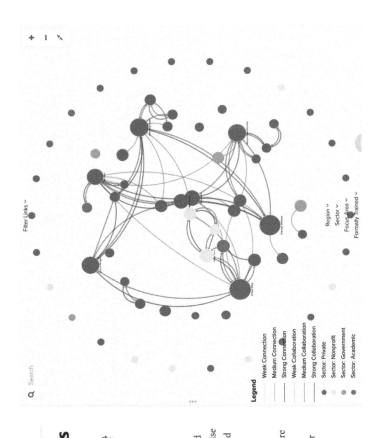

Welcome to the Aotearoa Futures Network Map

To close this description, click anywhere on the map. When on the map, you can access this description again by clicking the three vertical dots above the legend.

Purpose

Welcome to the Aotearoa Futures Network Map - a first step in exploring the futures ecosystem in New Zealand.

The purpose of this network is to visualise the relationships and interactions among futures practitioners so that we can maximise the potential for collaboration and alignment across sectors, and accelerate collective action toward a more just, equal and sustainable Aotearoa for future generations.

It is intended that the map provides the organising infrastructure to enable diverse groups of people to connect, coordinate and collaborate within and across organisations to do more together than is possible alone.

In practice, this might look like:

Figure 10.1 Aotearoa Futures Network.
Source: Courtesy of Victoria Mulligan

Afterword: Designing Your Sustainable Future

THE DSF DESIGN BRIEF

We propose a comprehensive framework for practitioners looking to navigate the intricate journey of creating impactful, sustainable initiatives. Crafted to align visionary goals with actionable strategies, this template serves as a valuable tool in structuring and guiding projects toward meaningful outcomes. It encompasses elements of mission planning, stakeholder engagement, and leadership style, all while integrating the principles of Futureback Leadership to ensure a balance between aspirational objectives and grounded, pragmatic steps. While acknowledging the complexity and multitude of factors influencing sustainable development, the template in Figure 10.2 aims to provide clarity and direction amid the challenges of shaping a sustainable future. Its connection to global sustainability goals further positions it as a potential instrument for guiding those committed to making a positive, enduring impact on their communities and beyond. Let's explore this in more detail.

"My Ambition" is crucial as it sets the foundational goal, guiding the entire sustainable future initiative. It articulates a clear, overarching objective, ensuring all decisions and strategies align with this central purpose. This clarity is vital for steering efforts,

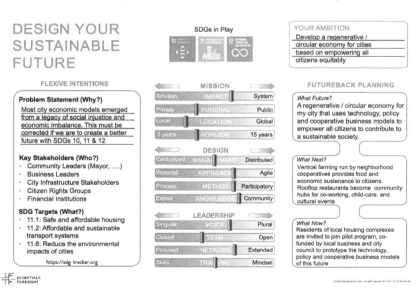

Figure 10.2 Design Your Sustainable Future Template.
Source: By authors.

efficiently utilizing resources, and communicating the initiative's purpose to stakeholders, thereby fostering engagement and support. For example, an ambition to develop a regenerative/circular economy for cities, focused on equitably empowering all citizens, envisions transforming urban economies into systems that replenish and restore resources based on social equity. By setting an ambition, you're committing to a holistic approach that tackles environmental sustainability while also addressing social equity – a dual focus that is increasingly recognized as essential for the long-term health and prosperity of urban communities. This ambition serves as a north star, guiding your initiative toward impactful and meaningful outcomes that resonate with a broad range of stakeholders.

The "Flexible Intentions" section is where you detail the specific aspects of your initiative, giving it shape and direction. This includes defining the problem statement, identifying key stakeholders, and setting specific targets aligned with Sustainable Development Goals (SDGs).

- Problem statement: The foundation of your initiative is understanding the "why." For example, recognizing that most city economic models have roots in social injustice and economic imbalance is crucial. Addressing these issues is essential to creating a future that aligns with SDGs 10, 11, and 12, focusing on reduced inequalities, sustainable cities and communities, and responsible consumption and production.

- Key stakeholders: Identifying "who" is involved or affected is key. This includes community leaders such as mayors, business leaders who can drive economic change, stakeholders in city infrastructure who can implement changes, citizen rights groups who advocate for equitable treatment, and financial institutions that can support funding for these initiatives.

- SDG targets: The "what" of your initiative should align with specific SDG targets. In this context, focusing on targets like 11.1 for safe and affordable housing, 11.2 for affordable and sustainable transport systems, and 11.6 for reducing the environmental impacts of cities. These targets provide clear, actionable goals that guide the initiative toward tangible, measurable outcomes.

By clearly defining these aspects in the Flexible Intentions section, you create a focused framework for your initiative, ensuring that every action taken is purposeful and aligned with your overarching ambition. This structure helps in setting a shared space for engaging stakeholders in designing a sustainable future.

Once the design space is outlined, defining the principles for designing a sustainable futures initiative is critical. Making these choices explicit increases the clarity on the "ways of working." Resonating with the mindset of thinking full spectrum, a range of choices are available for intentional decision-making:

1. Mission choices:
   - System vs. project-based approach: Choose a system-based approach for overarching city-wide integration, like implementing a city-wide sustainable transport system, when targeting holistic, long-term sustainability goals. Opt for a project-based approach for specific, localized projects, such as establishing community recycling centers, where immediate impact or targeted solutions are needed.
   - Impact type: For a systemic change approach, consider initiatives like revising city zoning laws to support sustainable development, recommended for fundamental restructuring of economic and social systems. Alternatively, a solution-focused impact might involve installing solar panels on public buildings, best when addressing specific issues with immediate, tangible outcomes.
   - Geographical scope: Select a local scope for initiatives focused on city-specific needs, like creating urban green spaces, and solutions. Choose a global scope for projects with international relevance, such as participating in global sustainability networks or adopting international green building standards.
   - Temporal scope: A short-term scope is suitable for projects aimed at quick wins, like launching a city-wide composting program, or immediate goals. A long-term scope is better for ambitious projects, such as transitioning to a fully renewable energy grid, requiring extensive planning and long-term commitment.

2. Design choices:
   - Management style: Use a centralized management style for uniform implementation and control in large-scale projects, like city-wide waste management systems, or opt for a distributed style to foster local innovation and community involvement, such as neighborhood-based sustainability initiatives.
   - Approach: A waterfall approach is preferable for projects with defined stages and minimal expected changes, like building a new public transit system. An agile approach is ideal for projects needing adaptability to evolving needs, such as developing community engagement programs for environmental awareness.
   - Method: Process-oriented methods are best for projects requiring strict adherence to guidelines, like establishing new environmental regulations. Participatory methods are crucial for initiatives where community engagement drives success, such as co-designing community green spaces.
   - Knowledge base: Choose an expert-led knowledge base for projects requiring specialized knowledge, like developing new green technologies. A community-based approach is invaluable for initiatives where local experiences and insights are crucial, like community-driven urban farming projects.
3. Leadership choices:
   - Voice: A singular voice is useful for clarity in decision-making, particularly in complex situations, like establishing a new city sustainability policy. A plural voice ensures inclusivity and collaborative decision-making with diverse perspectives, necessary for initiatives like community stakeholder meetings on urban development.
   - Openness: Opt for a closed team dynamic in specialized projects requiring focused expertise, such as technical research teams for sustainable infrastructure. An open dynamic benefits from a wide range of ideas and community engagement, like open forums for city sustainability planning.
   - Network: Focused networks are best for deep, specialized collaborations, such as partnerships with environmental NGOs for conservation projects. Extended networks are ideal

for projects benefiting from diverse insights, like international collaborations on climate change initiatives.

- Training approach: Skills development is crucial when specific competencies are needed for project implementation, such as training programs for green technology installation. A mindset fostering approach encourages sustainability-oriented thinking for long-term change, like workshops on sustainable living practices.

Integrating the choices of mission, design, and leadership is crucial for framing the intentions of a sustainable future initiative as it aligns operational strategies with core ambitions, ensuring coherence and feasibility. This integration tailors approaches to diverse stakeholder needs, operationalizes broad SDGs into specific, actionable strategies, and facilitates adaptive, responsive planning. Such coherence is essential in transforming high-level objectives into localized, achievable actions, guaranteeing that every element of the initiative, from management style to stakeholder involvement, directly contributes to achieving the defined goals in a realistic and effective manner.

An important pillar of the brief is outlining how leading futureback can shape the aspirations of a sustainable future initiative. As described in Chapter 9, and further detailed in Appendix II, each step opens an opportunity to imagine, design, and lead toward a better future:

- What future? This step involves defining a clear and ambitious future goal for the initiative. The purpose here is to set a visionary target that guides all subsequent actions and decisions. In this case, the envisioned future is a regenerative/circular economy for the city, leveraging technology, policy, and cooperative business models to empower all citizens. The benefit of this step is that it establishes a concrete, aspirational end state, serving as a north star for the initiative. It ensures that all efforts are consistently aligned toward a transformative and impactful goal.
- What next? Here, you identify the immediate, significant milestones that need to be achieved to progress toward the envisioned future. This step is about breaking down the overarching goal into more manageable, concrete projects or initiatives. The example of implementing vertical farming run

by neighborhood cooperatives, which also serve as community hubs, illustrates this step. The benefit of identifying these milestones is that they create a roadmap of tangible actions, making the ambitious future goal seem more attainable and providing clear focus areas for short-term efforts.

- What now? The final step is about taking immediate actions that set the stage for achieving the future vision. This involves initiating projects or activities that lay the groundwork for the larger goals. In the given example, it's about inviting residents to join a pilot program co-funded by local businesses and the city council to prototype the elements of the future vision. The purpose of this step is to kickstart the initiative with practical, achievable tasks that build momentum and start to bring the envisioned future into reality. The benefit is that it translates vision into action, mobilizing resources and stakeholders, and beginning the process of tangible change.

Leading futureback from a clearly defined future state aims to cultivate a shared understanding that is aspirational, yet grounded in the realities of complex socio-technical situations. It contributes an important perspective in designing sustainable futures initiatives and complements the template as a guide to navigating the complexities of sustainable future planning with clarity and confidence. While the approach aims to align all aspects, from overarching goals to specific actions, and tailors the initiative to diverse stakeholder needs and local contexts, practitioners know that there are many other factors influencing the success of any intervention in complex situations. A template like this is but one tool among many in the intricate process of driving change, particularly because the path to transformation is multifaceted and requires a multitude of approaches. Ideally, this or any similar template can increase clarity on intentions of designing sustainable futures, while humbly recognizing the broader, dynamic context in which these sustainable initiatives unfold.

YOUR ASTROLABE

In the journey of designing sustainable futures, the choices we make at personal, organizational, and community levels are intricately linked and profoundly impactful. Reminiscent of our Astrolabe guiding us throughout this journey, we envision a similar model to guide practitioners to be more aware, agile, and resilient along the journey (Figure 10.3). At the personal level, choices revolve around aligning one's values with actions, pursuing careers and lifestyles that contribute positively to societal and environmental well-being. For organizations, the focus shifts to embedding sustainability into their core strategies, ensuring that their operations and

Figure 10.3 My Astrolabe Model.

Source: By authors.

ethos resonate with the broader objectives of societal good and environmental stewardship. Community choices further expand this scope, encompassing public policies, communal initiatives, and collaborative efforts that foster a sustainable living environment for all inhabitants. Each choice, whether made as an individual, a member of an organization, or a citizen of a community, contributes to the tapestry of a sustainable and resilient future. These choices are distinct, so let's explore what they might be for anyone designing sustainable futures.

Myself

In the quest for a sustainable future, practitioners must navigate a complex landscape of personal and professional choices. These choices, deeply interwoven, span the realms of purpose, outcomes, environmental consciousness, and inclusivity.

Purposeful alignment in work and life stands at the core of impactful transformation. This involves integrating personal values and professional endeavors, ensuring that one's work contributes meaningfully to broader societal objectives. Such alignment leads to greater personal fulfillment and societal impact, as seen in careers in renewable energy or community development projects. The challenge lies in finding opportunities that align with personal values and offer professional growth. Staying informed about societal needs and flexible in adapting career paths is crucial for resilience and effectiveness.

Outcome-oriented strategies are equally vital. Redefining success to include positive social and environmental impacts alongside financial gains demands a shift in perspective. Advocating for corporate policies prioritizing sustainability and supporting ethical business practices are examples of how individuals can contribute to broader societal welfare. The difficulty here is balancing financial objectives with social and environmental responsibilities. Practitioners need to adapt their strategies to sustainable business practices and focus on long-term impacts over short-term gains.

Environmental consciousness is another key aspect. Individuals committing to sustainable practices like reducing waste and advocating for green policies in the workplace significantly contribute to environmental sustainability. The challenge is altering established habits and convenience-based practices. Staying informed about environmental issues and solutions, and being flexible in adopting more sustainable practices, enhances resilience in maintaining these commitments.

Lastly, a commitment to inclusivity is crucial. Creating diverse and inclusive environments in personal and professional spheres enhances creativity and problem-solving, vital for addressing sustainability challenges. Initiatives promoting inclusivity, such as diversity training and equitable decision-making processes, can overcome biases and change organizational cultures. Continuous education about diversity and inclusivity, adapting to new perspectives, and advocating for inclusivity, even when faced with resistance, are necessary for building a more equitable world.

For yourself, these interconnected areas of purpose, outcomes, environmental consciousness, and inclusivity can form the pillars on which to build a sustainable transformation. Practitioners must integrate these principles into their lives, overcoming challenges with resilience, awareness, and agility. In addition, they form a foundation for engaging your organization and community toward a more equitable and sustainable future.

My Organization

In guiding an organization toward a more sustainable future, a practitioner must thoughtfully integrate key aspects into the organization's ethos and operations. It starts by embedding a sense of purpose within an organization and is about aligning the company's mission with broader societal goals. This involves creating a work environment that addresses the basic needs of employees and also encourages them to find deeper meaning in their work. For instance, implementing policies that support social justice and community engagement demonstrates an organization's commitment to being more than just a profit-driven entity. The challenge lies in harmonizing individual purposes with the collective goals of the organization, which requires a willingness to continually question and adapt.

Advocating for an outcomes-focused approach means reevaluating the traditional metrics of success that balance profitability with the impact on employees, customers, and the wider community. For example, shifting toward shared social value involves transcending efficiency and control, to emphasize collaborative and equitable practices. The difficulty here is in redefining what success looks like for the organization, moving beyond short-term gains to long-term, holistic prosperity.

A practitioner should also champion environmental stewardship within the organization. This might involve adopting sustainable practices across operations, reducing the company's carbon footprint, or innovating in product design for minimal environmental impact. The challenge is integrating these practices into the core business strategy, making sustainability a key factor in every decision, from procurement to product development.

Finally, fostering a sense of belonging within the organization involves creating a culture that values and celebrates diversity. This could include developing inclusive hiring practices, promoting diversity in leadership, or creating programs that encourage understanding and appreciation of different cultures and backgrounds. The challenge is in breaking down existing biases and stereotypes and creating an environment where every employee feels valued and empowered.

For a practitioner, the journey of guiding an organization in designing a more sustainable future requires a nuanced understanding of these aspects. It's about creating a symbiosis between individual aspirations and the collective vision of the organization, ensuring that every strategy and decision contributes to a broader, more sustainable, and inclusive future.

My Community

Envisioning a sustainable future for communities requires a practitioner to integrate key elements into the community's ethos and operations, reflecting a similar approach taken in personal and organizational choices.

Purpose within a community context extends beyond basic amenities. Anticipating citizens' needs using futureback thinking prepares for challenges like climate change. Proactive policies and environments reflecting collective goals and values are crucial. For example, ensuring cost-free access to educational and recreational resources like the metaverse in public spaces is a step toward this purposeful approach.

In addressing climate impact, the community adopts practices contributing to the circular economy, crucial for sustainable living. Encouraging product lifecycle extension through repair, reuse, donation, and recycling creates an environment of active environmental stewardship. Aligning various stakeholders to adopt and maintain these practices consistently is a significant challenge. Fostering values that transcend financial goals is essential in outcomes-focused community development. Working with local businesses to encourage more equitable ownership models improves lives beyond financial profit by extending benefits to the entire community.

Creating an environment where diversity is celebrated and every individual feels valued is fundamental to fostering belonging in a community. Actively seeking different perspectives enhances problem-solving and innovation. Overcoming traditional norms and promoting inclusivity at every level are challenges that require creativity and courage. For a practitioner, guiding a community toward a sustainable future is about nurturing these elements and creating synergy between individual aspirations and collective vision. Building a community that is resilient, adaptable, and reflective of a broader, more inclusive, and sustainable future is the key objective.

A MANIFESTO

With a brief mapping of our journey and an astrolabe to assist us navigate the turbulent waters, a manifesto can act as a personal guiding star. Inspired by Alex Danchev's (2011) collection of 100 manifestos of artists from the last 100 years, we see this as an embodiment of our deepest convictions. Its written and visual content acts as a declaration of commitment toward a better future.

For practitioners of sustainable futures, each element outlined in Figure 10.4 of our suggested manifesto is both a commitment and a call to arms, that captures the essence of a personal and professional mission:

- "I would love to change…" This element of the manifesto represents the desire for transformation. It is a recognition of the current state and an expression of the need to evolve. For instance, stating "I would love to change the paralysis of climate anxiety" acknowledges a barrier to action and sets the stage for a proactive approach to overcoming it.

- "Because I believe…" This section provides the rationale behind the desire for change. It underpins the manifesto with a philosophy or a core value that drives the practitioner. "Because I believe storytelling positive futures will manifest a tangible

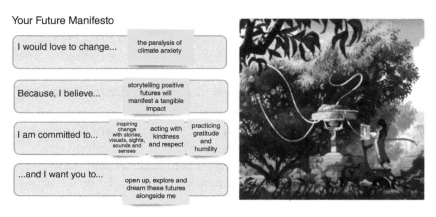

Figure 10.4 Futures manifesto, participant's work from the Designing Sustainable Futures course.

Source: By authors.

impact" conveys a conviction that narratives have power, that they can shape attitudes and provoke action toward those very futures.

- "I am committed to…" Here lies the pledge to take concrete steps. It's a declaration of the specific strategies and behaviors one is dedicated to pursuing. Commitments like "inspiring change with stories, visuals, sights, sounds, and senses" and "acting with kindness and respect" offer a clear course of action that aligns with the manifesto's purpose and beliefs.

- "And I want you to…" This is the collaborative aspect of the manifesto, extending an invitation to others to join the journey. It suggests an openness and a willingness to engage with a community of like-minded individuals. Saying "open up, explore and dream these futures alongside me" is more than a polite request; it is a communal invitation to build collective strength in a shared direction.

A manifesto's visual companion amplifies its message, and in Figure 10.4, the image's meaning is even more for the creator than the viewer. It shows a harmonious blend of technology and nature, reflecting a desire to move beyond climate anxiety through an inspiring illustration of a sustainable future. The flourishing greenery and solar-powered technology visually reaffirm a belief that envisioning and working toward positive outcomes is possible. The character, engrossed in their interaction with technology amidst nature, reflects a commitment to integrating sustainable practices into daily life. Although generative by AI, the sketch-like, painterly quality of the scene rather than photorealistic invites others to join in this sustainable journey, where a future is crafted through collective effort and shared dreams can create a future where community, technology, and the environment coalesce to create a vibrant, sustainable world.

Being reminded of one's manifesto acts as an anchor, keeping the practitioner grounded in their values and focused on their objectives amidst the distractions and challenges that arise. A manifesto is a source of inspiration and resilience, a tool to keep one aligned with their purpose, especially when the path gets arduous. By revisiting the manifesto, practitioners of sustainable futures reaffirm their commitments, rekindle their beliefs, and regenerate their collaborative spirit, ensuring they remain steadfast on the path to meaningful change.

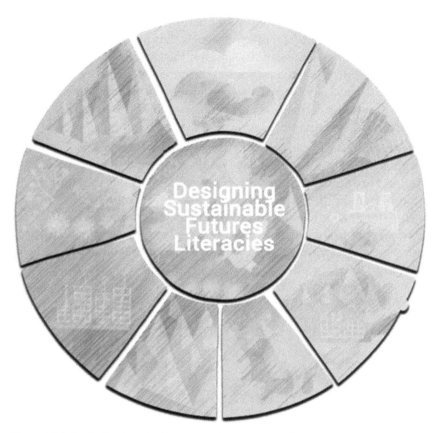

Figure 10.5 Designing Sustainable Futures Literacies Template.
Source: By authors.

Developing the nine designing sustainable futures literacies is a crucial investment in all our abilities to be ready to shape whatever world emerges. Use the template in Figure 10.5 to guide your development. In a world where change is the only constant, the ability to envision, speculate, and generate visions for sustainable futures empowers us to navigate uncertainty with confidence. By building worlds that prioritize sustainability, shaping systems that account for ecological balance, and designing fictions that foster empathy and collaboration, we are laying the groundwork for a more resilient and equitable society. Cultivating collaboration and making stories that challenge the status quo encourage us to reflect on our values and the impact of our actions. Mobilizing leadership in this context means stepping into roles that have the power to inspire and enact change, ensuring that the future we dream of can become a reality. These literacies are not mere skills; they fortify the mindset to guide us toward a sustainable world where innovation, empathy, and leadership converge to create environments that thrive on diversity, sustainability, and collective well-being.

In the end, these and any other tools can increase more awareness, agility, and resilience on the journey to a sustainable future. However, when the noisy present drowns out the sounds of a preferred future, the only key is a commitment to holistic well-being for individuals, organizations, and communities. By making conscious, purposeful, and shared choices at every level, can we collectively steer design futures that are sustainable, resilient, and flourishing for all.

Buon Viaggio

Afterword: Designing Your Sustainable Future

Acknowledgments

This book, and the course, is the result of envisioning an integrated initiative, creating engaging educational experiences, and cultivating a community to make our collective vision a reality. This book would not have been possible without the support of Lyn Jeffery of IFTF and Cabirio Cautela of POLI.design – they made the partnership for *Designing Sustainable Futures* possible, and we thank them deeply for their commitment. Our pilot course was an incredible learning opportunity for all, and we look forward to continuing and improving it in the coming years. Cindy Baskin was just as essential, and through her guidance and actions, we were able to make this experiment happen. Similarly, working with Roberta Gorno of POLI.design allowed us to define and agree on the parameters of our partnership.

The foundation of this partnership is the faculty and expert contributors listed at the beginning of this book. Manuela, Victoria, and I are all very appreciative of their contributions and our learning throughout the journey. In addition to the expert team, the input and feedback from Jake Dunagan and Stuart Candy were critical to strengthening our ideas through the writing process.

Collaborating closely with the POLI.design marketing team of Barbara Casati, Paola Galdi, and Luca Mautone, Cindy was also instrumental in securing our pilot cohort of students. A huge acknowledgment goes to them for their active participation and important contributions to both the content and pedagogy of designing sustainable futures:

- Kimberley Frecon
- Yuke Huang
- Mark Teo
- Carine Chisu
- Joni Chan

- Clay Bunyard
- Katy Cooper
- Keith Webster
- Pratibha Mistry
- Debora Kantt
- Rodney Frederickson
- Tina Jailani
- Crystal Campbell
- Diarmaid Upton
- Sandra Niehaus

Under the guidance of Ayca Guralp from IFTF, Victoria Rodriguez Schon and Silvia Torri did an incredible job, delivering the experience, enabling us to reflect, and revise the overall approach, key insights, and content.

Because of the high level of delivery excellence, we were able to pivot this experience into a book. As in all book writing, collaboration is essential. Reviewers Lev Gorelov and Beate Stiehler-Mulder helped us to clarify the content, while Natasia Taylor and Lara Cocciuti created incredible graphics to help tell the story.

While the course provided much insight and inspiration, designing sustainable futures can always benefit from looking across the multitude of practices and practitioners.

It was an honor for us to have Sohail Inayatullah write the forward to this book. As he always does, his connecting us to his PhD student Shakil Ahmed evolved into the signature store of the book. His expert insights and edits contributed to shining a meaningful futures spotlight on the story of his country. Together with Anir Chowdhury, who shared his incredible story about a2i, both provided valuable context for Bangladesh's transformation journey, which we all hope will continue on a positive trajectory.

Many other storymakers join this collective effort. Starting with Taqi Shaheen for sharing his experiences with gaming better futures. Cherry-Ann Davis shared her story of hybrid ethnography and Pan-African narratives. Elise Talgorn and Harald Tepper shared their stories and insights on storymaking at Philips. We are gracious of the contributions at the leading edge of designing sustainable futures from Rosanna Vitiello and Marcus Willcocks.

A huge thanks is due to Meredith Norwich, Bethany Nelson, and the rest of the Routledge team for their patience and commitment to seeing this book to fruition.

Finally, to our family members whose resilience supported the writing of another book. From Joseph to my parents Mimi and Pepe, partner Rachel, and our children Ori, Anäelle, Nati, and Elia. From Manuela to my parents for encouragement, to my daughter Sofia, whose fresh perspective allows me to see reality with new eyes, and to my extended family of relatives and friends across the globe whose ongoing inspiration fuels my journey.

Author and Faculty Profiles

CO-AUTHOR AND GUIDE THROUGH CHAPTER 9: MOBILIZING LEADERSHIP

Vice-Dean and Professor Joseph Press, Co-author and Co-founder of the IDeaLs research lab, serves as our compass in navigating the concept of futureback leadership. His experience and writing on leadership began with his role at the Center for Creative Leadership (CCL), where he held the position of Strategic Advisor to the CEO. At CCL, a global frontrunner in leadership development, Joseph designed crafted programs that ingeniously integrated futures, design, and change methodologies. These programs, offering fresh insights and tools, set a new standard in leadership training. Concurrently, he co-established the aforementioned research lab, IDeaLs.

At the Institute for The Future (IFTF), he engages organizations as a futures architect. He partners with leaders to conceptualize improved futures, curate meaningful experiences, and foster leadership that triggers systemic change. As a co-founder of MakeOurFuture.coop, he guides sustainable transitions worldwide.

His co-authored books delve into the modern workplace, entrepreneurial spirit, and transformational strategies, with a significant focus on the understanding of leadership and its crucial role in these domains. Joseph's commitment to education is evident in his teaching roles at the Politecnico di Milano and Parsons The New School for Design, where he continues to learn about the interplay of innovation, design, and leadership.

CO-AUTHOR AND GUIDE THROUGH CHAPTER 2: SPECULATING FUTURES

Professor Manuela Celi, Associate Professor at the Design Department of Politecnico di Milano, contributes her wealth of knowledge to this book, as an expert on the chapter's topic and as one of its distinguished authors. In addition to her role as the lead researcher of FUEL, she also teaches in the Metadesign and Design Futures courses at the Design School of Politecnico di Milano. Professor Celi's prominence in the field of future studies and anticipation is well-recognized, as having co-chaired the design and anticipation special session at the Anticipation Conference in Trento in 2015.

Her research journey began with an emphasis on design-related knowledge forms and their applications in learning systems to enhance metacognitive abilities. Over time, she expanded her research to encompass advanced design processes, fostering a transdisciplinary approach that intertwines design with humanities and social sciences. This cross-disciplinary viewpoint guides her investigations into the creation of intermediate or semi-finished design products imbued with rich cultural content, such as trends and scenarios.

Committed to bridging the gap between research and education, Professor Celi continually innovates her teaching methodologies. She delivers pioneering content in her courses and runs experimental learning activities for her students which are closely tied to foundational research. Her academic contributions have been featured in prestigious academic publications including *Futures, The Design Journal, DIID–Disegno Industriale Industrial Design, The Design Management Journal*, and *The Strategic Design Journal*.

OUR GUIDE THROUGH CHAPTER 1: EXPERIENCING FORESIGHT

Dr. Jake Dunagan is the director of Design Futures at the Institute for The Future (IFTF), where he applies his knowledge of strategic foresight to the intersection of emerging technologies, societal transformations, and governance design. His cutting-edge approaches to foresight and extensive experience lend weight to our exploration of sustainable futures. The IFTF, an independent nonprofit research organization, has a 55+-year track record in foresight and future thinking. Its contribution to the field has helped myriad organizations navigate complex future scenarios, enabling them to make more informed and strategic decisions. Dunagan's work and the broader efforts of the IFTF provide key insights and tools in our quest for a more sustainable future. Their emphasis on long-term thinking and strategic action resonates strongly with our sustainability objectives, making their perspective indispensable to our journey of designing sustainable futures.

OUR GUIDE THROUGH CHAPTER 3: GENERATING VISIONS

Jeremy Kirshbaum is a leading strategist and entrepreneur guiding organizations on responsibly leveraging generative AI. Jeremy founded Handshake, an innovation consultancy helping clients like Deloitte, the International Rescue Committee, and many others be early movers on AI. He also launched Library of Babel, a platform for collaborative exploration of AI's creative potential. With over 15 years of experience building ventures, Jeremy has his finger on the pulse of emerging technologies. He has advised governments, businesses, and nonprofits on generating value from AI while addressing risks. Jeremy is a prominent voice on AI ethics, as an advisor for AI and Faith and other AI ethics organizations.

Jeremy uses a wide variety of generative AI models and tools in his work. Of course, the heavy-hitters like Claude and GPT-4 are favorites, but often more niche or open source models like GPT-Neo-X, Llama 2, or Falcon are called for. Each model comes with its own strengths and weaknesses, and its own biases to navigate. Weaving together their outputs with rich context and collaborative human process, it's possible to quickly, cheaply, and provocatively create visions of the future with ease and facility that would never before have been possible.

OUR GUIDE THROUGH CHAPTER 4: BUILDING WORLDS

Jacques Barcia is currently a research fellow at the Institute for The Future, where his work delves into the intricate relationship between future narratives and the evolution of storytelling. The co-founder of Futuring Today, Jacques Barcia holds a master's degree in design, which highlights his profound comprehension of the creative process. He also serves as a futurist-in-residence at Porto Digital, a non-profit science and technology park in Brazil, where he imparts his expertise to startups, steering them toward innovation for the upcoming decade. Furthermore, he is a fellow at the Centre for Postnormal Policy and Futures Studies and a Design Futures lecturer at Cesar School. His extensive research spans a variety of fields such as energy, work, entrepreneurship, cities, media, and grief.

Barcia's fiction, which is deeply ingrained in his understanding of future trends, has been showcased in respected publications like Shine: An Anthology of Optimistic Science Fiction and The Apex Book of World Science Fiction. His non-fiction work, which centers on technology, economics, crime, and human rights, has been featured in several Brazilian newspapers. Barcia's unique blend of expertise positions him as a crucial source of information for this chapter's topic; world-building, demonstrating his ability to both conceive and articulate comprehensive and plausible future worlds.

OUR GUIDE THROUGH CHAPTER 5: SHAPING SYSTEMS

Professor Silvia Barbero, the founding member of Sys Lab research group at Politecnico di Torino, focuses on the application and research of systemic methodologies to tackle complex societal and environmental challenges. She brings a multidisciplinary background that encompasses design, engineering, circular economies, and sustainability science to systemic design. Elected as chair of the Systemic Design Association (SDA) in 2018, Professor Barbero is a leading figure in the field of systemic design for sustainability.

The Sys Lab has been instrumental in advancing the field of systemic design, particularly in the context of sustainability. Sys Lab integrates various perspectives, from technological to social, into the framework of systemic thinking. In this manner, the Sys Lab approach extends the foundational theories of systems thinking into the design sphere, with a focus on their application in creating sustainable solutions for complex societal challenges. Sys Lab has become a hub for innovation and a catalyst for change, working closely with a variety of public and private, local, and international stakeholders from academia, industry, and policy-making sectors, toward building a more sustainable world.

OUR GUIDE THROUGH CHAPTER 6: DESIGNING FICTIONS

Victoria Rodriguez Schon is a PhD student in design at Politecnico di Milano, her research regards applying a pluriversal perspective to design futures, through the decolonization of methodologies such as trend research and signal hunting. With a master's in integrated product design from Politecnico di Milano and a bachelor's in industrial design from the University of Buenos Aires, her work critically examines how post-colonial theories may inform futures making, specifically in technological and product-based contexts. She conducts her research as a part of the Fashion in Process (FiP) Research Laboratory from the Design Department at Politecnico di Milano, a multidisciplinary collective that works with innovative and culture intensive industries, applying a design-driven approach to research and consultancy projects that aim to sustainably develop creative industries. Victoria has also pursued diverse teaching roles as Assistant and Lecturer in industrial design and fashion courses, both at Politecnico and the University of Buenos Aires. Her academic pursuits and professional experience such as the Government of the City of Buenos Aires, reflect her commitment to challenging the conventional paradigms of modernity and innovation in design, striving for futures that embrace plural perspectives.

OUR GUIDE THROUGH CHAPTER 7: CULTIVATING COLLABORATION

To provide expertise in this chapter, we introduce Professor Anna Meroni, an architect, PhD in design, and Associate Professor in the Department of Design at Politecnico di Milano. Her focus is on service and strategic design, with a particular interest in how design can facilitate social innovation and sustainability. Professor Meroni heads the Product Service System Design Master's program and also coordinates the Polimi Desis Lab. She has developed specific methods and tools for co-design and is recognized for introducing the concept of community-centered design. In addition to her academic role, Anna serves as the Deputy Dean of the School of Design at Politecnico di Milano and participates in international research and teaching.

The Polimi Desis Lab is a research lab dedicated to design for social innovation and sustainability. Located in the Department of Design at Politecnico di Milano, the lab specializes in collaborative services aimed at enhancing local development. This encompasses areas such as food systems, urban mobility, and manufacturing.

The Lab possesses unique skills in identifying and supporting social innovation. It integrates contributions from various disciplines like economics, sociology, and planning to develop holistic solutions. The Lab also emphasizes training, offering postgraduate courses in service design, and participating in local and international research projects.

OUR GUIDE THROUGH CHAPTER 8: MAKING STORIES

Tommaso Buganza is a Full Professor of Leadership and Innovation at the School of Management at Politecnico di Milano, where he co-founded LEADIN'Lab, the Laboratory for Leadership, Design, and Innovation, and serves as the scientific director of IDeaLs, a research platform focused on human engagement in transformative processes. He lectures in Innovation Management and Project Management, oversees the Project Management Academy, and coordinates the innovation and training area at Polimi GSOM. He also chairs the Product Development Management Conference EIASM-IPDMC. Professor Buganza's extensive experience in innovation management and design thinking is further showcased through his prominent presence on platforms like Coursera, where he educates and equips professionals and students with the necessary tools to innovate and lead. His role in establishing the IDeaLs research lab at Politecnico di Milano emphasizes the intersection of design and leadership, promoting design-led innovation to address societal challenges. This initiative fosters a multidisciplinary approach, advocating the synergy of design, innovation, and leadership to engage stakeholders for a more equitable and sustainable future.

OUR GUIDE TO ILLUSTRATING FUTURES

June Chow is a registered architect in Malaysia with over a decade of experience in the building industry. In 2023, she founded her own practice, distinguished by a unique approach that merges innovative design with artificial intelligence. As a certified Green Building Index facilitator, she leverages her expertise to create environmentally friendly architectural solutions. June's skills transcend traditional design; she actively investigates AI's potential to amplify creativity and efficiency. Her dedication to sustainability is complemented by her ability to connect with a global clientele, a skill enhanced by her proficiency in multiple languages.

A trailblazer in applying AI in architecture, June empowers professionals across various disciplines, offering coaching and collaborating with designers on a project basis.

Appendix I: Anticipating Futures with AI

1. **Train** (upload scenario, describe expected output/audience/ publication, etc.)

   - **Focus on the Future:** Your prompt should direct attention toward the future. For example, "Imagine how advancements in technology might reshape our society in the next 20 years."

   - **Influence with Your Preferred Future:** While exploring various scenarios, it's important to also consider what you would like the future to look like. This is often referred to as your "preferred future" in the alternative futures model. For instance, "Given the various scenarios we've explored, which elements align most closely with our future goals and values?"

   - **Encourage Broad Thinking:** Make sure your prompt is open-ended to allow for a wide range of possibilities. For instance, "Consider the various ways climate change could impact global economies."

2. **Try** (prompt the AI to generate a headline from this future)

   - **Highlight Uncertainty:** Emphasize the unpredictable nature of the future in your prompt. For instance, "Given the uncertainty of global health trends, what could healthcare systems look like in 2040?"

   - **Incorporate STEEP Factors:** Your prompt should inspire thoughts around social, technological, economic, environmental, and political factors. For example, "How might political shifts influence technological innovation over the next decade?"

- **Think in Systems:** Encourage an understanding of how different elements interact within a whole. For example, "Explore how changes in environmental policy might affect both the economy and societal behaviors."
- **Emphasize Plausibility, Not Probability:** Your prompt should stress the exploration of plausible scenarios, not only probable ones. For instance, "What could be the implications of a significant breakthrough in renewable energy, even if it seems unlikely right now?"

3. **Reflect** (critique the output)
   - **Encourage Storytelling:** Promote the creation of detailed narratives. For example, "Describe a day in the life of a city dweller in 2050 under a scenario where autonomous vehicles have replaced personal car ownership."
   - **Seek Diverse Perspectives:** Highlight the value of different viewpoints. For instance, "How might the future of work look from the perspective of employees, employers, and regulators?"
   - **Promote Critical Thinking:** Encourage questioning of assumptions. For example, "What would happen if the trend towards urbanization reverses and people start moving back to rural areas?"
   - **Reflect on Implications:** Stress the need to consider the implications of each scenario. For instance, "What would be the potential impacts on our organization if a global digital currency were to become the norm?" Specificity is key: The more specific your prompt, the more tailored the output will be. For instance, "Explore the potential uses of renewable energy to mitigate the impacts of climate change in Germany by 2035" will yield more focused results than a broad question like "What is the future of energy?"

4. **Refine** (adjust the prompt and retry)
   - **Iterate and Refine:** Don't settle for the first output. Provide feedback to the AI on what you'd like to see more of in the scenario, or what aspects you feel were overlooked. For example, "Expand on the economic implications of this scenario" or "Provide specific examples of how societal behaviors might change."

- **Summon Diverse Perspectives, Not AI Opinions:** Remember, the AI doesn't have personal opinions. However, it can generate perspectives from different types of individuals. For instance, "Describe this future scenario from the viewpoint of a renewable energy startup founder, a government policy maker, and a rural farmer."

- **Critique and Recreate:** Once you have a scenario you like, ask the AI to identify potential flaws or criticisms. You can also ask it to reimagine the scenario in different formats. For example, "Rewrite this scenario as a news headline" or "How might this scenario unfold as a plot in a science fiction movie?"

Bonus: Tips for Augmenting Artifact Design:

By generating artifacts from envisioned futures, we can step into the shoes of forward-thinking archaeologists. While GenAI will exponentially change with unforeseen impacts on design processes, a few fundamentals will help you begin designing with emerging technologies:

1. Start with Scenarios: Start with a scenario to train the AI by describing the scene, including the specifications of the design brief.

2. Be Inspired by References: Refer to a reference photo for the AI to draw inspiration from something with symbolic importance for the potential users.

3. Generate a Collection: GenAI can create representations for a series of artifacts. The more visual imagery the better the design dialog.

4. Visualize the Variety: Describe the initial style as more sketch-like, in order to invite more conversation and inspiration rather than a finished image. Continue to experiment with style/mood and just as when generating scenarios (Chapter 3), continually learn, iterate, and refine.

Appendix II: Leading Futureback

Based on the approach in *Office Shock: Creating Better Futures for Living and Working*, futureback leadership can enhance your ability to envision, experience, and enact more sustainable futures.

By asking three simple questions, you can chart a pathway to your preferred future by making choices that steer you consistently in that direction:

1. *What future do you prefer?* This is exploring Horizon 3, the edges of our aspirations for more purpose and prosperity.
2. *What's next for you in that future?* This is experiencing Horizon 2, where everything we touch and feel is meaningful.
3. *What do you choose to do now?* This is enhancing Horizon 2, with choices and actions that turn the present into a glimpse of the future.

The key is to think in reverse – start by defining your purposeful vision for the future, then work backward to determine logical steps today. However, we are hard-wired to think present-forward. It's what got us here, for both the good and the bad.

The future belongs to the dreamers and doers. To begin, ask yourself:

1. **First things first:** Who wants to make the future better? Yourself, Your Organization, or Your Community.
2. **Second is best:** What do you want to change?

STEP 1 – WHAT FUTURE? ENVISION YOUR PREFERRED FUTURE

The first step in futureback leadership is to unleash your imagination. First disconnect from the present, then ask the question: What

Future? Think big and bold, so you can paint a vivid picture of the life and world you want to create ten years from now.

Expand your imagination to unlock the future you want. Get super detailed – what does your ideal future look, feel, sound, and taste like? What possibilities excite and energize you? Fully describe your future self and the positive impact you want to make. Be fully present with who you will become. Capture your most purposeful goals for people, the planet, and prosperity. This vision will be your guiding North Star toward creating a better future for yourself, your organization, and your community.

Wherever you ask "what future?," try these tools to envision your preferred world:

Time travel visualization: This guided visualization transports you to imagine your ideal future self and life ten years from now in vivid detail. The immersive first-person experience unlocks creativity, provides clarity of purpose, and generates a touchstone vision to guide your decisions and persist through obstacles.

1. Set a timer for 15–20 minutes so that you can fully immerse yourself without interruption. Sit comfortably in a quiet space. Minimize distractions.
2. Take a few deep, centering breaths to relax. Close your eyes. Release stress and negative thoughts with each long exhale.
3. Picture yourself precisely ten years in the future on a specific date. How old are you? What do you look like? What are you wearing?
4. Mentally view your future life in rich detail – your job, relationships, home, passions, accomplishments. Let your imagination flow unrestricted. Engage all your senses.
5. Imagine your typical day. What is your morning routine? Who do you interact with? What do you accomplish?
6. When the timer ends, immediately write down every sensory detail you envisioned. Capture this extensive snapshot of your future self and life.
7. Alternatively, use an AI tool to expand your visualization by generating additional sensory details about your future scenario.
8. Review your vision regularly to crystallize it and check your alignment. Use a journal, vision board, or audio notes.

Time travel visualization gives you a glimpse of your future life by unlocking present-bound imagination to inspire a sense of purpose. By experiencing your future self, you gain clarity to make decisions in the present that align with your vision. This exercise helps overcome status quo bias that tricks our brain into thinking the future will resemble the past. In reality, the future is ours to create. Time traveling liberates you from the past by transporting your mind into the realm of possibility.

Purposeful goal setting: Define three purposeful goals rooted in bringing meaning to people, the planet, and prosperity. These will drive your future vision.

1. Review your visualization and reflect on what brought your future self joy, purpose, and meaning.
2. Extract three core goals that align with your highest values for people, planet, and prosperity.
3. Phrase as "I will..." statements describing measurable outcomes. For example, "I will provide clean water access to 100,000 people."
4. Check that each goal expands positive impact beyond yourself. If not, rework until purposeful.
5. Write your finalized purposeful goals on a card to carry with you. Let them guide major decisions.

   Purposeful goal setting crystallizes your vision while activating a sense of meaning. They provide a moral compass for navigating trade-offs and obstacles on your path ahead. You overcome short-term bias by defining ambitious goals requiring sustained effort. Most importantly, purposeful goals connect your future to making a difference in the lives of others.

Vision board: Create a visual map of your future vision using inspiring images, quotes, and objects. Display it where you will see it often.

1. Gather images, words, and objects that represent your future vision – use magazines, websites, or personal photos.
2. Arrange elements creatively on a board. Use bold colors and visual metaphors to deepen the meaning.

3. Place your vision board where you will frequently see it – your office, kitchen, or community center.
4. Alternatively, use an AI image generation to create representations of your vision to add to your board.
5. Revisit your board often to crystallize your ideal future and check your alignment.
6. Modify your board as your vision evolves. This is your visual map – keep it energizing!

Your *vision board* will be a vibrant, 3D manifestation of your future dreams and purpose. Translating your vision into images and metaphors unlocks creativity and new insights. Displaying it prominently keeps you immersed in your preferred future. Your vision board helps overcome temporal myopia by surrounding you with symbolic representations of your ten-year vision every day. This strengthens neural connections to your future self.

Future self-letter: Write a letter dated ten years in the future offering insights into your present self. Seal it and open it ten years later!

1. Set a timer for 15 minutes. Imagine yourself ten years in the future on a specific date.
2. Alternatively, use an AI writing assistant to generate your future self letter or an AI art generator to generate a picture of your future self.
3. Seal the letter in an envelope marked with the future date. Open and read it ten years from now.
4. As an alternative, email yourself a dated future letter – it will magically appear ten years later!

Future self-letter is a powerful visualization that crystallizes your future vision. Writing wisdom from your future self provides perspective. It builds anticipation for the person you will become. Sealing the letter makes your vision tangible. This ritual overcomes present bias by strengthening your emotional connection to your future self. Opening and reading the letter ten years from now will be an incredible experience!

Shared vision mapping: Bring together family, friends, or colleagues to co-create a shared map of your collective future vision.

1. Individually, complete the time travel visualization exercise to envision your future self and goals.
2. Come together in a workshop setting without distractions. Have each person share their future vision. Identify common themes and differences.
3. As a group, discuss how you might collaborate to support each other's purposeful goals. Sketch a mind map showing connections.
4. Create a large, visual display capturing highlights of your shared future vision and how your dreams intersect. Place this reminder in a visible gathering space.
5. Have your group ask an AI for unique prompts to spark creative ideas for collaborative goal synergies.
6. Reconvene periodically to update your map as your individual and shared visions evolve. Celebrate progress made together.

Shared vision mapping leverages the power of collective wisdom to enhance individual perspectives. It builds excitement for the future you will create together. Combining complementary strengths makes your purposeful goals feel within reach. This collaboration overcomes isolated thinking by aligning your vision with people who energize you. Shared dreams manifest faster.

Envisioning your preferred world is the first step in futureback leadership. It will guide your choices to create the future you want to experience. Your creativity and imagination are the only limits to envisioning a purpose-driven future. Begin shaping your boldest dreams into reality today. The future belongs to the visionaries who can experience that preferred future, so now let's ask the question *What Next?*

STEP 2 – WHAT NEXT? EXPERIENCE YOUR PREFERRED FUTURE

Now envision how your preferred future will feel, and what experiences it will bring for you personally, your organization, and your community when shaped by purpose. Create vivid scenes that bring your preferred future to life. Make it vivid! What will you see, hear, touch, taste? Who will you spend time with? What will technology enable you to do? Where will you be? How will you feel emotionally? How will you spend your time?

These experiences will guide the decisions needed to translate your dreams into reality. They reveal insights into your values and purpose. Keep referring to these visions to check that your daily choices align.

Wherever you ask "what next?", try these tools to experience your future:

Purposeful experience mapping: Imagine and describe sensory experiences of achieving your purposeful goals to make them tangible.

1. For each purposeful goal, close your eyes and visualize accomplishing it. Engage all your senses.
2. Write a detailed description of how it looks, sounds, and feels. Where are you? Who is with you? How did you get there? How do you feel?
3. Give each experience snapshot a title to summarize the key emotion or insight.
4. When facing obstacles, re-read your experience maps to reconnect with how accomplishing your purpose will feel.
5. Use an AI tool to transform your written descriptions into vivid sensory videos or images to make the experiences even more immersive.

   Purposeful experience mapping translates your future into tangible experiences, and they become more attainable. Imagining purposeful success activates your motivation. You overcome superficial thinking by emotionally engaging your future success. Your purpose propels you through present difficulties.

Future vision simulation: Use all five senses to imagine and record an immersive multi-sensory vision of your preferred future.

1. Choose a purposeful goal scene. Set a timer for 15 minutes. Get comfortable and close your eyes.
2. Mentally immerse yourself using all five senses. See vivid colors, feel textures, hear sounds, smell scents, and taste flavors.
3. When the timer ends, write out the full sensory experience. Capture all rich details.

4. Re-read your sensory experience to feel reconnected with your purposeful vision.
5. Employ AI to generate additional sensory details to expand and enrich your future vision simulation.

Future vision simulation vividly engages all your senses and strengthens neural connections to your vision as attainable. Sensory details also unlock creativity and insights. By feeling your purposeful vision, you light your way forward.

Organizational impact scenario: Envision your future organization to fulfill its purpose and reveal directions for transformation.

1. Imagine your organization ten years from now. How has it evolved to better serve its purpose?
2. Journey through this future organization. What do you see? How do people interact? What is the culture? How has the business model changed?
3. Record detailed observations about the organization, employees, and customers in this preferred future.
4. Have an AI system analyze your observations and propose principles for organizational changes needed to realize this future vision.

Organizational Impact Scenario inspires insights into how to transform your organization. It reveals where to pilot changes that move you toward this vision. Envisioning liberates you from past constraints. Your organization's purpose becomes actionable when you see how it can manifest.

Future day immersion: Writing a detailed script of a future day creates an immersive glimpse of the future.

1. Visualize your typical weekday ten years in the future, from sunrise to bedtime.
2. Write out your full schedule including activities, conversations, locations, emotions, and sensations. Make it vivid.
3. Give your future day a creative title capturing the theme or feeling of that day.

4. When you need clarity or inspiration, re-read your future day and re-experience how it feels.

5. Input your future day description into an AI tool to create an engaging video reenactment.

Future day immersion makes your envisioned routine and accomplishments feel more tangible and achievable. It reveals insights about your values, priorities, and purpose in action. Re-reading your future day provides inspiration and motivation to align with your present.

Local community quest: Take a mental walk into the future to envision a thriving local community.

1. Imagine walking through your local area ten years in the future. What has changed for the better? Who do you see? How are people interacting?

2. Visually explore new opportunities, convening spaces, businesses, and technology-enabling connections. What is now possible for the community?

3. Use AI to transcribe your narration into vivid text descriptions to tangibly document your community vision.

4. Distill your future walk into principles for manifesting this vision of a purpose-driven, connected community.

Local Community Quest immerses yourself in an aspirational future for your local area. It activates thinking about new possibilities for community interaction and change-making collaborations.

Shared visions workshop: Host an interactive workshop to co-create enriched visions of your shared future.

1. Individually complete the Time Travel Visualization exercise. Have participants record details to share.

2. In a circle, have each person share their vision summary. Identify commonalities and differences. Discuss.

3. As a group, co-design collaborations to support each other's purposeful goals. Visually map synergies. Identify group norms.

4. Ask an AI to identify commonalities and gaps across your group to identify opportunities to collaborate and converge on each other's purposeful goals.

5. Document your Shared Visions Workshop with photos, videos, and notes. Keep building on each other's dreams.

Shared Visions Workshop combines complementary perspectives to make your purposeful visions feel attainable. Shared accountability provides momentum. Mutual support combats isolation and self-doubt. Our collective future shines brighter through the synergy of our dreams.

Experiencing your preferred future is the second step in futureback leadership. It will guide your choices to make the decisions today to help you realize the future you want. Immerse yourself in it. These visions will guide you to take action today to create the change you wish to see. Your purposeful future awaits – begin laying the bricks to build it!

The future belongs to the leaders who can make decisions to bring the preferred future closer to the present, so now let's ask the question *What Now?*

STEP 3 – WHAT NOW? MAKE FUTUREBACK CHOICES

You now have a vivid vision and experience of your preferred future. With your eyes on the horizon, make daily choices aligned with your purpose. What actions can you take right now to steer yourself toward your dreams? How will you navigate obstacles along the way?

Use your future visions to guide decisions today. By constantly checking that your daily decisions align with your future vision, you ensure steady progress to realize that vision.

Embrace the journey, while remembering that small steps compound over time into large leaps. You may need to periodically adjust course but stay firmly rooted in your values and fixed on your North Stars.

When you ask "what now?" try these tools to make futureback decisions:

Backcasting: Working backward from a future milestone to the present reveals the logical steps to achieve your vision.

1. Choose a meaningful future milestone or purposeful experience from your vision.
2. Brainstorm pathways back to the present that would enable this future achievement.
3. Outline actionable steps and key milestones from the future back to now. Identify dependencies.
4. Use an AI assistant to analyze your backcast and propose optimizations to accelerate your pathway.
5. Review and adjust your backcast regularly as conditions change. Maintain flexibility while moving forward.

   Backcasting creates a navigational chart guiding your decisions toward your future vision. It makes your purpose attainable by breaking it down into logical, sequential steps you can take now. Having a plan reduces uncertainty and builds self-efficacy to stay the course.

If-then planning: Target likely obstacles and make customized if–then plans to overcome them.

1. Identify three to five obstacles that could hinder achieving your future vision. Consider technical barriers, resource limitations, distractions, and self-doubts.
2. For each obstacle, write an "if–then" plan detailing your positive response. For example, "If I feel discouraged, then I will review my vision board."
3. Visualize yourself implementing these plans using mental rehearsal. This neurologically primes you to act on these plans when obstacles occur.
4. Use an AI tool to analyze your if-then plans and suggest additional responses tailored to your strengths.
5. Modify your if-then plans as needed when new obstacles emerge on your journey. Be prepared, not paranoid!

   If-then planning dramatically increases the likelihood you will overcome obstacles successfully. Mentally rehearsing your customized plans activates neural pathways to stay resilient when challenges arise. You shift from reactive to responsive.

Action milestones calendar: Plot meaningful actions on a calendar to create accountability for steady progress.

1. Break down your backcasted plan into concrete weekly actions. Prioritize by ease of implementation and impact.
2. Add these action steps to your calendar on specific days with set reminders. Integrate into your routine.
3. Share your calendar with a trusted accountability partner. Meet regularly to celebrate progress and troubleshoot hurdles.
4. Use an AI productivity assistant to optimize your calendar and suggest additional impactful actions aligned with your purpose.
5. Check your calendar often! Completing these milestones moves you toward your future vision.

    The action milestones calendar commits actions to your calendar and provides structure to stay focused amidst distractions. Sharing it with others creates accountability. Regular achievement of purposeful milestones builds momentum – you actively create your vision instead of passively dreaming it.

Purpose alignment check: Pause before decisions to check alignment with your future vision.

1. Set hourly reminders to ask yourself throughout the day: "Is this aligned with my purposeful future vision?"
2. Before finalizing any significant decision or commitment, pause and reflect on whether it moves you toward your vision.
3. If misaligned, reconsider the decision. Ask yourself: In ten years will this choice still enrich my life and legacy?
4. Use an AI tool to analyze your calendar and highlight any activities not aligned with your purpose and future vision.
5. Make course corrections when needed to keep moving steadily in the right direction. Progress isn't always linear.

    Purpose alignment check offers regular check-ins for self-awareness to notice potential misalignment early. Questioning decisions against your future vision priorities keeps you focused on what matters most. Even small misalignments compound over time into major detours. Developing this habit is your safety net.

Future journey sketchbook: Create a sketchbook chronicling your future journey to guide in-the-moment decisions from a big-picture perspective.

1. Craft a physical or digital sketchbook to document your future journey. Include inspiration, visions, plans, and milestones achieved.
2. Refer to your sketchbook frequently when making decisions to reconnect with your North Star and progress made.
3. Before finalizing commitments, review relevant pages in your sketchbook to check alignment.
4. When facing obstacles, re-read your sketchbook for motivation to persist. See how far you've come!
5. Update with learnings, new inspirations, and modified goals. This is the living logbook of your purpose journey.

    Your future journey sketchbook provides an unfolding visual record of your future path, centered around purpose. Reviewing it frequently strengthens connections between present decisions and your long-term vision. You avoid veering off course and losing momentum. Each new entry documents your progress toward your ideal future.

Embrace your network: Share your future with trusted individuals who can uplift and empower you.

1. Identify three to five individuals passionate about your purpose who energize you. These are your anchors.
2. Meet with each person to share your future vision and request their support when you feel discouraged.
3. Gather your network for regular check-ins. Report progress, share challenges, and ask for insights.
4. Use an AI life coach to track your mood and reach out to your support network when you need motivation.

5. Offer support to others when you can. Mutual sharing of purpose deepens bonds that raise you higher.

   Embrace your network energizes you to navigate the obstacles with supportive companions cheering you on the journey. Shared accountability provides strength when conviction wavers. Your community believes in you until you can believe fully again in yourself. We rise higher together.

READY TO WRITE YOUR FUTURE?

You now have the tools to envision, experience, and enact the future you want. Consistently apply futureback leadership and you can make choices today to write your destiny. Stay committed to your values and keep your eyes on the horizon you imagined. Before you know it, your small acts will compound into the very future you envisioned.

Your future story is yours to write, by leading futureback you can make y(our) future better.

Bibliography

INTRODUCTION

A2I mission: Future of education. https://a2i.gov.bd/a2i-missions/future-of-education/#:~:text=Keeping%20pace%20with%20the%20changing,of%20both%20learners%20and%20teachers.

A2I website. www.a2i.gov.bd.

Ahlborg, H., Ruiz-Mercado, I., Molander, S., & Masera, O. (2019). Bringing technology into social-ecological systems research—motivations for a socio-technical-ecological systems approach. Sustainability.

Amatullo, M., Boyer, B., May, J., & Shea, A. (Eds.) (2021). *Design for social innovation: Case studies from around the world.* Routledge.

Ambasz, E. (Ed.). (1972). *Italy: The New Domestic Landscape: Achievements and Problems of Italian Design* (Museum of Modern Art). Distributed by New York Graphic Society, Greenwich, Conn. https://assets.moma.org/documents/moma_catalogue_1783_300062429.pdf

Angheloiu, C. (2019). Design x futures = design futures? *Future Tense*, Jun 21, 2019. https://medium.com/the-shape-of-things-to-come/design-x-futures-design-futures-26e47b43775d.

Baghai, M., Coley, S., & White, D. (1999). *The alchemy of growth: Practical insights for building the enduring enterprise.* Perseus Books.

Barbero, S. (2017) *A circular Europe on the way.* Turin: Allemandi. P146. https://projects2014-2020.interregeurope.eu/retrace/news/news-article/1772/retrace-method-guide-for-policymaking/

Bell, W. (1997). *Foundations of futures studies: Human science for a new era.* Transaction Publishers.

Bijker, W.E., Hughes, T.P., & Pinch, T. (1989). The Social Construction of Technological Systems: New Directions in the Sociology and History of Technology.

Brown, T. (2009). *Change by design: How design thinking transforms organizations and inspires innovation.* HarperCollins.

Burley Farr, K., Song, K., Yeo, Z. Y. et al. (2023). Cities and regions tackle climate change mitigation but often focus on less effective solutions. *Communications Earth & Environment*, 4, 439. https://doi.org/10.1038/s43247-023-01108-6

Cagnin, C., et al. (2015). *Developing futures literacy: Embracing complexity and navigating uncertainty.* UNESCO Publications.

Carboni, Joel. (2017). Thoughts on project management and climate change. Project Management Research and Practice. 4. 1. 10.5130/pmrp.v4i0.5462.

Chowdhury, A. (2021). *Digital Bangladesh to innovative Bangladesh: The road to 2041.* United Nations Development Programme (undp.org).

Cooper, R. G. (1990). Stage-gate systems: A new tool for managing new products. *Business Horizons, 33*(3), 44–54.

Corner, A., & Clarke, J. (2016). *Talking climate: From research to practice in public engagement* (pp. 1–146). Palgrave Macmillan.

Crownhart, C. (2024, June 14). These board games want you to beat climate change. *MIT Technology Review*. Retrieved from https://www.technologyreview.com/2024/06/14/board-games-beat-climate-change/

Drath, Wilfred & Mccauley, Cynthia & Palus, Charles & Van Velsor, Ellen & O'Connor, Patricia & Mcguire, John. (2008). Direction, Alignment, Commitment: Toward a More Integrative Ontology of Leadership. The Leadership Quarterly. 19. 635–653. 10.1016/j.leaqua.2008.09.003.

Damhof, L., & Gulmans, J. (2023). Imagining the impossible: An act of radical hope. *Possibility Studies & Society*, 1(1–2), 51–55. https://doi.org/10.1177/27538699231174821.

Dator, J. (2009). Alternative futures at the Manoa school. *Journal of Futures Studies*, 14(2), 1–18.

Dunne, A., & Raby, F. (2013). *Speculative Everything: Design, Fiction, and Social Dreaming*. Mit Press.

Ehrlichman, D., Sawyer, D., & Wei-Skillern, J. (2015). *The most impactful leaders you have never heard of*. Stanford Social Innovation Review. https://doi.org/10.48558/76ZG-JV21

Figueres, C., & Rivett-Carnac, T. (2020). *The future we choose: surviving the climate crisis*. Alfred A. Knopf.

Inayatullah, S. (2022). Causal Layered Analysis: Theory, Conceptual Framework and Method. In CLA 3.0—Thirty Years of Transformative Research. Tamkang University Press.

Smillie, I. (2009). Freedom from want: The remarkable success story of BRAC, the global grassroots organization that's winning the fight against poverty. Kumarian Press.

Folke, Carl & Hahn, Thomas & Olsson, Per & Norberg, Jon. (2005). Adaptive Governance of Social-Ecological Systems. *Annu. Rev. Environ. Resour.* 15. 441–73. 10.1146/annurev.energy.30.050504.144511.

Future of Education in Bangladesh Envisioning 2041. (2019). https://a2i.gov.bd/a2i-publications/futures-of-education-in-bangladesh-2041-report/

Gaziulusoy, İ., & Oztekin, E. (2019). Design for sustainability transitions: Origins, attitudes and future directions. *Sustainability*, 11, 3601.

Geels, F.W. (2004). From sectoral systems of innovation to socio-technical systems: Insights about dynamics and change from sociology and institutional theory. *Research Policy*, 33, 897–920.

Hancock, T., & Bezold, C. (1994). Possible futures, preferable futures. *Healthcare Forum Journal*, 37(2), 23–29.

Hutchins, G., & Storm, L. (2019). Regenerative leadership: the DNA of life-affirming 21st century organizations. Wordzworth Publishing.

MacMillan, S. (2022). Hope over fate: Fazle Hasan Abed and the science of ending global poverty (2022). Rowman & Littlefield Publishers.

Inayatullah, S. (1998). Causal layered analysis: Poststructuralism as method. *Futures*, 30(8), 815–829.

Inayatullah, S. (2004). *The causal layered analysis (CLA) reader: Theory and case studies of an integrative and transformative methodology*. Tamkang University Press.

Inayatullah, S. (2008). Six pillars: Futures thinking for transforming. *Foresight*, 10(1), 4–21.

Inayatullah, S. (2015). *What works: Case studies in the practice of foresight*. Tamkang University Press.

Irwin, T., Kossoff, G., & Tonkinwise, C. (2015). Transition design: A proposal for a new area of design practice, study, and research. *Design and Culture*, 7(2), 229–246.

Johansen, R., Press, J., & Bullen, C. V. (2023). *Office shock: creating better futures for working and living*. Berrett-Koehler Publishers.

Kotchen, M., Rising, J., & Wagner, G. (2023). The costs of 'Costless' climate mitigation. *CBS Insights* (columbia.edu). Columbia Business School Insights.

Kotter, J. P. (1995). Leading change: Why transformation efforts fail. *Harvard Business Review*, 73(2), 59–67.

Kristof, N. (2021). What can Biden's plan do for poverty? Look to Bangladesh. https://www.nytimes.com/2021/03/10/opinion/biden-child-poverty-bangladesh.html

Larsen, N., Mortensen, J. K., & Miller, R. (2020, February 11). What is 'Futures literacy' and why is it important? *On overcoming blind resistance to change and poverty of the imagination*. https://medium.com/copenhagen-institute-for-futures-studies/what-is-futures-literacy-and-why-is-it-important-a27f24b983d8

Fikret Berkes and Carl Folke, eds. (1999). Linking Social and Ecological Systems. Management Practices and Social Mechanisms for Building Resilience. *Environment and Development Economics*. 4(2): 237–242. doi:10.1017/S1355770X99220165

Malena-Chan, R. A. (2019). Making climate change meaningful: Narrative dissonance and the gap between knowledge and action. Master thesis, University of Saskatchewan, Canada.

Miller, R. (2007). Futures literacy: A hybrid strategic scenario method. *Futures, 39(4)*, 341–362.

Miller, R. (Ed.) (2018). *Transforming the future: Anticipation in the 21st century*. UNESCO & Routledge.

Moore, G. A. (1991). *Crossing the chasm: Marketing and selling high-tech products to mainstream customers*. HarperBusiness.

Morozov, E. (2013). To save Everything, Click Here; the Folly of Technological Solutionism. London: PublicAffairs.

Moser, S. C. (2016). Reflections on climate change communication research and practice in the second decade of the 21st century: What more is there to say? *WIREs Climate Change*, 7(3), 345–369.

NESTA. (2019). Our futures: by the people, for the people. https://media.nesta.org.uk/documents/Our_futures_by_the_people_for_the_people_WEB_v5.pdf

Norman, D. A. (2023). *Design for a better world: Meaningful, sustainable, humanity centered*. The MIT Press.

Papanek, V. (1971). *Design for the real world: Human ecology and social change*. Pantheon Books.

Press, J., Bellis, P., Tommaso Buganza, Magnanini, S., Trabucchi, D., Rami, A. B., Verganti, R., & Federico Paolo Zasa. (2021). IDeaLs (Innovation and Design as Leadership). Emerald Group Publishing.

Ramos, J., Sweeney, J. A., & Peach, K. (2019). *Our futures: By the people, for the people*. NESTA.

Raworth, K. (2017). Doughnut economics: Seven ways to think like a 21st-century economist. https://www.kateraworth.com/doughnut/.

Rittel, H. and Webber, M. (1973). Dilemmas in a General Theory of Planning, Policy Sciences, 4(2), 155–169.

Ruiz Manuel, I., & Blok, K. (2023). Quantitative evaluation of large corporate climate action initiatives shows mixed progress in their first half-decade. *Nature Communications,* 14, 3487. https://doi.org/10.1038/s41467-023-38989-2.

Sharifi, A. (2023). Resilience of urban social-ecological-technological systems (SETS): A review. Sustainable Cities and Society, 99, id 104910. https://doi.org/10.1016/j.scs.2023.104910

Slaughter, R. A. (1995). *The foresight principle: Cultural recovery in the 21st century.* Adamantine Press.

Starr, S. L. (1989). The structure of ill-structured solutions: Boundary objects and heterogeneous distributed problem solving. In *Distributed artificial intelligence* (Vol. 2, pp. 37–54). Morgan Kaufmann. https://doi.org/10.1016/B978-1-55860-092-8.50006-X

Stead, M., Coulton, P., & Lindley, J. (2019). The future is metahistory: Using spime-based design fiction as a research lens for designing sustainable internet of things devices. In M. Evans, A. Shaw, & J. H. Na (Eds.), International Association of Societies of Design Research Conference 2019 (IASDR 2019): Design Revolutions. Manchester School of Art, Manchester Metropolitan University.

Stockholm Resilience Centre. (n.d.). The wedding cake model of the sustainable development goals. https://www.stockholmresilience.org/research/research-news/2016-06-14-applying-a-wedding-cake-to-the-sdgs.html.

The AGI journey: Making digital innovation work for the poor (2022). https://a2i.gov.bd/a2i-publications/the-a2i-journey/

United Nations. (n.d.). The 17 goals.

United Nations. (1972). *Report of the United Nations conference on the human environment.* United Nations

United Nations. (2000). *United Nations millennium declaration.* United Nations.

United Nations. (2015). *Transforming our world: The 2030 agenda for sustainable development.* United Nations.

United Nations. (2023). New Analysis of National Climate Plans: Insufficient Progress Made, COP28 Must Set Stage for Immediate Action. https://unfccc.int/news/new-analysis-of-national-climate-plans-insufficient-progress-made-cop28-must-set-stage-for-immediate

United Nations Conference on Environment and Development. (1992). *Agenda 21.* Rio de Janeiro. Agenda 21. Retrieved from: https://www.un.org/esa/dsd/agenda21/res_agenda21_00.shtml

United Nations Conference on Sustainable Development. (2012). *The future we want.* Rio de Janeiro. Retrieved from: https://sustainabledevelopment.un.org/futurewewant.html

UNESCO. (n.d.). Sensing and making sense of futures literacy. http://en.unesco.org/about-us/how-we-work.

UNESCO. (n.d.). *Futures literacy.* https://en.unesco.org/futuresliteracy/about

White, E. (2022). What is climate change adaptation and why is it vital? *World Economic Forum* (weforum.org). https://www.weforum.org/agenda/2022/10/climate-change-adaptation-cop27/

World Bank. (2023). *Social Dimensions of Climate Change*. https://www.worldbank. org/en/topic/social-dimensions-of-climate-change

World Commission on Environment and Development. (1987). *Our common future (The Brundtland Report)*. Oxford University Press.

World Economic Forum. (2023). *The Global Risks*. https://www3.weforum.org/docs/ WEF_Global_Risks_Report_2023.pdf

Zunaid Ahmed Palak, Z. (2023). Digital Bangladesh: A story of transformation, resilience, and sustainability. *The Daily Star*, Jan 16, 2023. https://www.weforum.org/agenda/2023/05/six-elements-accelerating-education-for- a-smart-bangladesh-and-a-smart-world/.

Additional Inspiration

Better World—Ultimate Guide to Sustainability. https://www.betterworld.info/ sustainability

GLESI—How to reach the UN SDGs. https://www.glesi.org/.

Project Drawdown. https://www.drawdown.org/.

SDG in Progress. https://sdginprogress.com/.

Sustainable Engineer. http://www.sustainableengineer.org/.

Sustainable World. http://thebritishgeographer.weebly.com/sustainable-world.html.

CHAPTER 1

Abrahamson, D., & Sánchez-García, R. (2016). Learning is moving in new ways: The ecological dynamics of mathematics education. *Journal of the Learning Sciences*, 25(2), 203–239.

Anab Jain. *TED talk: Why we need to imagine different futures*. https://www.ted.com/ talks/anab_jain_why_we_need_to_imagine_different_futures.

Ballew, M. T., Marlon, J. R., Goldberg, M. H., Maibach, E. W., Rosenthal, S. A., Aiken, E., et al. (2022). Changing minds about global warming: Vicarious experience predicts self-reported opinion change in the USA. *Climatic Change*, 173(3), 1–25.

BBC Podcast, (2022). https://www.bing.com/ck/a?!&&p=572e54061a8636feJmltd HM9MTcxODQ5NjAwMCZpZ3V pZD0wZGY4NzI5OC04 ZjZlLTYzZGItM2U2YS02NmQyOGU2ODYyYWUmaW5zaWQ9NTE4MA& ptn=3&ver=2&hsh=3&fclid=0df87298-8f6e-63db-36a-66d28e6862ae&psq= Taqi+Shaheen+and+Sara+Khan+Pathan+bbc+podcast&u= a1aHR0cHM6Ly9nZW5vWUuY2guYmJjLmNvLnVrL3czY3QzN3Mx&ntb=1

Candy, S. (2010). The futures of everyday life: Politics and the design of experiential scenarios (Publication No. 10.13140/RG.2.1.1840.0248) [Doctoral dissertation, University of Hawai'i at Mānoa]. https://doi.org/10.13140/RG.2.1.1840.0248

Candy, S., & Dunagan, J. (2016). The experiential turn. *Human Futures*, 26–29. https:// futuryst.blogspot.com/2016/12/the-experiential-turn.html.

Candy, S., & Dunagan, J. (2017). Designing an experiential scenario: The people who vanished. *Futures*, 86, 136–153. https://doi.org/10.1016/j.futures.2016.05.006.

Candy, S., & Kornet Weber, K. (2017). A field guide to ethnographic experiential futures. *Journal of Futures Studies*. https://www.researchgate.net/publication/ 331857932

Chakrabarti, Ronika & Mason, Katy. (2014). Designing better markets for people at the bottom of the pyramid: Bottom-up market design. 10.4337/9781782549758.00014.

Chapin, F. S., Weber, E. U., Bennett, E. M., et al. (2022). Earth stewardship: Shaping a sustainable future through interacting policy and norm shifts. *Ambio*, 51, 1907–1920. https://doi.org/10.1007/s13280-022-01721-3.

Eagleman, D. (2015). *The brain: The story of you*. Pantheon Books.

Hayward, P., & Candy, S. (2017). The Polak Game, or: Where do you stand? *Journal of Futures Studies*, 22(2), 5–14. https://doi.org/10.6531/JFS.2017.22(2).A5

Hensel, M., Bryan, J., McCarthy, C., et al. (2023). Participatory approaches enhance a sense of urgency and collective efficacy about climate change: Qualitative evidence from the *world climate* simulation. *Journal of Geoscience Education*, 71(2), 177–191. https://doi.org/10.1080/10899995.2022.2066927.

Jain, A. (2017). Why we need to imagine different futures. www.ted.com. https://www.ted.com/talks/anab_jain_why_we_need_to_imagine_different_futures/transcript

Kahn, H. (1960). *On thermonuclear war*. Princeton University Press.

Kahn, H. (1962). *Thinking about the unthinkable*. Horizon Press.

Kahneman, D. (2011). *Thinking, fast and slow*. Farrar, Straus and Giroux.

Lakoff, G. (2008). The neural theory of metaphor. In Gibbs, R. (Ed.). *The Cambridge handbook of metaphor and thought* (pp. 17–38). Cambridge University Press.

McGonagil. (2022). Imaginable: how to see the future coming and feel ready for anything–even things that seem impossible today. Spiegel And Grau.

Meadows, D. H., Meadows, D. L., Randers, J., & Behrens, W. W. (1972). *The limits to growth*. Universe Books.

Polak, F. (1961). *The image of the future* (E. Boulding, Trans.). Oceana Publications.

Schwartz, P. (1991). The art of the long view: Planning for the future in an uncertain world

Shapiro, L. (2019). *Embodied cognition*. Routledge.

Slaughter, R. A. (1991). Changing images of futures in the 20th century. *Futures*, 23(5), 499–514. https://doi.org/10.1016/0016-3287(91)90085-Y.

Solnit, R. 2016 [2004]. *Hope in the dark: Untold histories. Wild possibilities* (Updated ed.). Haymarket Books.

Toffler, A. (1970). *Future shock*. Random House.

Verne, J. (1865). *From the earth to the moon*. Pierre-Jules Hetzel.

Wells, H. G. (1895). *The time machine*. William Heinemann.

Wiener, N. (1948). *Cybernetics; or, control and communication in the animal and the machine*. MIT Press.

Wilson, A. D., & Golonka, S. (2013). Embodied cognition is not what you think it is. *Frontiers in Psychology*, 4, 58.

World Economic Forum. The climate progress survey: business & consumer worries & hopes. https://www3.weforum.org/docs/SAP_WEF_Sustainability_Report.pdf.

World Economic Forum. (2023). *The Global Risks*. 18th Edition. https://www3.weforum.org/docs/WEF_Global_Risks_Report_2023.pdf

CHAPTER 2

Benjamin, R. (2019). *Race after technology: Abolitionist tools for the new Jim code*. Polity.

Bleecker, J. (2009). *Design fiction: A short essay on design, science, fact and fiction.* Near Future Laboratory.

Bush, D., & Ambush, E. (Eds.) (1975). Italy: The new domestic landscape: Achievements and problems of Italian design. *The Museum of Modern Art.* New York Graphic Society. Retrieved from: https://assets.moma.org/documents/moma_catalogue_1783_300062429.pdf

Candy, S., & Dunagan, J. (2017). Designing an experiential scenario: The People Who Vanished. Futures, 86, 136–153. https://doi.org/10.1016/j.futures.2016.05.006

Celi, M. (Ed.) (2015). *Advanced design cultures, long-term perspective and continuous innovation.* Springer.

Celi, M., & Formia, E. (Eds.) (2016). *Humanities and design lab. Le culture del progetto e le scienze umane e sociali.* Maggioli Ed.

Celi, M., & Formia, E. (2017). Aesthetics of futures. Shaping shared visions of tomorrow. *The Design Journal,* 20(Suppl. 1), S63–S76.

Design Council. (2018). *The design economy* [Report]. Design Council. https://www.designcouncil.org.uk/our-work/research-insight/design-economy-report/

Dunne, A., & Raby, F. (2013). *Speculative everything: design, fiction, and social dreaming.* MIT Press.

Fischer, G., & Giaccardi, E. (2006). Meta-design: A framework for the future of end user development. In H. Lieberman, F. Paternò, & V. Wulf (Eds.), *End user development—Empowering people to flexibly employ advanced information and communication technology* (pp. 427–457). Kluwer Academic Publishers.

Fletcher, H. (2006). The principles of inclusive design. (They include you.). https://www.designcouncil.org.uk/fileadmin/uploads/dc/Documents/the-principles-of-inclusive-design.pdf

Gombrich, E. H. (1961). *Art and illusion.* Pantheon Books.

Maughan, T. (2020). *How big tech hijacked its sharpest, funniest critics.* MIT Technology Review. https://www.technologyreview.com/2020/02/21/905817/how-big-tech-hijacked-its-sharpest-funniest-critics/

Judah, H. (2017, November 24). Ungender, deprogram, urinate: Improve your life with post-cyber international feminism! *The Guardian.* https://www.theguardian.com/artanddesign/2017/nov/24/ica-ungender-deprogram-urinate-how-post-cyber-international-feminism-can-improve-your-life.

Maggic, M. (2016). *Egstrogen farms [Video].* Vimeo. https://vimeo.com/149112412

Malpass, M. (2017). *Critical design in context: History, theory, and practices.* Bloomsbury Publishing.

Margolin, V. (2007). Design, the future and the human spirit. *Design Issues,* 23(3), 4–15.

Meadows, D. H., Meadows, D. L., Randers, J., & Behrens, W. W. (1972). *The limits to growth.* Universe Books.

Schultz, W. (2018). Mapping the emergence of design in policymaking: Design skills in Australian and Danish central governments. *CoDesign,* 14(4), 359–374.

Simon, H. A. (1996). *The sciences of the artificial* (3rd ed.). MIT Press.

Sterling, B. (2005). *Shaping things.* The MIT Press.

Tonkinwise, C. (2014). How we intend to future: Review of anthony dunne and fiona raby, speculative everything: Design, fiction, and social dreaming. *Design Philosophy Papers,* 12(2), 169–187.

Yelavich, S., & Adams, B. (2014). *Design as future-making.* Bloomsbury Academic.

CHAPTER 3

Anadol, R. (2022). *Unsupervised* [Exhibition]. Museum of Modern Art, New York.

Anthropic. (2022). *AI for the people, by the people*. https://www.anthropic.com.

Bayes Impact. (2022). *Simulanis*. https://www.bayesimpact.org/simulanis.

Benjamin, W. (1968). *Illuminations*. Harcourt, Brace & World.

Brown, T. (2020). *Human-centered design*. Design for good. https://designforgood.info/human-centered-design/

Bruno, C. (2022). Digital Creativity Dimension: A New Domain for Creativity. In: Creativity in the Design Process. Springer Series in Design and Innovation, vol. 18. Springer, Cham. https://doi.org/10.1007/978-3-030-87258-8_3

Cambria, E., & White, B. (2014). Jumping NLP curves: A review of natural language processing research. *IEEE Computational Intelligence Magazine, 9*(2), 48–57.

Cassidy, M. (2022). "We are Froggies": Using Anthropic's AI assistant to simulate a children's story. Anthropic blog. https://www.anthropic.com/blog/we-are-froggies.

Cohen, H. (1973). *Aaron*. http://www.aaronshome.com/aaron/index.html.

Eisenstein, S. (1980). *Film form: Essays in film theory*. Harcourt Brace Jovanovich.

Elgammal, A., Liu, B., Elhoseiny, M., & Mazzone, M. (2017). *CAN: Creative adversarial networks, generating art by learning about styles and deviating from style norms*. ICCC.

Floridi, L., Cowls, J., Beltrametti, M., Chatila, R., Chazerand, P., Dignum, V., et al. (2018). AI4People—An Ethical Framework for a Good AI Society: Opportunities, Risks, Principles, and Recommendations. Minds & Machines 28, 689–707. https://doi.org/10.1007/s11023-018-9482-5

Fuentes, A. (2017). The *creative spark: How imagination made humans exceptional*. Dutton.

Goodfellow, I., Pouget-Abadie, J., Mirza, M., Xu, B., Warde-Farley, D., Ozair, S., et al. (2014). *Generative adversarial nets*. NIPS.

Goodman, N. (1982). *Languages of art: An approach to a theory of symbols*. Hackett Publishing Company.

Hockney, D. (2010). *David Hockney: Fleurs fraîches: Drawings on iPhone and iPad*. Fondation Pierre Bergé—Yves Saint Laurent

Jobin, A., Ienca, M., & Vayena, E. (2019). The global landscape of AI ethics guidelines. *Nature Machine Intelligence, 1*(9), 389–399.

Kar, S. (2021). A brief history of artificial intelligence. *Medium*. https://medium.com/the-innovation/a-brief-history-of-artificial-intelligence-cf4ce6e8a70f.

Leeson, L. H. (2001). *Agent ruby*. http://art.stanford.edu/agentruby/.

Malakuti, S. (2019). Beyond human-centered design: Designing for society, the environment, and the future. Medium. https://uxdesign.cc/beyond-human-centred-design-anning-for-society-the-environment-and-the-future-9758bc6c5053.

Mori, M. (1970). The uncanny valley. *Energy, 7*(4), 33–35.

Nilsson, N. J. (2009). *The quest for artificial intelligence: A history of ideas and achievements*. Cambridge University Press.

Oxman, N. (2016). *Material ecology*. [Exhibit]. Museum of Modern Art, New York.

Paglen, T., & Crawford, K. (2019). ImageNet roulette. https://imagenet-roulette.paglen.com/.

Perrault, R., Shoham, Y., Brynjolfsson, E., Clark, J., Etchemendy, J., Grosz, B., et al. (2019). The AI Index 2019 annual report. AI Index Steering Committee, Human-Centered AI Institute, Stanford University.

Raviola, E., Barile, L., Cebrian, M., Cerda, J., Surana, K., Ben-Akiva, M., et al. (2022). Crowdsourcing systems thinking using sociotechnical simulations. *Proceedings of the National Academy of Sciences,* 119(15), 152–163.

Rea, N. (2021). How did AI art evolve? *Artnet News.* https://news.artnet.com/art-world/ai-art-history-timeline-2034873.

Russell, S. J., & Norvig, P. (2021). *Artificial intelligence: A modern approach.* Pearson.

Samuel, A. L. (1959). Some studies in machine learning using the game of checkers. *IBM Journal of Research and Development,* 3(3), 210–229.

Schmidhuber, J. (2015). Deep learning in neural networks: An overview. *Neural Networks,* 61, 85–117.

Stanford HAI. (n.d.). *Artificial intelligence and life in 2030.* Stanford Human-Centered Artificial Intelligence. https://hai.stanford.edu/research/ai-and-life-2030

Sutherland, I. E. (1963). *Sketchpad: A man-machine graphical communication system.* Massachusetts Institute of Technology.

Szeliski, R. (2010). *Computer vision: Algorithms and applications.* Springer Science & Business Media.

van den Berg, R. (2022). AI-driven design tools: A world of possibility and peril. Adobe Blog. https://blog.adobe.com/en/publish/2022/03/01/ai-driven-design-tools-a-world-of-possibility-and-peril

Vitiello, R., & Willcocks, M. (2021). How the city speaks to us and how we speak back: Rewriting the relationship between people and place. In Courage, Courage et al. (Eds.), *The Routledge handbook of placemaking.* Routledge.

Wang C, Burris MA. (1997). Photovoice: Concept, Methodology, and Use for Participatory Needs Assessment. *Health Education & Behavior.* 24(3): 369–387. doi:10.1177/109019819702400309

Wilson, H. J., Daugherty, P. R., & Morini-Bianzino, N. (2017). The jobs that artificial intelligence will create. *MIT Sloan Management Review,* 58(4), 14–16.

Winkelmann, M. (Beeple). (2021). *Everydays: The first 5000 days.* [Digital artwork]. Christie's Auction House.

Zhong, R. Y., Xu, X., Klotz, E., & Newman, S. T. (2020). Intelligent manufacturing in the context of industry 4.0: A review. *Engineering,* 6(5), 616–630.

CHAPTER 4

Aguilar, F. (1967). *Scanning the Business Environment.* Macmillan.

Bruner, J. (2002). *Making stories: Law, literature, life.* Harvard University Press.

Bussey, M. P., & Barcia, J. (2018). Marginalia and the ethnosphere. *Text,* 22(Special Issue 52), 1–10. https://doi.org/10.52086/001c.25561.

Callenbach, E. (1975). *Ecotopia: The notebooks and reports of William Weston.* Banyan Tree Books.

Calvino, I. (2012). *Lezioni Americane.* Mondadori Milano.

Carroll, J. (2000). Five reasons for scenario-based design. *Interacting with Computers,* 13(1), 43–60.

Celi, M. (2013). Gli scenari come narrazione. In A. Penati (Ed.), *Il design costruisce mondi* (pp. 49–61). Mimesis edizioni.

Chabria, P. S., Fujii, T., & Taneja, S. (Eds.). (2021). *Multispecies cities: Solarpunk urban futures*. World Weaver Press.

Delistraty, C. C. (2014). The psychological comforts of storytelling. The Atlantic. Retrieved from https://www.theatlantic.com/health/archive/2014/11/the-psychological-comforts-of-storytelling/381964/

Dunne, A., & Raby, F. (2013). *Speculative everything: Design, fiction, and social dreaming*. MIT Press.

Glenn, J. (1972). Futurizing teaching vs. futures courses. *Social Science Record, 9*(3), 26–29.

Holling, C. S. (2001). Understanding the complexity of economic, ecological, and social systems. *Ecosystems, 4*(5), 390–405. http://www.jstor.org/stable/3658800.

Inayatullah, S. (2004). Causal layered analysis: Theory, historical context, and case studies. In S. Inayatullah (Ed.), *The causal layered analysis (CLA) reader* (pp.8–49). Tamkang University Press.

Irwin, T. (2015). Transition design: A proposal for a new area of design practice, study, and research. *Design and Culture, 7*(2), 229–246. https://doi.org/10.1080/17547075. 2015.1051829.

Kahn, H. (1960). *On thermonuclear war*. Princeton University Press.

Kahn, H. (1962). *Thinking about the unthinkable*. Horizon Press.

Kerkez, M. (2014). Childs shares how science fiction might inform urban design. *Inside UNM*. http://news.unm.edu/news/childs-shares-how-science-fiction-might-inform-urban-design.

Le Guin, U. K. (1985). *Always coming home*. Harper & Row.

Lodi-Ribeiro, G., Spindler, R., Orsi, C., Marcal, T., Martins, R., Costa, A. L. M. C., et al. (2013). *Solarpunk: Histórias ecológicas e fantásticas em um mundo sustentável*. Editora Draco.

Raven, P. G., & Elahi, S. (2015). The new narrative. *Futures, 74*, 49–61.

Robinson, K. S. (1990). *Pacific edge*. Tom Doherty Associates.

Robinson, K. S. (2022). *The ministry for the future: A novel*. Orbit.

Schwartz, P. (1991). The art of the long view: Planning for the future in an uncertain world. Currency Doubleday.

Slaughter, R. A. (2002). From forecasting and scenarios to social construction: Changing methodological paradigms in futures studies. *Foresight, 4*(3), 26–31.

Stein, J. (2014). *Design fiction and speculative futures*. USC School of Cinematic Arts. http://cinema.usc.edu/announcements/announcement.cfm?id=14713.

Suvin, D. (1979). *Metamorphoses of science fiction: On the poetics and history of a literary genre*. Yale University Press.

The Guardian (2021). https://www.theguardian.com/world/2021/jan/12/bangladeshi-man-with-asthma-wins-france-deportation-fight#:~:text=A%20Bangladeshi%20man%20with%20asthma,of%20pollution%20in%20his%20homeland.

VanderMeer, J. (2013). *Wonderbook: The Illustrated guide to creating imaginative fiction*. Trade Paperback.

VanderMeer, J. and Zerfoss, J. (2018). *Wonderbook: an illustrated guide to creating imaginative fiction*. New York: Abrams Image.

von Stackelberg, P., & Jones, R. E. (2014). Tales of our tomorrows: Transmedia storytelling and communicating about the future. *Journal of Futures Studies, 18*(3), 57–76.

von Stackelberg, P., & McDowell, A. (2015). What in the world? Storyworlds, science fiction, and futures studies. *Journal of Futures Studies*, 20(2), 25–46.

Weick, K. E. (1995). *Sensemaking in organizations*. Sage Publications.

Weines, J., & Borit, M. (2021). Better game worlds by design: The gas framework for designing and analyzing games based on socio-ecological systems thinking, demonstrated on nusfjord (2017). *Games and Culture*, 17(2), 262–283. https://doi.org/10.1177/15554120211027109

Womack, Y. L. (2013). *Afrofuturism: The world of black sci-fi and fantasy culture*. Chicago Review Press, Incorporated.

Zaidi, L. (2017). *Building brave new worlds: Science fiction and transition design*. Unpublished master's thesis. OCAD University.

Zaidi, L. (2019). Worldbuilding in science fiction, foresight, and design. *Journal of Futures Studies*, 23(4), 2–12. https://doi.org/10.6531/JFS.201906_23(4).0003.

CHAPTER 5

Barbero, S., & Bicocca, M. (2017). *RETRACE: A systemic design approach to territorial policies*. Interreg Europe.

Battistoni, C., Giraldo Nohra, C., & Barbero, S. (2019). A systemic design method to approach future complex scenarios and research towards sustainability: A holistic diagnosis tool. *Sustainability*, 11(16), 4458. https://doi.org/10.3390/su11164458.

Capra, F., & Luisi, P. L. (2014). *The systems view of life: A unifying vision*. Cambridge University Press.

Jones, P., & Ael, K. V. (2022). *Design journeys through complex systems*. BIS Publishers.

Meadows, D. H. (2008). *Thinking in systems: A primer*. Chelsea Green Publishing.

Meadows, D. H., Meadows, D. L., Randers, J., & Behrens III, W. W. (1972). *Limits to growth*. Universe Books [Digital scan version]. https://1a0c26.p3cdn2.secureserver.net/wp-content/userfiles/Limits-to-Growth-digital-scan-version.pdf.

Norman, D. (2023). Design for a Better World–Meaningful, Sustainable, Humanity Centered. MIT Press.

Papanek, V. (1971). Design for the Rearl World–Human Ecology and Social Change Pantheon Books, New York 1971.

Ryan, A. J. (2014). A framework for systemic design. *FORMakademisk*, 7(4), 1–14. https://doi.org/10.7577/formakademisk.755.

Sevaldson, B. (2022). *Designing complexity: The methodology and practice of systems oriented design*. Common Ground Research Networks.

Stroh, D. P. (2015). *Systems thinking for social change*. Chelsea Green Publishing.

Swat, J., Sevaldson, B., & Luthe, T. (2019). When is systemic design regenerative? Values, direction and currencies in systemic design methodology. In Peter Jones, Jananda Lima, Ana Matic, and Goran Matic (eds) *Proceedings of relating systems thinking and design (RSD8) 2019 symposium*, CAD University.

Wahl, D. C. (2016). *Designing regenerative cultures*. Triarchy Press.

CHAPTER 6

Anzaldua, G. (1987). How to Tame a Wild Tongue. In Borderlands La Frontera: The New Mestiza. 53–64. San Francisco: Aunt Lute Books.

Berger, P. L., & Luckmann, T. (1966). *The social construction of reality: A treatise in the sociology of knowledge*. Anchor Books.

Bhabha, H. K. (1994). *The location of culture*. Routledge.

Bleecker, J. (2009). *Design Fiction: A short essay on design, science, fact and fiction*. Near Future Laboratory.

Braidotti, R. (2013). Posthuman Humanities. *European Educational Research Journal*, 12(1), 1–19. https://doi.org/10.2304/eerj.2013.12.1.1

Bronfenbrenner, U. (1979). *The ecology of human development: Experiments by nature and design*. Harvard University Press.

Butler, J. (1990). *Gender trouble: Feminism and the subversion of identity*. Routledge.

Candy, S. (2010). The futures of everyday life: Politics and the design of experiential scenarios [Doctoral dissertation, University of Hawai'i at Mānoa]. https://doi.org/10.13140/RG.2.1.1840.0248.

Candy, S., & Dunagan, J. (2017). Designing an experiential scenario: The people who vanished. *Futures*, 86, 136–153. https://doi.org/10.1016/j.futures.2016.05.006.

Candy, S., & Kornet, K. (2019). Turning foresight inside out: An Introduction to ethnographic experiential futures. *Journal of Futures Studies*, 23, 3–22. https://doi.org/10.6531/JFS.201903_23(3).0002.

Candy, S., & Watson, J. (2018). *The thing from the future* (2nd ed.). Situation Lab.

Celi, M., & Formia, E. (2017). Aesthetics of futures. Shaping shared visions of tomorrow. *The Design Journal*, 20, S63–S76. https://doi.org/10.1080/14606925.2017.1353039.

Climate change and human behaviour. (2022). Nat Hum Behav, 6, 1441–1442. https://doi.org/10.1038/s41562-022-01490-9

Costanza-Chock, S. (2020). *Design justice: Community-Led practices to build the worlds we need*. MIT Press.

De Beauvoir, S. (1949). *The second sex*. Vintage Books.

Dunne, A., & Raby, F. (2013). *Speculative everything: Design, fiction, and social dreaming*. The MIT Press.

Dunne, A., & Raby, F. (n.d.). United Micro Kingdoms. http://unitedmicrokingdoms.org/

Escobar, A. (2018). *Designs for the pluriverse: Radical interdependence, autonomy, and the making of worlds*. Duke University Press.

Escobar, A. (2019). *Autonomía y diseño: La realización de lo comunal* (C. Gnecco, Trans., 1st ed.). Universidad del Cauca. https://doi.org/10.2307/j.ctvpv50jd.

Fanon, F. (1963). The wretched of the earth (C. Farrington, Trans.). Grove Press.

Foucault, M. (1966). The order of things (2nd ed.). Routledge.

Fraser, N. (1990). Rethinking the public sphere: A contribution to the critique of actually existing democracy. *Social Text*, (25/26), 56–80. https://carbonfarm.us/amap/fraser_public.pdf

Gergen, K. J. (2009). *An invitation to social construction* (2nd ed.). Sage Publications.

Ginsberg, A. D. (n.d.). The sixth extinction. http://www.daisyginsberg.com/work/the-sixth-extinction

Haraway, D. (1985). A cyborg manifesto: Science, technology, and socialist-feminism in the late twentieth century. In *Simians, cyborgs, and women: The reinvention of nature* (pp. 149–181). Routledge.

Horkheimer, M., & Adorno, T. W. (1947). *Dialectic of enlightenment*. Social Studies Association, Inc.

Horkheimer, M. (1937). "Traditionelle und kritische Theorie", Zeitschrift für Sozialforschung, 6(2): 245–294; translated as "Traditional and Critical Theory",

Matthew J. O'Connell (trans.), in Max Horkheimer, Critical Theory: Selected Essays, New York: Continuum, 1972, pp. 188–243.

Maughan, T. (2020). How big tech hijacked its sharpest, funniest critics. MIT Technology Review.

McGonigal, J. *Our puny human brains are terrible at thinking about the future.* https://slate.com/technology/2017/04/why-people-are-so-bad-at-thinking-about-the-future.html

Mitchell, J. (2000). *Mad men and medusas: Reclaiming hysteria.* Basic Books.

Papanek, V. (1971). *Design for the real world: Human ecology and social change.* Pantheon Books.

Pendleton-Jullian, A. M., & Brown, J. S. (2016). *Pragmatic imagination: Single from design unbound.* Blurb (Self-Publishing Platform).

Popper, K. (2002). *The logic of scientific discovery* (2nd ed.). Routledge. (Original work published 1959).

Said, Edward W. (1977). *Orientalism. Penguin Modern Classics.* London, England: Penguin Classics.

Schultz, T., Abdulla, D., Ansari, A., Canlı, E., Keshavarz, M., Kiem, M., et al. (2018). What is at stake with decolonizing design? *A Roundtable. Design and Culture,* 10(1), 81–101. https://doi.org/10.1080/17547075.2018.1434368

Sterling, B. (2005). *Shaping things.* The MIT Press.

Studio Drift. (n.d.). *Work.* https://www.studiodrift.com/work/.

Superflux. (n.d.). *Mitigation of shock.* https://superflux.in/index.php/work/mitigation-of-shock-london/.

Superflux. (n.d.). *Projects.* https://superflux.in/index.php/projects/.

Wakkary, R., Odom, W., Hauser, S., Hertz, G. D., & Lin, H. W. J. (2015). Material speculation: actual artifacts for critical inquiry. *Aarhus Series on Human Centered Computing,* 1(1). https://doi.org/10.7146/aahcc.v1i1.21299. In Aarhus 2015: Critical alternatives 2015 (Vol. Aarhus Series on Human Centered Computing). Aarhus, Copenhagen.

Wikipedia Contributors. (n.d.). *Speculative design.* Wikipedia. https://en.wikipedia.org/wiki/Speculative_design

Yelavich, S., & Adams, B. (2014). *Design as future-making.* Bloomsbury Academic.

CHAPTER 7

Dam, R. F., & Siang, T. Y. (2022). *Stakeholder mapping: The complete guide to stakeholder maps.* Interaction Design Foundation. https://www.interaction-design.org/literature/article/map-the-stakeholders

Ehn, P. (2008). Participation in design things. In D. Hakken, J. Simonsen, & T. Robertson (Eds.), *Proceedings of the tenth conference on participatory design, PDC 2008* (pp. 1–4). Bloomington. https://doi.org/10.1145/1795234.1795248.

Giordano, F. B., Morelli, N., De Götzen, A., & Hunziker, J. (2018). The stakeholder map: A conversation tool for designing people-led public services. In A. Meroni, A. M. O. Medina, & B. Villari (Eds.), *ServDes.2018 conference: Service design proof of concept.* Linköping University Electronic Press. Linköping Electronic Conference Proceedings No. 150. http://www.servdes.org/wp/wp-content/uploads/2018/07/48.pd.

Hyvärinen, J., Lee, J., & Mattelmäki, T. (2014). Fragile liaison—opportunities and challenges in cross organisational service networks. In D. Sangiorgi, D. Hands, & E. Murphy (Eds.), *ServDes.2014 service future* (pp. 354–364). Linköping University Electronic Press; Linköpings universitet. http://www.ep.liu.se/ecp/article. asp?issue=099&article=034&volume=.

Johnson, M. P., Ballie, J., Thorup, T., & Brooks, E. (2017). Living on the edge: Design artefacts as boundary objects. *The Design Journal*, 20(Suppl. 1), S219–S235.

Manzini, E. (2015). *Design, when everybody designs: An introduction to design for social innovation* (1st ed.). The MIT Press.

Manzini, E. (2016). Design culture and dialogic design. *Design Issues*, 32(1), 52–59.

Manzini, E., Jégou, F., & Meroni, A. (2009). *Design oriented scenarios: Generating new shared vision of sustainable product service systems.* In M. Crul, J. C. Dielh, & C. Ryan (Eds.), Design for sustainability: A step-by-step approach. United Nations Environment Programme, Delft University of Technology.

Meroni, A., & Sangiorgi, D. (2011). *Design for services.* Gower Publishing.

Meroni, A., Selloni, D., & Rossi, M. (2018). *Massive codesign.* A proposal for a collaborative design framework [Text.Chapter]. FrancoAngeli Series—Open Access. https://series.francoangeli.it/index.php/oa/catalog/view/303/106/1409.

Morelli, N., & Tollestrup, C. (2007). New representation techniques for designing in a systemic perspective. In *Design inquiries, Nordes 07 conference.* Konstfack, University College of Arts, Crafts and Design, Stockholm, Sweden, May 27–30.

Schindler, T. (2023). Embracing participatory futures: The synthesis of collective human creativity & AI in envisioning tomorrow. https://www.linkedin.com/pulse/ embracing-participatory-futures-synthesis-collective-human-schindler/.

Star, S. L. (1989). The structure of Ill-structured solutions: Boundary objects and heterogeneous distributed problem solving. In L. Gasser, & M. Huhns (Eds.), *Distributed artificial intelligence* (Vol. 2, pp. 37–54). Morgan Kaufman.

Steen, M. (2013). Co-design as a process of joint inquiry and imagination. *Design Issues*, 29(2), 16–28. http://www.jstor.org/stable/24266991.

Stickdorn, M., & Schneider, J. (2010). *This is service design thinking.* BIS Publishers.

CHAPTER 8

Bamberg, M., & Andrews, M. (Eds.) (2004). *Considering counter-narratives: Narrating, resisting, making sense.* John Benjamins Publishing.

Boje, D. M. (1991). *The storytelling organization: A study of story performance in an office-supply firm.* Administrative Science Quarterly, 36(1), 106–126. https://doi. org/10.2307/2393432

Brown, T. (2009). *Change by design: How design thinking transforms organizations and inspires innovation.* HarperBusiness.

Bruner, J. (1990). *Acts of meaning.* Harvard University Press.

BSR. (2019). Sustainability storytelling: Creating a narrative that matters. [Blog post]. https://www.bsr.org/en/blog/sustainability-storytelling-creating-a-narrative-that-matters.

Buganza, T., Bellis, P., Magnanini, S., Press, J., Shani, A. B., Trabucchi, D., et al. (2021). *Storymaking: How organizations can engage people to make innovation happen.* Routledge.

Burnes, B. (2020). The origins of Lewin's three-step model of change. *The Journal of Applied Behavioral Science, 56*(1), 32–59.

Bushe, G. R., & Marshak, R. J. (2015). Dialogic organization development. In W. J. Rothwell, J. Stravros, R. Sullivan, & A. Naquin (Eds.), *Practicing organization development* (4th ed., pp. 407–418). Wiley.

Carlin, S. (2010). Getting to the heart of climate change through stories. In W. L. Filho (Ed.), *Universities and climate change.* Springer.

Carson, L., Köninger, T., MacNeill, J., & Bentzen, N. (2022). Combining mini-publics with democratic innovations: Theoretical foundations and practical considerations. *Policy Sciences, 55*(1), 3–32.

Colville, I., Pye, A., & Carter, M. (2013). Organizing to counter terrorism: Sensemaking amidst dynamic complexity. *Human Relations, 66*(9), 1201–1223.

Corner, A., & Clarke, J. (2016). *Talking climate: From research to practice in public engagement* (pp. 1–146). Palgrave Macmillan.

Couldry, N. (2008). Mediatization or mediation? Alternative understandings of the emergent space of digital storytelling. *New Media & Society, 10*(3), 373–391.

Cronon, W. (1992). A place for stories: Nature, history, and narrative. *The Journal of American History, 78*(4), 1347–1376.

Davis, J. (2002). Narrative and social movements. *Stories of Change: Narrative and Social Movements, 3*, 35.

Denning, S. (2006). *Effective storytelling: Strategic business narrative techniques.* Strategy & Leadership.

de Jong, M. D. T., Huluba, G., & Beldad, A. D. (2020). Different Shades of Greenwashing: Consumers' Reactions to Environmental Lies, Half-Lies, and Organizations Taking Credit for Following Legal Obligations. *Journal of Business and Technical Communication, 34*(1), 38–76. https://doi.org/10.1177/1050651919874105

Ecosystem Restoration Camps. (n.d.). John D. Liu—Our Founder. https://www.ecosystemrestorationcamps.org/john-d-liu.

Environmental Education Media Project. (n.d.). Green gold documentary films with John D. Liu. https://eemp.org/green-gold-documentary/.

Fab Foundation. (n.d.). Fab labs. https://fabfoundation.org/fab-labs/.

Füller, J., Mühlbacher, H., Matzler, K., & Jawecki, G. (2009). Consumer empowerment through internet-based co-creation. *Journal of Management Information Systems, 26*, 71–102. https://doi.org/10.2753/MIS0742-1222260303

Gabriel, Y. (2000). *Storytelling in organizations: Facts, fictions, and fantasies.* Oxford University Press.

Gersie, A. (2015). *Storytelling for a greener world.* Hawthorn Press.

Harari, Y. N. (2015). *Sapiens: A brief history of humankind.* Harper.

Hickman, G.R. (2010). Leading Change in Multiple Contexts: Concepts and Practices in Organizational, Community, Political, Social, and Global Change Settings. 10.4135/9781452274706.

Hobbs, W., Bai, X., & Wilson Miller, M. L. (2020). Changing the agricultural narrative: The transformative vision and potentials of John D. Liu's ecological knowledge. *Agriculture and Human Values.* https://doi.org/10.1007/s10460-020-10173-0.

Hopkins, R. (2019). *From what is to what if: Unleashing the power of imagination to create the future we want*. Chelsea Green Publishing.

Ivankova, N. V. (2014). *Mixed methods applications in action research*. SAGE Publications.

Kassawmar, T., Friedrich, T., Kassa, H., Kiesel, J., & Asmamaw, L. (2020). The long-term sustainability of integrated watershed rehabilitation: Evidence from Tigray in Northern Ethiopia. *World Development Perspectives*, 18. https://doi.org/10.1016/j.wdp.2020.100211.

Knez, I. (2013). How concerned, afraid and hopeful are we? Effects of egoism and altruism on climate change related issues. *Psychology*, 4, 744–752.

Kotter, J. P. (1996). *Leading change*. Harvard Business Press.

Küpers, W. M. (2013). *Embodied transformative metaphors and narratives in organisational learning*. Learning Organization.

Lakoff, G. (2010). Why it matters how we frame the environment. *Environmental Communication*, 4, 70–81.

Leiserowitz, A. (2006). Climate change risk perception and policy preferences: The role of affect, imagery, and values. *Climatic Change*, 77(1), 45–72.

Lipmanowicz, H., & McCandless, K. (2020). *Liberating structures: Including and unleashing everyone*. Eburon Academic Publishers.

Liu, J. D. (Director). (2001). Green gold: Sustaining national heritage [Film]. TVE; EEMP.

Liu, J. D. (2015). *John D. Liu: The healing power of ecosystems*. Radio Ecoshock. https://www.ecoshock.org/2015/04/john-d-liu-healing-power-of-ecosystems.html.

Malena-Chan, R. A. (2019). Making climate change meaningful: Narrative dissonance and the gap between knowledge and action. Master thesis, University of Saskatchewan, Canada.

Maniates, M. F. (2001). Individualization: Plant a tree, buy a bike, save the world?. *Global Environmental Politics*, 1(3), 31–52.

Manovich, L. (2001). *The language of new media*. MIT Press.

Markowitz, E. M., & Guckian, M. L. (2018). Climate change communication: Challenges, insights, and opportunities. In S. Clayton & C. Manning (Eds.), *Human perceptions, impacts, and responses* (pp. 35–63). Elsevier Academic Press. https://doi.org/10.1016/B978-0-12-813130-5.00003-5

McKee, R., & Fryer, B. (2003). Storytelling that moves people. *Harvard Business Review*, 81(6), 54–61.

MIT D-Lab. (n.d.). Developing technologies to improve the lives of people living in poverty. https://d-lab.mit.edu/.

Moser, S. C. (2016). Reflections on climate change communication research and practice in the second decade of the 21st century: What more is there to say? *WIREs Climate Change*, 7(3), 345–369.

Morel, E. (2017). The storyworld accord: Econarratology and postcolonial narratives. By Erin James. *ISLE: Interdisciplinary Studies in Literature and Environment*, 24(2), 373–374.

Mumby, D. K. (1987). The political function of narrative in organizations. *Communication Monographs*, 54(2), 113–127.

Nabi, R. L., Gustafson, A., & Jensen, R. (2018). Framing climate change: Exploring the role of emotion in generating advocacy behavior. *Science Communication*, 40(4), 442–468.

Nanson, A. (2021). *Storytelling and ecology: Empathy, enchantment and emergence in the use of oral narratives*. Bloomsbury Publishing.

Naughton, L. (2014). Geographical narratives of social capital and place attachment: Using oral history in local planning. *Planning Theory & Practice, 15*(4), 515–530.

Noffke, S., & Somekh, B. (2005). Action research. In B. Somekh & C. Lewin (Eds.), *Research methods in the social sciences* (pp. 89–96). SAGE Publications Ltd.

O'Neill, S. J., Boykoff, M., Niemeyer, S., & Day, S. A. (2013). On the use of imagery for climate change engagement. *Global Environmental Change, 23*(2), 413–421.

Owen, H. (2008). *Open space technology: A user's guide.* Berrett-Koehler Publishers.

Paschen, J. A., & Ison, R. (2014). Narrative research in climate change adaptation— Exploring a complementary paradigm for research and governance. *Research Policy, 43*(6), 1083–1092.

Perkowitz, B., Speiser, M., Harp, G., Hodge, C., & Krygsman, K. (2014). *American climate values 2014: Psychographic and demographic insights.*

Prosci. (n.d.). ADKAR change management model overview, Washington, DC: Strategic Business Insights and ecoAmerica. https://www.prosci.com/adkar/adkar-model.

Rigby, D. K, Sutherland, J., & Takeuchi, H. (2016). Embracing agile. *Harvard Business Review, 94*(5), 40–50.

Rost, J. C. (1993). *Leadership for the twenty-first century.* Praeger.

Rotmann, S. (2017). "Once upon a time…" Eliciting energy and behaviour change stories using a fairy tale story spine. *Energy Research & Social Science, 31,* 303–310.

Salmon, C. (2002). *Storytelling: Bewitching the modern mind.* Verso.

Schein, E. H. (1996). Kurt Lewin's change theory in the field and in the classroom: Notes toward a model of managed learning. *Systems Practice, 9*(1), 27–47.

Scharmer, O., & Kaufer, K. (2013). *Leading from the emerging future: From ego-system to eco-system economies.* Berrett-Koehler Publishers.

Senge, P. M. (2006). *The fifth discipline: The art and practice of the learning organization.* Broadway Business.

Shaw, P. (2002). *Changing conversations in organizations: A complexity approach to change.* Routledge.

Shell. (2020). *Shell sustainability report 2020.* Shell Global.

Sinclair, A. (2007). *Leadership for the disillusioned: Moving beyond myths and heroes to leading that liberates.* Allen & Unwin.

Singh, S., & Sonnenburg, S. (2012). Brand performances in social media. *Journal of Interactive Marketing, 26*(4), 189–197.

Smith, N. C., & Langford, P. (2009). Evaluating the role of fairness in consumer boycotts. *Journal of Business Research, 62*(10), 1001–1008.

Sterman, J. D. (2002). All models are wrong: Reflections on becoming a systems scientist. *System Dynamics Review: The Journal of the System Dynamics Society, 18*(4), 501–531.

Talgorn, E., Hendriks, M., Geurts, L., & Bakker, C. (2022). A storytelling methodology to facilitate user-centered co-ideation between scientists and designers. *Sustainability, 14*(7), 4132.

Talgorn, E., & Ullerup, H. (2023). Invoking 'Empathy for the Planet' through participatory ecological storytelling: From human-centered to planet-centered design. *Sustainability, 15*(10), 7794. https://doi.org/10.3390/su15107794.

Teshome, A. (2014). An evaluation of watershed management in Ethiopia. *Kasetsart Journal of Social Sciences, 35*(3), 669–679.

Thomashow, M. (1996). *Ecological identity: Becoming a reflective environmentalist.* MIT Press.

Uhl-Bien, M. (2006). Relational leadership theory: Exploring the social processes of leadership and organizing. *The Leadership Quarterly,* 17(6), 654–676.

Veland, S., Scoville-Simonds, M., Gram-Hanssen, I., Schorre, A., Khoury, A., Nordbø, M., et al. (2018). Narrative matters for sustainability: The transformative role of storytelling in realizing 1.5°C futures. *Current Opinion in Environmental Sustainability,* 31, 41–47.

Wang, C. C., & Burris, M. A. (1997). Photovoice: Concept, methodology, and use for participatory needs assessment. *Health Education & Behavior,* 24(3), 369–387.

Watkins, J. M., Mohr, B. J., & Kelly, R. (2011). *Appreciative inquiry: Change at the speed of imagination.* Wiley.

Weber, E. U. (2016). What shapes perceptions of climate change? New research since 2010. *Wiley Interdisciplinary Reviews: Climate Change,* 7(1), 125–134. https://doi.org/10.1002/wcc.377

Weick, K. E. (1995). *Sensemaking in organizations.* SAGE Publications.

Weisbord, M. R., & Janoff, S. (2010). *Future search: Getting the whole system in the room for vision, commitment, and action.* Berrett-Koehler Publishers.

Wittmayer, J. M., Avelino, F., van Steenbergen, F., & Loorbach, D. (2017). Actor roles in transition: Insights from sociological perspectives. *Environmental Innovation and Societal Transitions,* 24, 45–56.

CHAPTER 9

Abouleish, I. (2005). *Sekem: A sustainable community in the Egyptian desert.* Floris Books.

Aguilera, R. V., Rupp, D. E., Williams, C. A., & Ganapathi, J. (2007). Putting the S back in corporate social responsibility: A multilevel theory of social change in organizations. *Academy of Management Review,* 32(3), 836–863. https://doi.org/10.5465/AMR.2007.25275678.

Amini, M., & Bienstock, C. C. (2014). Corporate sustainability: An integrative definition and framework to evaluate corporate practice and guide academic research. *Journal of Cleaner Production,* 76, 12–19. https://doi.org/10.1016/j.jclepro.2014.02.016.

Avolio, B. J., Walumbwa, F. O., & Weber, T. J. (2009). Leadership: Current theories, research, and future directions. *Annual Review of Psychology,* 60, 421–449.

Bass, B. M., Waldman, D. A., Atwater, L., & Avolio, B. J. (2016). *The nature of leadership.* Sage Publications.

Battilana, J., Sengul, M., Pache, A. C., & Model, J. (2022). Five essential organizational capabilities for implementing commitment to purpose. *MIT Sloan Management Review,* 63(4), 1–6. https://sloanreview.mit.edu/article/five-essential-organizational-capabilities-for-implementing-commitment-to-purpose/.

Battiston, F., Guillon, M., Chavez, M., Latora, V., & Moreno, Y. (2020). Taking turns in the spotlight: Leadership dynamics in creative teams. *Scientific Reports,* 10, 6058.

Baumgartner, R. J., & Rauter, R. (2017). Strategic perspectives of corporate sustainability management to develop a sustainable organization. *Journal of Cleaner Production,* 140, 81–92. https://doi.org/10.1016/j.jclepro.2016.04.146.

Bolton, R., & Landells, T. (2022). Towards regenerative business models: Insights from the circular economy and bio-economy spaces. *Journal of Cleaner Production,* 38, 372–388. https://doi.org/10.1016/j.jclepro.2022.144430

Bolton, Dianne & Landells, Terry. (2023). Storytelling, sensemaking and sustainability agendas. 10.4324/9781003225508-19.

Boyatzis, R. E., Rochford, K., & Jack, A. I. (2014). Antagonistic neural networks underlying differentiated leadership roles. *Frontiers in Human Neuroscience*, 8, 114.

Boyd, B. (2009). On *the origin of stories: Evolution, cognition, and fiction*. Harvard University Press.

Christensen, L. J., Peirce, E., Hartman, L. P., Hoffman, W. M., & Carrier, J. (2007). Ethics, CSR, and sustainability education in the Financial Times top 50 global business schools: Baseline data and future research directions. *Journal of Business Ethics*, 73(4), 347–368. https://doi.org/10.1007/s10551-006-9211-5.

Cozolino, L. (2006). *The neuroscience of human relationships: Attachment and the developing social brain*. WW Norton & Company.

Cloutier, Caroline & Oktaei, Parnian & Lehoux, Nadia. (2019). Collaborative mechanisms for sustainability-oriented supply chain initiatives: state of the art, role assessment and research opportunities. *International Journal of Production Research*. 58. 1–15. 10.1080/00207543.2019.1660821.

Drath, W. (2001). *The deep blue sea: Rethinking the source of leadership*. Jossey-Bass and Center for Creative Leadership.

Drath, W. H., McCauley, C. D., Palus, C. J., Van Velsor, E., O'Connor, P. M., & McGuire, J. B. (2008). Direction, alignment, commitment: Toward a more integrative ontology of leadership. *The Leadership Quarterly*, 19(6), 635–653.

Drath, W., & Palus, C. (1994). *Making common sense: Leadership as meaning-making in a community of practice*. Center for Creative Leadership.

Drath, W. H., & Palus, C. J. (1994). Making common sense: Leadership as meaning-making in a community of practice. *Consulting Psychology Journal: Practice and Research*, 46(1), 19–32. https://doi.org/10.1037/1061-4087.46.1.19.

Dweck, C. S., & Yeager, D. S. (2019). Mindsets: A View From Two Eras. *Perspectives on Psychological Science*, 14(3), 481–496. https://doi.org/10.1177/1745691618804166

Elkington, J. (1999). Triple bottom line revolution: Reporting for the third millennium. *Australian CPA*, 69(11), 75–76.

Falk, E. B., & Bassett, D. S. (2017). Brain and social networks: Fundamental building blocks of human experience. *Trends in Cognitive Sciences*, 21(9), 674–690.

Francis, C. (2024). The Future We Choose: Surviving the Climate Crisis, New York.

Frias-Aceituno, J. V., Rodríguez-Ariza, L., & Garcia-Sánchez, I. M. (2013). Is integrated reporting determined by a country's legal system? An exploratory study. *Journal of Cleaner Production*, 44, 45–55. https://doi.org/10.1016/j.jclepro.2012.12.006

Ford, J., Ford, L., & Polin, B. (2021). Leadership in the Implementation of Change: Functions, Sources, and Requisite Variety. Journal of Change Management, 21(1), 87–119. https://doi.org/10.1080/14697017.2021.1861697

Furr, N., Dyer, J., & Nel, K. (2018). *Leading transformation: Applying neuroscience to leadership*, Harvard business review press.

Ghadiri, F., Habermacher, A., & Peters, T. (2020). *Neuroleadership: A journey through the brain for business leaders*. Springer.

Hannah, S. T., Balthazard, P. A., Waldman, D. A., Jennings, P. L., & Thatcher, R. W. (2013). The psychological and neurological bases of leader self-complexity and effects on adaptive decision-making. *Journal of Applied Psychology*, 98(3), 393.

Harris, A. (2008). Distributed leadership: According to the evidence. *Journal of Educational Administration*, 46(2), 172–188. https://doi.org/10.1108/09578230810863253

Hörisch, Jacob & Tenner, Isabell & Schaltegger, Stefan. (2019). The influence of feedback and awareness of consequences on the development of corporate sustainability action over time. *Business Strategy and the Environment*. 29. 10.1002/bse.2394.

Johansen, B. (2020). Full-Spectrum Thinking: How to Escape Boxes in a Post-Categorical Future. Berrett-Koehler Publishers.

Laloux, F. (2014). *Reinventing organizations: A guide to creating organizations inspired by the next stage in human consciousness*. Nelson Parker.

Mar, R. A., & Oatley, K. (2008). The function of fiction is the abstraction and simulation of social experience. *Perspectives on Psychological Science*, 3(3), 173–192.

McCauley, C., & Palus, C. J. (2021). Developing the theory and practice of leadership development: A relational view. *The Leadership Quarterly*, 32(5), 101456. https://doi.org/10.1016/j.leaqua.2020.101456

Manzini, Ezio. (2015). Design, When Everybody Designs: An Introduction to Design for Social Innovation. 10.7551/mitpress/9873.001.0001.

Menges, J. I., & Kilduff, M. (2015). Group emotions: Cutting the Gordian knots concerning terms, levels of analysis, and processes. *Academy of Management Annals*, 9(1), 845–928.

Metcalf, L., & Benn, S. (2013). Leadership for sustainability: An evolution of leadership ability. *Journal of Business Ethics*, 112(3), 369–384.

Palus, C. J., & Drath, W. H. (2001). Putting something in the middle: An approach to dialogue. *Reflections*, 3(2), 28–39.

Palus, C. J., & Horth, D. M. (2002). *The Leader's edge: Six creative competencies for navigating complex challenges*. Jossey-Bass.

Pearce, Eiluned & Wlodarski, Rafael & Machin, Anna & Dunbar, Robin. (2019). Exploring the links between dispositions, romantic relationships, support networks and community inclusion in men and women. PLOS ONE. 14. e0216210. 10.1371/journal.pone.0216210.

Polman, P., & Winston, A. S. (2021). *Net positive: How courageous companies thrive by giving more than they take*. Harvard Business Review Press.

Press, J., Bellis, P., Buganza, T., Magnanini, S., Trabucchi, D., Shani, A. B. (Rami), et al. (2021). *IDeaLs (Innovation and Design as Leadership): Transformation in the digital era* (1st ed.). Emerald Publishing Limited.

Sabbab, S., & Ahmed, S. (2024, January 21). *Restructuring climate education in Bangladesh*. Dhaka Tribune. https://www.dhakatribune.com/opinion/op-ed/337332/restructuring-climate-education-in-bangladesh?fbclid=IwAR02DFJaj-r481ED0bTsGinoWQdmciLz_3sdyRSTBK7S2xL0yc_PmgaFQlg.

Schacter, D. L., & Madore, K. P. (2016). Remembering the past and imagining the future: Identifying and enhancing the contribution of episodic memory. *Memory Studies*, 9(3), 245–255. https://doi.org/10.1177/1750698016645230

Scharmer, O. (2009). *Theory U: Leading from the future as it emerges*. Berrett-Koehler Publishers.

Scharmer, C. & K.Kaufer,. (2013). *Leading From the Emerging Future: From Ego-system to Eco-system Economies*.

Schaltegger, Stefan & Hörisch, Jacob & Loorbach, Derk. (2020). Corporate and entrepreneurial contributions to sustainability transitions. Business Strategy and the Environment. 29. 10.1002/bse.2454.

Schoemaker, Paul & Heaton, Sohvi & Teece, David. (2018). Innovation, Dynamic Capabilities, and Leadership. *California Management Review*. 61. 000812561879024. 10.1177/0008125618790246.

Sekem. (2021). Sekem website. https://www.sekem.com/.

Sekem. (2021). Sekem Sustainability Report 2020. https://www.sekem.com/wp-content/uploads/2021/09/Sekem_SR2020_en_single-1.pdf

Senge, P., Smith, B. and Kruschwitz, N. (2008). The Next Industrial Imperative

Facing up to climate change requires a revolution in business thinking. Smith, J. (2018). Futureback thinking: A transformative approach to leadership. *Leadership Quarterly*, 29(4), 423–436.

Smit, J., & Watson, J. (2023). *The lonely quest of Unilever's CEO -Paul Polman*. Anthem Press.

Stephens, G. J., Silbert, L. J., & Hasson, U. (2010). Speaker–listener neural coupling underlies successful communication. *Proceedings of the National Academy of Sciences*, 107(32), 14425–14430.

Tetlock, P. E., & Gardner, D. (2015). Superforecasting: The art and science of prediction. Crown Publishers/Random House.

Trost, W., Frühholz, S., Schön, D., Labbé, C., Pichon, S., Grandjean, D., et al. (2015). Getting the beat: Entrainment of brain activity by musical rhythm and pleasantness. *Neuroimage*, 103, 55–64.

Uhl-Bien, M., Marion, R., & McKelvey, B. (2007). Complexity leadership theory: Shifting leadership from the industrial age to the knowledge era. *The Leadership Quarterly*, 18(4), 298–318.

Verganti, R. (2017). *Design-driven innovation: Changing the rules of competition by radically innovating what things mean*. Harvard Business Review Press.

Vygotsky, L. S. (1978). *Mind in society: The development of higher psychological processes*. Harvard University Press.

Wahl, D. C. (2016). *Designing regenerative cultures*. Triarchy Press.

Wahl, D. C. (2017). The potential of developmental evaluation and action research in the context of regenerative sustainability projects and initiatives. *Action Research*, 15(4), 377–395. https://doi.org/10.1177/1476750317698037.

Wahl, D. C. (2018). Integral development realising the transformative potential in groups, organisations and social systems. In R. Ingle & A. Nicholls (Eds.), *Social entrepreneurship: Agency, context, performance* (pp. 205–238). Edward Elgar.

Wahl, D. C. (2021). *The regenerative business: Redesign work, cultivate human potential, achieve extraordinary outcomes*. Emerge.

Waldman, D. A., Balthazard, P. A., & Peterson, S. J. (2011). Leadership and neuroscience: Can we revolutionize the way that inspirational leaders are identified and developed? *Academy of Management Perspectives*, 25(1), 60–74.

Wenger, E. (1998). *Communities of practice: Learning, meaning, and identity*. Cambridge University Press.

CONCLUSION

Danchev, A. (2011). *100 artists' manifestos: From the futurists to the stuckists*. Penguin UK.

How to create your own manifesto: with 3 gorgeous examples to inspire you. *Visual Journal Studio*.

What is a manifesto? How to write a manifesto. MasterClass (2024)

Index

Design Council (2018) 68
design-driven dialog 7, *7–9*
designer's role 171, 183
design fiction 21, 24, *157*, 158,
   253–254; abstract artifacts to embodied
   experiences 139–141; artifacts *see*
   artifacts; arts and crafts of 145–156;
   experiential futures ladder 140, *141*;
   futures literacy 157, *157*; speculative
   design and 61, 66–70, 139–141;
   success of 140; sustainable futures 104;
   transformative power 69; The Thing
   from the Future 145–147, *146*
*Design for the Real World - Human
   Ecology and Social Change* (Papanek) 10
Design Futures 61–62, 251, 252
Designing Regenerative Cultures (Wahl)
   122
designing sustainable futures: Aotearoa
   Futures Network 231, *232*; artifacts
   see artifacts; Astrolabe to navigate seas
   18–21, *19*; for Bangladesh 14–18, 212;
   collaboration 138; community 242;
   critical dimensions of 4; facilitators/
   curators role 231; futures literacy
   see futures literacy (FL); integrating
   disciplines with sustainability 3;
   manifesto 243–246, *245*; organization
   241–242; personal and professional
   choices 239–240; practitioners of
   243, *245*; scenarios 102–103; STES
   (Socio-Technical-Ecological Systems)
   10–11, *12–13*; stories 43; storytelling
   in 103; template 233, *233*; territorial
   map 19, *20*
*Design Justice: Community-Led
   Practices to Build the Worlds We Need*
   (Costanza-Chock) 111
develop phase, double diamond scheme
   169, 170
dialogic organization development (OD) 189
Digital Bangladesh Vision 14
digital twin 80, 88
discovery phase, double diamond scheme
   169, 169–170
Distribute Impact 89
diversity 3, 258, *259*; communities 144;
   and inclusivity 240; participants from
   organizations 191; in shaping futures 67;
   stakeholders 89, 134, 207; visualizing
   perspectives 53
Donut Model 6
double diamond model 169, *169*, 181
Drath, W. H. 208
DSF design brief 233–238
Dunagan, J. (Director of Design Futures at
   the Institute for The Future) 19, 29, 36,
   39, 41, 47, 247, 251

Dunne, A. 65, 66; *Speculative
   Everything: Design, Fiction, and Social
   Dreaming* 65

Earth 2050 82
Earth stewardship 43
ecological design: environmental
   sustainability 80, 234; Life Cycle Design
   (LCA) 129; Systemic Design 120, 122
Ecotopia (Callenbach) 107
education: futures thinking in 16–18, 213;
   leadership for better future 15–18
egstrogen farms *70*, 70–71, *71*
Elahi, S. 104
embodied cognition 41
embodied experiences 36, 41; abstract
   artifacts to 139–141
empowerment 226–227
engagement, storymaking for *187*,
   187–190
Enterprise Development Centre (EDC) 225
Environmental Asylum 114–115
environmental consciousness 240
environmental, social, and governance
   (ESG) 39, 198–199
environmental sustainability: diversity and
   inclusivity 240; generative AI (GenAI)
   80; individual commitment 240; and
   social equity 234; wicked problems 10
envisioning preferred future 260–264;
   future self-letter 263; purposeful goal
   setting 262; shared vision mapping
   263–264; time travel visualization
   261–262; vision board 262–263
envisioning sustainable futures 38, 82,
   237–238; for Bangladesh 14; generative
   AI (GenAI) *see* generative artificial
   intelligence (GenAI); regenerative/
   circular economy 237; through
   embodied metaphor 41
epistemology 7, 54, 58, 60, 140
ethics 37, 66, 90, 252
Ethiopian farmers stories 188
Ethnographic Experiential Foresight 44
expanded experiential futures ladder *see*
   experiential futures ladder
experiences: in building industry 255–256;
   embodied 36, 42, 139–141; foresight
   see foresight; immersive 55; for
   participants 44–45; preferred future
   264–268; provocative 44; shared 36, 95;
   sustainable *see* sustainable experiences
   creation; Systemic Design 130
experiential futures: embodied experiences
   36, 42, 139–141; experiential futures
   ladder 41–43, *42*
experiential futures ladder 41–43, *42*;
   design fiction 140, *141*; expanded 102,

For Product Safety Concerns and Information please contact our EU
representative GPSR@taylorandfrancis.com
Taylor & Francis Verlag GmbH, Kaufingerstraße 24, 80331 München, Germany